A Teaching Guide for Law Enforcement and Others

Talking With Youth About Prevention

Conflict • Drugs • Traffic Safety • Violence • Assault • Gangs • Vandalism • Bias • Property Crime • Sexual Assault

and ideas for —

• Effective Presentations • Youth-Led Projects • and more!

The National Crime Prevention Council is a private, nonprofit tax-exempt [501(c)(3)] corporation whose principal mission is to enable people to prevent crime and build safer, more caring communities. In addition to this book, NCPC publishes kits of camera-ready program materials, posters, and informational and policy reports on a variety of crime prevention and community-building subjects. NCPC offers training, technical assistance, and national focus for crime prevention; it acts as secretariat for the Crime Prevention Coalition of America, more than 136 national, federal, and state organizations committed to preventing crime. It also operates demonstration programs and takes a major leadership role in youth crime prevention. NCPC manages the McGruff "Take A Bite Out Of Crime" public service advertising campaign, which is substantially funded by the Bureau of Justice Assistance, Office of Justice Programs, U.S. Department of Justice.

This publication was made possible through Cooperative Funding Agreement No. 86-MU-CX-K002 from the Bureau of Justice Assistance, Office of Justice Programs, U.S. Department of Justice. Opinions are those of NCPC or cited sources and do not necessarily reflect U.S. Department of Justice policy or positions. The Bureau of Justice Assistance is a component of the Office of Justice Programs, which also includes the Bureau of Justice Statistics, the National Institute of Justice, the Office of Juvenile Justice and Delinquency Prevention, and the Office for Victims of Crime.

Copyright 1992
National Crime Prevention Council
Reprinted 1997, Cooperative Agreement No. 95-DD-BX-K003

All rights reserved except that copies of portions of this book may be made with proper attribution for nonprofit use and not for sale.

ISBN 0-934513-30-9

Acknowledgments

This document represents the work of more than two dozen people. They took the vision created by NCPC staff and transmuted it into a document that is, we hope, user-friendly and truly helpful to those seeking to talk with young people about prevention.

Key NCPC staff in this project:

S. Joanna Wild, *Director of Youth Development*
Jean F. O'Neil, *Managing Editor and Director of Research*
Judith Kirby, *Special Assistant for Youth Programs*

They were critical in numerous ways to the creation and quality of this document.

Other NCPC staff and consultants: Fay Pattee of NCPC developed the cover design and assisted in polishing up artwork; Jacqueline Aker helped in the final proofing and document assembly; Marty Pociask oversaw production. John A. Calhoun, Executive Director, was supportive and constructive throughout a difficult project gestation. Terrence W. Modglin, Director of Youth Programs, championed the original concept. Janet Erickson, a consultant to NCPC, prepared many of the early drafts of chapters; Sarah Hay, also a consultant, provided extensive editing, rewriting, and original text that pervades the entire document. Mike Ferrans, interning at NCPC during the summers of 1991 and 1992, did an enormous amount of research and substantial writing on this project. Tara Epstein, interning during the summer of 1991, also helped. Diane Alexander assisted with research; Diana Engel provided word processing support.

The Document Development Group that met in April 1991 to explore the frame and scope of this Guide included Artemus Carter (Cleveland Marshall School of Law, Cleveland, Ohio), Maria Cedeno (Dade County Public Schools, Miami, Florida), Rita Dysart (Police Department, Kansas City, Missouri), Marti English (Montgomery County Public Schools, Wheaton, Maryland), Dot Price (Dekalb County Police Department, Decatur, Georgia), Ken Rosenberg (Arlington County Police Department, Arlington, Virginia), Steve Rutzebeck (Maryland State Police, Pikesville, Maryland), and Jerry Skrzypiec (Maryland State Police, Pikesville, Maryland).

At the Bureau of Justice Assistance, Office of Justice Programs, U.S. Department of Justice, Robert H. (Bob) Brown, Jr., was a tower of patience and support for what has been a challenging project.

The knowledge, ideas, and activities contained in this document would not have been possible without the contributions of many thinkers and doers over the past decades. In many senses the content reflects what NCPC perceived as the most current or leading thought on the subject. *Talking With Youth* draws heavily on NCPC's past work, of course, but we gratefully acknowledge the contributions noted below and thank the authors for permission to use them:

- Virginia Public Schools, City of Charlottesville, TIPs Curriculum for "Observing Road Signs" and "Laws and the Crazy Elephant."
- Community Board of San Francisco for "Elementary Conflict Management."
- Creative Conflict Resolution: More Than 200 Activities for Keeping Peace in the Classroom for "The Lorax" and the "The Bug Board."
- Young Lawyers Section of the Bar Association of the District of Columbia for "Are You a Good Witness?"
- Center to Prevent Handgun Violence, STAR Curriculum, for "Feelings" and "Understanding Anger."
- Youth Force of Citizen's Committee for New York City for "Attitude Check."

Table of Contents

Introduction
    How This Guide is Organized 2
    Using This Guide 2
    In Performance 3
    Your Reward 3
    For the Future 3

Self Protection, Grades K-6 5
    Crime Prevention and Personal Safety 5
    The Latchkey Child 5
    Establishing a Routine 6
    Learning to Use the Phone 6
    Learning Door Answering Safety 6
    Commonsense Personal Safety Rules 7
    Child Abuse and Touching Problems 7
    Approaches Used To Attract Children 8
    Why Children Don't Tell Adults About a Touching Problem 9
    Strangers 9
    Messages For Parents 9
    Sample Materials and Activities 10
    Resources 14

Police, Their Job, and Respect for the Law, Grades K-6 15
    An Effective Partnership 15
    Overcoming Negative Attitudes and Stereotypes 15
    Developing a Positive Relationship With Youth 16
    Understanding the Police Officer's Job 16
    Rules and Laws 17
    Messages For Parents 17
    Sample Materials and Activities 18
    Resources 20

Traffic Responsibility, Grades K-6 21
    Pedestrian Responsibility 21
    Pedestrian Safety Rules 22
    Myths and Facts About Pedestrian Responsibility 22
    Bicycle Responsibility 22
    Bicycling Rules 23
    Preventing Theft 23
    Responsible Use of Tricycles and Other Riding Toys 24
    Skateboarding Wisely 24
    Roller Skating Responsibility 24
    Buckling Up is the Law 25
    Messages for Parents 26
    Sample Materials and Activities 26
    Resources 29

Table of Contents

Alcohol and Other Drug Use Prevention, Grades K-6.......31
Youthful Substance Abuse.................32
What Children Think About Alcohol and Other Drugs............32
Risk Factors.................32
Why Some People Use Drugs.................32
Understanding the Five- to Eight-Year Old.................33
Drugs That Heal and Drugs That Harm.................33
Understanding the Nine- to 11-Year Old.................33
Resisting Peer Pressure.................34
Understanding the Effects of Alcohol and Other Drugs.................34
"I Saw Someone Using Drugs. What Should I Do?".................35
Community-Building Alternatives to Drug Use.................35
Other Alternatives to Drug Use.................35
Messages for Parents.................36
Sample Materials and Activities.................37
Resources.................41

Conflict Management, Grades K-6.................43
Causes of Conflict.................43
Methods of Managing Conflict.................44
Messages for Parents.................44
Sample Materials and Activities.................44
Resources.................47

Gangs, Grades 4-6.................49
Gangs and Youth.................50
Profile of a Preteen Gang Member.................50
Why Preteens Join Gangs.................50
Gang Criminal Activities.................51
Signs of Gangs.................51
Consequences of Gang Membership.................51
Keeping Children From Joining Gangs.................52
Messages for Parents.................52
Sample Materials and Activities.................53
Resources.................53

Property Crime and Vandalism, Grades 4-8.................55
What is Property?.................55
Property Crime.................56
Myths and Facts About Property Crimes.................56
What is Vandalism?.................57
Who is the Vandal?.................57
Who Are the Victims of Vandalism?.................57
Vandalism Costs.................58
Preventing Vandalism.................58
Other Property Crimes.................58
Youth Can Help Prevent Property Crime.................58
Messages for Parents.................59
Sample Materials and Activities.................60
Resources.................64

Personal Protection Against Crime, Grades 7-12.................65
What is Crime?.................65
Teenage Crime Victims.................66
The Effects of Crime.................66

How Victims Respond	67
The Effects of Crime on the Community	67
Help for Victims	67
Victims' Rights	67
How Teens Can Reduce Teen Victimization	68
How To Report a Crime	69
How To Help a Friend Who is a Crime Victim	69
Community Crime Prevention Strategies	70
If You're Confronted	70
Messages for Parents	71
Sample Materials and Activities	71
Resources	75

Sexual Assault and Acquaintance Rape Prevention, Grades 7-12 . . . 77

Sexual Assault	78
Rape	78
Myths and Facts About Sexual Assaults	78
Acquaintance Rape	80
Facts About Rapists	80
Reducing Your Risks	80
If Rape Happens	81
Effects of Rape on the Survivor	82
Helping a Friend Who Has Been Raped	82
Messages for Parents	83
Sample Materials and Activities	84
Resources	93

Alcohol and Other Drug Use Prevention, Grades 7-12 . . . 95

What is a Drug?	96
Why Teens Need Anti-Drug Education	96
Know the Drug Problem in Your Community	98
How Drug Use Affects a Community	98
How Drug Use Affects Teens	99
Drugs and Sexually Transmitted Diseases	99
Drugs and Pregnancy	99
Who Abuses Drugs?	99
Reasons Teens Give for Using Drugs	100
Signs of Drug Use	100
How To Help a Friend Who is Using Drugs	101
Community Building Equals Drug Prevention	102
Other Alternatives to Drug Use	102
Messages for Parents	103
Sample Materials and Activities	104
Resources	109

Motor Vehicle Responsibility, Grades 7-12 . . . 111

The Number One Problem	111
Why Teens Drink	112
The Effect of Alcohol on Driving	112
Factors Affecting Levels of Impairment	113
There is no Quick Way To Sober Up	113
Other Drugs	113
How To Recognize Drunk or Drugged Drivers	114
Encountering an Impaired Driver	114
Consequences of Drunk or Drugged Driving	114

Table of Contents

    Strategies To Reduce Drunk or Drugged Driving 115
    Seat Belts Really Do Save Lives 115
    Why People Don't Use Seat Belts. 116
    Messages for Parents 116
    Sample Materials and Activities 117
    Resources 121

Cults and Gangs, Grades 7-12 123

    What Do Gangs Do? 124
    Gangs: Myth and Reality. 124
    Why Teens Join Gangs 124
    Profile of a Teen Gang Member 125
    Types of Gangs 125
    Other Characteristics of Gangs 125
    Consequences of Gang Membership 126
    Are Gangs in Your Community? 126
    How To Report Gang Activity. 126
    What Are Cults and Who Joins Them? 126
    Warning Signs of Cult Behavior 127
    Alternatives to Gang and Cult Membership. 127
    Messages for Parents 128
    Sample Materials and Activities 128
    Resources 130

Bias-Motivated Violence, Grades 7-12. 131

    What is Bias-Motivated Violence? 131
    Who Are the Targets of Bias-Motivated Violence? 132
    What Generates Bias-Motivated Violence? 133
    Strategies To Stop or Reduce Bias-Motivated Violence 133
    Be Intolerant of Intolerance 134
    Messages for Parents 135
    Sample Materials and Activities 135
    Resources 138

Conflict Management, Grades 7-12. 141

    What Is Conflict? 141
    Conflict Role Models 142
    Inhibitors of Effective Conflict Management 142
    Triggers. 142
    Classes of Conflict 143
    Negotiating: Interest, Not Position 143
    Reaching Agreement 144
    Skills for Conflict Resolution 144
    Leaving Judgments Out of the Process 145
    Tips on De-Escalating Conflict 145
    Messages for Parents 146
    Sample Materials and Activities 146
    Resources 148

Building Blocks: Developing an Effective Presentation . . . 151

    About Learning 151
    How Children Learn. 151
    Experiential Learning Appeals to Teens. 153
    The Role of the Presenter. 153
    How To Be the Best — A Summary. 156
    Asking Questions of Your Audience 156

Table of Contents

    Choosing Activities for Your Presentation 156
    Case Studies 157
    Role-Playing 157
    Interactive Lecture 158
    Small Group Activities/Discussions 159
    Audio-Visual Materials 159
    Preparation Checklist 161
    Presentation Overview 161

Building Blocks: Youth-Led Projects 163
    Crime and the Community 164
    Building a Stronger Community Through Partnership 164
    Attitudes and Stereotypes: Barriers to Success 165
    The Needs and Task of Adolescence 165
    Youth-Led Projects Are Making a Difference 166
    The Four Rs of Successful Programs 166
    Calling All Teens: Recruiting Youth 168
    Planning for Success 168
    Don't Forget 170
    Publicizing Your Project 170
    Sample Materials and Activities 171
    Resources 174

Building Blocks: When a Youth Reports a Crime 175
    Why Many Young People Don't Report Crime 175
    The Trauma of Victimization 176
    Recovery From Victimization 176
    Responses of Adult Victims 176
    Responses of Child Victims 177
    Reacting to a Disclosure in the Classroom 177
    A Checklist 177
    Back in the Classroom 179
    Providing Appropriate Referrals 180
    The Presenter's Reaction 180

General Resources 181

Introduction

Talking With Youth About Prevention is intended to help law enforcement officers — and others everywhere who care about and work with youth — do the best job they possibly can in doing just what its name implies — talking with young people about the value of prevention, how to practice prevention, and how to lead prevention efforts. Youth as disproportionate victims of violence and other crimes in our communities need to know how to help themselves, each other, and the community. This *Guide* is designed to help you in your effort to help them.

Who should be talking with youth about prevention? Parents, school officials, religious leaders, civic leaders, older siblings, grandparents, neighbors — to name just a few. A large measure of the job, however, falls to law enforcement professionals. That is why this book is designed for them as the primary audience, but all those who share the task of bringing up children can benefit from the information in the book.

Talking With Youth About Prevention arose out of a clear need for a comprehensive reference for people who must make presentations to children in the kindergarten through 12th grade age group. Many excellent curricula, workbooks, brochures, coloring books, and other materials exist in specific subject areas or for specific age groups. But the essentials were not collected anywhere in a generally available form.

It was also clear that high turnover, reduced training budgets, and retirements of senior personnel in police agencies combined with a heightened concern by communities for the safety and well-being of their young people had created a need for solid information that a reasonably informed professional could work from, whether giving a 20-minute presentation or a series of classroom talks. The National Crime Prevention Council saw the need and took on the challenge. NCPC's network is wide. It has learned a great deal in working with practitioners around the country in school settings, in youth groups, and in general community-police relationships; its reproducible materials are widely regarded as among the best.

The topics were hard to select because requests for presentations run the gamut. One day, an officer may be talking to high school juniors and seniors about preventing date rape; the next day that same person may be talking with second graders about responsible bike riding. But the Document Development group helped us focus on key areas, which made an overwhelming prospect manageable.

How the *Guide* Is Organized

A survey of practitioners combined with the work of the Document Development Group of experienced professionals helped enormously in shaping the format of this *Guide*. It became apparent that the "K-6" and "7-12" categories were most readily useful. That is how the *Guide* breaks out substantive materials for presentations to youth with two exceptions. There was also a need for information on working together with youth on projects, on dealing with victimization disclosures, and on constructing the best presentation for a particular setting.

That is why the *Guide* is divided into three major sections. The first section contains materials for students in grades K-6 on self-protection, alcohol and other drug use, property crime and vandalism, gangs, traffic responsibility, and respect for police and the law. The next section, materials for students in grades 7-12, covers some shared territory but at an age-appropriate level: alcohol and other drugs, cults and gangs, motor vehicle responsibility, personal protection, sexual assault prevention. The third section consists of building blocks — information on how to make presentations, how to handle disclosures of victimizations, etc.

Within each chapter, you will find a summary, a general discussion of the subject and points to teach children, and detailed information on key issues, as appropriate. "Messages for Parents," is designed to help you shape presentations to adults about helping their children grow up safer and more secure. "Sample Materials and Activities" provide starter ideas; the "Resources" sections point to sources of further help.

Using This *Guide*

If you have made presentations to children before, you will probably be ready to go directly to subject-specific sections to review information and materials that can help you modify or enhance your talks. If you are relatively unfamiliar with — or unaccustomed to — working with youth, you might find some of the "Building Blocks" materials handy in helping you to develop your framework.

By having a fairly clear idea of your audience and what is being asked of you in terms of time and content, you can decide what points are most important to emphasize in your presentation. Repetition and discussion are important tools for learning; allow time for your audience to digest your points and explore their meaning. Any one chapter in this book has enough material for at least three or four presentations; select thoughtfully and don't feel the need to cover every point. Better that the young people learn two or three key points well than get confused in the flood of information!

The sample materials and activities are just that — samples. There are dozens, if not hundreds, of brochures, booklets, videos, and other materials that can augment any given subject. Moreover, your experience may suggest additions or improvements. Both the "General Resources" chapter and the specialized resources noted at the end of each chapter offer a wealth of information on how to find materials and activities that are relevant. Some of the materials are free; others are offered at low cost.

We hope you will feel free to update or augment materials in the *Guide*. There is no feasible way to bring you all the material that might have been helpful. If you're going to want to give in-depth talks on particular subjects, get more information, by all means. Try your department's crime analysis unit, the local library, a local criminal justice planning agency, or a nearby criminology or sociology department of a college or university, to name just a few resources beyond those spelled out in this guide.

In Performance

It's difficult to put into words the secrets of success in talking with young people about the sometimes scary, sometimes sensitive range of topics that crime prevention covers. If we were to offer you five general pieces of advice, they would be these:

- **Be yourself** — an adult, not another kid — but relax. Lecturing at attention won't invite the children to relax and open up to your messages.

- **Remember that children's fears and concerns are real,** no matter how silly or inconsequential they may seem from an adult perspective.

- **Show that you care.** Young people need direct signals that you are concerned about and care about them as people. They are not skilled at reading subtle signs and body language.

- **Repeat, re-emphasize, and ask for feedback.** Even older youth need to hear the point you're making and give it back in their own words — or better still practice it — in order for it to become knowledge they can actually use.

- **Give positive feedback.** It's been proved over and over that children learn more, and learn more quickly, if their successes are praised and their failures seen as opportunities for learning, not as personal disasters.

Your Reward

One of the best things about talking with children about prevention is that you are shaping the future — creating a future with more people who understand how crime can be prevented, more people who want to work together to build and sustain safer communities, and more people who have a positive understanding of the value and role of law enforcement. Best of all, you're helping to reduce the chances that these young people will become victims of crime or drugs.

For the Future

This book has been a monumental task; there are many ideas we did not hear and many choices we had to make. Please feel free to let us know what you think, what worked for you, and what you did that worked better! Write National Crime Prevention Council, Attention: Talking Feedback, 1700 K Street, NW, Second floor, Washington, DC 20006-3817. We'd like to hear from you.

Introduction

Self-Protection

Grades K–6

It is important that we begin teaching crime prevention to children when they are young — when habits are more easily established and we can most significantly influence the odds in their favor.

Using the information in this chapter, you will be able to teach young people to:

- avoid dangerous situations;
- be safe when they are home alone;
- be observant and report dangerous situations; and
- use the telephone properly

Crime Prevention and Personal Safety

Many of the more than 26 million children between the ages of five and 13 are left to care for themselves (and possibly younger brothers and sisters as well) without adult supervision at various times during the day or week.

To reduce their risks of becoming crime victims, children need self-protection information at an early age, reinforced and expanded throughout their childhoods. Children who are well-grounded in crime prevention and practice sound self-protection techniques are more likely to continue to use these throughout their lives.

The Latchkey Child

Latchkey child refers to children left to care for themselves — and sometimes for younger siblings — without adult supervision. There are more latchkey children now than ever before because of the increase in women working outside the home, the increase in the number of single-parent families, the decline of extended families, the absence of neighborhood connections, and the shortage of affordable child care.

Many children enjoy having the chance to take care of themselves and feel grown up when trusted with responsibility. Others may feel less confident. All of them at some time feel lonely, bored, or scared.

Statistics suggest that children at home alone are at greater risk of being involved in accidents; of being harmed by strangers, siblings, and friends; and of committing delinquent acts. It is especially important that they learn and practice personal safety techniques. There are a variety of skills discussed below that can help them reduce their risk of victimization.

Establishing a Routine

Teaching latchkey children to establish a routine will help them avoid feeling lost or abandoned; it allows them to plan activities that will keep them productively occupied and entertained.

Morning schedules may include such things as wake-up, time for breakfast, time to get dressed, time to complete chores, and time to leave for school. An after-school schedule may include such things as time to check in with a parent or other adult, time to eat a snack, time for homework, time for recreation (specifying where and with whom), time for chores, and time the parent will arrive home.

Learning To Use the Phone

For a child home alone, the telephone is the link to the outside. It can be used to alleviate fears and, most importantly, to report emergencies. But improper use can also increase a child's chance for victimization by people who may call to see if the house is empty or the child is home alone. All children should become comfortable with basic telephone skills. They should:

- know how to use all types of telephones, including rotary, dial, push button, and pay phone;
- know by memory their home phone number (including the area code), a parent's work number, and a friend's number;
- know how to dial the correct emergency number and the five basic steps to report an emergency:
    — Speak loudly, slowly, and clearly so the other person can hear and understand them.
    — Say "I have an emergency."
    — Tell the operator their name, the address where they are, and the phone number where they are.
    — Say why they need help.
    — Know not to hang up until the person they're talking to says it's OK.
- keep a list of emergency phone numbers posted by all the phones in the house;
- be prepared to use "safe statements" when they are home alone and answer the phone. Examples of such safe statements include:
    — "My mother is busy right now. Can she call you back?"
    — "My dad can't come to the phone right now. Can he call you back?"
    — "My mom is talking to the neighbor. Can I have her call you back?"

Learning Door Answering Safety

Children need to know what to do when someone comes to the door while they are home alone. Generally, it is advisable not to allow anyone — adult or child — inside the house; but if there are exceptions, they should be clear and written. The child should be able to see who is outside the door without opening it. Most importantly, a child should learn what to say without letting the person at the door know that he or she is home alone.

Basic door safety tips for children include:

- Always keep the door locked.
- When someone comes to the door, see who is there without opening the door.
- Look through the viewer or window to see if the person is a stranger or someone you know — never open the door for someone you don't know.
- Ask "Who is it?" without opening the door.
- Never tell anyone you are alone. Use a safe statement such as:
    — "My mother is busy right now."
    — "My father can't come to the door."
- Never hide a house key outside the house — someone else may find it.
- Never wear your house key outside your clothing for others to see.

- Discuss with your parents what you should do if you lose your key and can't get into the house.

Common Sense Personal Safety Rules

At Home

- Check the outside of your home for signs of anything unusual before you go in. If something doesn't look right, don't go in. Go to a neighbor's house or a pay phone to call the police.
- Be sure all the doors and windows are locked.
- When you go out, always be sure that you take your key and that the doors and windows are locked before you leave.
- Turn on the outside lights (such as the porch light) when it starts to get dark.
- If you go out after dark, leave a light on inside your home.
- Keep your bike and toys inside your home when you're not using them.

At School

- Always take the same route to and from school.
- Know where there are McGruff Houses (or similar block parent homes or designated, community-sponsored "Safe Places" such as fire departments) on or near your school route.
- Notice where there are pay phones on your school route in case you have to make a call in an emergency.
- If you ride your bike to school, keep it locked with a sturdy lock in the school bicycle rack.
- Put your name on your personal possessions so you can identify them if they are stolen or lost.
- Keep your money in your pocket or backpack until you need it.
- Don't leave anything you care a lot about in your desk, especially overnight.
- Keep away from strangers — especially in areas where you are away from others, whether around the bathrooms, playground, or outside the building. Report suspicious people or activity to a teacher immediately.

- Never accept a ride from anyone, unless your parents personally told you it was OK to ride with that person at that time.
- Go straight home after school, unless your parents specifically gave you permission to go somewhere else.

Out and About

- Keep your money safely concealed except when you're paying for something.
- Always try to walk or play with friends rather than by yourself.
- Let the adult responsible for you know where you are at all times.
- Don't take short cuts through areas where there aren't a lot of people.
- If someone follows you don't go near them. Change direction or cross the street. If they still follow you or if you feel scared, run to the nearest person you can find and ask them to help you. If they won't help you, keep running to the next person.
- If someone tries to grab you, run away and scream — make lots of noise.
- If you're in a public place like a shopping mall and get separated from your parent, don't go looking for him or her. Go to the nearest store counter and tell the employee that you have lost your mom or dad and you need help finding them.

Child Abuse and Touching Problems

According to the National Committee for Prevention of Child Abuse, most states' definitions of child abuse include the following:

- **physical violence:** intentional injury that may include severe beating, burns, strangulation, or human bites;
- **emotional cruelty and deprivation:** unreasonable demands on a child to perform above his or her capabilities and does so in an excessive or aggressive manner — examples include constant teasing, belittling, verbal attacks, and a lack of love, support, or guidance; and
- **physical neglect:** the failure to provide a child with

food, clothing, shelter, or medical care.

It's important that children learn to recognize situations that are abusive, know that they have the right to say no to behaviors that make them uncomfortable, to tell someone about what happened to them, and to expect corrective action.

Children are often taught about "stranger danger," but the reality is that most danger lies not with strangers but with someone the child knows. In most cases of child abuse, including sexual abuse and abduction, the offender is a family member, relative, or some other person the child knows and trusts. When this trust is violated, the child feels confused and does not know what to do. Particularly in the case of sexual contact, the child may not know that what has happened is not only wrong, but it is a crime; that he or she is not at fault; and that it's OK to talk about it.

- An estimated three million suspected child abuse incidents are reported every year in the United States.
- The average age of a child abuse victim is 7.9 years.
- Each year, an estimated 1,000 children die from child abuse, and those who survive often suffer lasting pain and even disability from serious injuries and emotional trauma.
- Abused children are at high risk for becoming involved with alcohol and other drugs; they are more likely to run away or to become involved in crime and violence.

Sometimes there are no easily discernible signs of child abuse. However, according to the American Academy of Child and Adolescent Psychiatry, the following symptoms may serve as signals of abuse:

- sleep problems and nightmares;
- depression or withdrawal from family or friends;
- seductiveness;
- statements that their bodies are dirty or damaged, or expressed fear that something is wrong in their genital area;
- refusal to go to school;
- delinquency;
- secretiveness;
- unusual interest in, or avoidance of, all things sexual;
- suggestions of sexual molestation in drawings, games, or fantasies;
- unusual aggressiveness; and
- suicidal behavior.

A note of caution: Some of these symptoms may be signals of other problems in a young person. If a child is unusually aggressive or depressed, it doesn't necessarily mean that he or she is suffering from abuse. Children with symptoms should be referred to a professional for accurate diagnosis of the problem.

Approaches Used To Attract Children

According to the Rape Crisis Network, there are nine types of approaches and techniques used by child molesters:

- **Bribes** (offender is usually known to the child):
    - "I'll give you a present (money, toy, etc.)."
    - "I'll take you to the amusement park."

- **Games and fun** (offender is usually known to the child; games lead to intimate body contact):
    - tickling;
    - hide under the blanket;
    - play doctor;
    - hide items under clothes.

- **Emergency** (offender is usually a stranger):
    - "Your mom is sick, and she asked me to bring you to the hospital."

- **Lure of opportunity** (offender is usually a stranger):
    - Offender may offer the child a modeling career or some other exciting job and then take pornographic pictures or engage in molestation.

- **Authority** (offender may be known to the child and takes advantage of the respect a child has for authority):
    - a stranger tells the child he is a policeman and

may even wear a uniform, carry a badge, and have a flashing light in the car;
— a relative may use position as a family member to trick a child into sex games;
— a teacher may use his or her authority to abuse a child.

- **Assistance** (offender is usually a stranger):
  — "My dog is lost; will you help me find it?"
  — "I'm lost, will you show me _____?" (often a popular landmark, school, or big building).

- **Attention/affection** (offender is usually known to the child):
  — "I won't like you anymore if you don't … "

- **Threats/fear** (offender is usually known to the child):
  — "I'll go to jail if you tell."
  — "No one will believe you if you tell."

- **Psychological manipulation** (offender is usually known to the child):
  — "I'm doing this because I love you."
  — "What we're doing is all right — everyone does it."
  — "We're special friends. This is our little secret."

Why Children Don't Tell Adults About a Touching Problem

There are a variety of reasons why children don't tell. They include:

- They are afraid that no one will believe them.
- They believe that it's their fault and that they will get into trouble.
- They are frightened by threats made by the offender about what will happen if they tell someone.
- They have tried to tell an adult but didn't know the right words, or may have described the situation in a way that the adult didn't understand what they were talking about.

- They may not know that the sexual activity was wrong.

Open and honest communication between caring adults and children about their bodies and the difference between acceptable and unacceptable touching can lesson many of these fears and help children feel more comfortable about asking for help. Children should fully understand these key concepts:

- No one has the right to ask a child to keep secrets from his or her parents. Presents and surprise parties are OK, because the child knows when the secret stops.
- No one has the right to touch a child in a way that hurts him or her or makes him or her feel uncomfortable.
- No one has the right to ask a child to touch them is a way that makes him or her feel uncomfortable.
- Children have the right to say no, even to an adult.

Strangers

While most child abuse is committed by someone the child knows, it is also important that children learn to use suitable caution with strangers. Children should use special caution when approached by a stranger and be familiar with common tricks and lures that a stranger might use to win their trust or friendship.

Messages for Parents

- Children think in literal terms. For example, parents may find them playing with other knives after they have been instructed not to play with a specific knife. Be very specific about what you tell and ask them.
- Set limits, rules, and policies that are best for your family, not what you are told other parents allow.
- Be clear and consistent.
- When teaching personal safety skills, parents should work to build confidence rather than use scare tactics.
- Playing "what if" with a variety of scenarios can assist in improving the child's judgment. Switch roles sometimes.

Self-Protection • Grades K–6

- Parents need to know their children's friends, their habits, and where they tend to hang out.
- Working to keep communication lines open can be rewarding:
  — children need to feel free to come to parents about anything;
  — work to frame ideas as positive messages; and
  — work to build personal communication skills.
- Work with the child to rehearse and anticipate concerns and potential problems. Look at typical daily situations, such as:
  — what to do when traveling to and from school;
  — what to do when arriving home;
  — what to say if someone comes to the door or telephones;
  — what to do in the event of negative peer pressure; and
  — how to cope with emergencies.

Sample Materials and Activities

Coming and Going

Objective:
To identify ways to tell if your home looks safe to enter and ways to demonstrate responsibility when leaving home.

Time:
30 minutes.

Materials:
None.

When left home alone, children must understand the concepts of responsibility and safety. Role-play situations in which the children are home alone. Ask them to list situations they think it's important to know about. Focus the activity on steps they should take when entering and leaving a house or apartment.

Brainstorm a list of things to check before they walk in the door: Include looking for signs of anything unusual like broken windows, open doors, a strange car in the driveway, or an unusual light being turned on. Discuss what a child should do if he or she notices anything unusual.

Also, discuss what children should do before they leave their home. Include such things as locking windows and doors, turning lights on or off, and telling someone where they are going. To conclude the activity, ask for volunteers to practice techniques to use when leaving home. Ask children to enter the classroom as if it were their home and apply the techniques that you have discussed with the class. Have several students repeat the exercise until the class feels comfortable with the techniques.

Door Answering Safety

Objective:
To identify rules for door safety.

Time:
30 minutes.

Materials:
None.

Define door safety and explain that the door helps keep a home secure; however, it works only if it is kept shut and locked. If the door is opened to a stranger, a child is vulnerable to danger. (See "Learning Door Safety" and "Commonsense Personal Safety Rules" sections in this chapter.)

Sample activities: The following scenarios should be acted out with a child playing the role of "door answerer" and you as the "person at the door." Reverse roles and recruit children to play both roles.

1. A stranger comes to the door and identifies himself as a delivery man. He says he has a package for your mother and needs a signature to verify delivery. Ask for a volunteer and act out the scenario. At this point, the children should already be familiar with the rules on door safety. Practice ways the participants can respond to someone at the door without opening the door or revealing any personal information.

2. When the child answers the door and asks who is there, a man replies: "I'm a friend of your mother's. I've come by to drop off a cake." Again, you will play the role of the stranger.

3. A person who says she is selling subscriptions to children's magazines knocks at the door and wants to offer you a special deal. Act out this scenario and make it clear to the children that no matter how appealing such an offer is never open the door. Instead, ask them to come back later.

Wrap-up: Repeat the rules of door safety.

Telephone Skills

Objective:
To familiarize children with the telephone.

Time:
15 minutes each.

Materials:
"Calling for Help" handout.

Use the "Calling for Help" handout to teach children the basic concepts of using the telephone.

Children should memorize their area code and telephone number. Have them point it out on the mock-up phone. Children should also know where pay phones are along their routes to and from school, the store, the library, and places they play, and they should know how to use a pay phone. They should understand that if they don't have a quarter for the call, a combination of nickels and dimes will work, and that they can call the operator or 911 without any coins (assuming that this applies in their area).

Practice answering the phone as though the children were at home, remembering two important rules:

- Never tell anyone you are home alone.

- Never give any personal or family information over the telephone. Use safe statements whenever necessary.

Practice what to do with an obscene phone call or a caller who won't hang up. Remind children that they don't have to talk to strangers, even over the phone.

Discuss emergencies. These include crimes, fires, or accidents that involve injuries. What's not an emergency? What should they be able to be able to tell about the emergency? (Their name, their location, the phone number they are calling from, what happened, and whether someone is hurt. See "Learning To Use the Phone" section in this chapter.)

Have children describe two or three emergencies and role-play them encountering the emergency and making the appropriate call.

Self-Protection • Grades K–6

Calling for Help

Remember to

- Stay calm.
- Speak slowly.
- Give your full name.
- State the problem clearly.
- Explain where you are and where the problem is.
- Follow the emergency operator's instructions carefully.

In many areas, 9–1–1 is the all-purpose emergency number.

The emergency number where I live is

_____ (Police)

_____ (Fire)

_____ (Rescue)

Self-Protection • Grades K–6

McGRUFF™ SAYS– Here are 5 ways to play it safe!

When you're playing, alone, or with a friend, remember to be smart, and be safe. Follow my directions, and play it safe!

1. Never get into a car with a stranger, or someone you don't trust.

2. Never open a door to a stranger, or someone you don't trust.

3. Never let anyone touch you who makes you feel unsafe.

4. Remember to always lock your doors at home—and remind your parents, too!

5. One more tip—keep your bicycle locked up whenever you leave it—so it'll be there when you get back!

TAKE A BITE OUT OF CRIME®

© 1985 The Advertising Council, Inc.

A message from the Crime Prevention Coalition and the Ad Council.

Resources

State and Local Contacts

Boy Scouts
Girl Scouts
Local Kiwanis International chapter
Local child abuse prevention chapter
Local Campfire, Inc., chapter
Local victim assistance organization
Local public and private schools
Local libraries
YMCA/YWCA
4-H clubs

National Contacts

American Bar Association
740 15th Street, NW, Ninth Floor
Washington, DC 20005
202-662-1000

A national legal resource center for child advocacy and protection.

Children's Defense Fund
25 E Street, NW
Washington, DC 20001
202-628-8787

Provides a strong and effective voice for the children of America who cannot vote, lobby, or speak up for themselves. CDF pays particular attention to the needs of poor, minority, and disabled children. Its goal is to educate the nation about the needs of children and encourage preventive investment in children before they get sick, drop out of school, or get into trouble. An extensive publication catalog is available at no cost.

Child Welfare League of America
440 First Street, NW, Third Floor
Washington, DC 20001-2085
202-638-2952

A federation of over 650 public and voluntary child welfare agencies, community-based and regionally organized, who work with children and their families on critical issues such as child abuse, adolescent pregnancy, adoption, out-of-home care, child day care, and homelessness.

National Center for Missing and Exploited Children
2101 Wilson Boulevard, Suite 550
Arlington, VA 22201
703-235-3900 or 800-843-5678

Serves as a clearinghouse for information on missing and exploited children, provides technical assistance to citizens and law enforcement agencies, and offers training to law enforcement. A number of publications are available at no charge.

National Coalition Against Sexual Assault
912 North Second Street
Harrisburg, PA 17102
717-728-9764

Crisis intervention and long-term counseling; provides group and individual counseling. Works with all age groups.

National Committee for the Prevention of Child Abuse
332 South Michigan Avenue, Suite 1600
Chicago, IL 60604
312-663-3520

A volunteer-based organization that is dedicated to involving all concerned citizens to prevent child abuse. Sponsors public awareness and chapters located in all 50 states provide services, education and training, conducts research and evaluation, and provides state and national level programs.

National Crime Prevention Council
See "General Resources" section.

Publications

Massachusetts Committee for Children and Youth. *Preventing Child Abuse: A Resource for Policy Makers and Advocates.* 1987. Available from National Committee for Prevention of Child Abuse, 312-663-3520.

National Crime Prevention Council. *Keeping Kids Safe Kit.* 1997. Available from NCPC, 202-466-6272.

National Safe Kids Campaign. *National Safe Kids Campaign.* 1997. Available from the Campaign, 202-662-0600.

Police, Their Job, and Respect for the Law

Grades K–6

This chapter examines the role of police officers in the community, discusses common attitudes and stereotypes that block communication between police and youth, and provides tips for improving communication and developing rapport with youth. It will help you teach children ages five to 11 to:

- name at least two things that law enforcement officers do as a part of their jobs;
- develop a good rapport with law enforcement officers;
- know how to signal or stop someone if they need assistance; and
- understand the benefits of rules and laws to a community.

An Effective Partnership

The partnerships among law enforcement, schools, and other youth-serving agencies are important. Police officers in the community can provide a variety of important services:

- advice and counsel on crime prevention to agency administrators working with youth;
- crime prevention education directly to youth;
- greater public understanding of the role of law enforcement; and
- positive relationships with youth.

Overcoming Negative Attitudes and Stereotypes

Developing a positive relationship between police officers and youth is key to helping young people prevent crime. Basic to this relationship is mutual respect and open communication.

A variety of factors influence the perceptions of police officers by youth including:

- news media;
- popular movies and television programs;
- perceptions of parents and other adults;
- perceptions of older siblings; and
- perception of peers.

A Teaching Guide for Law Enforcement and Others

Unfortunately, many of the contacts that youth have with police officers are negative. For example:

- A parent uses the police officer to threaten children into behaving: "You'd better … , or I'm going to tell that police officer to come over here and … "

- Children hear their parents complain about having received a traffic ticket, accompanied by highly negative remarks about all police.

- An elementary school child hears an angry battle between his parents and police officers who were called to intervene in a domestic dispute.

- A youth hears accusations of police brutality in television reports.

- Parents who emigrated from a country where police officers were agents of government suppression and brutality may convey to their children feelings that police should be feared and distrusted.

- A child overhears a neighbor who was the victim of a burglary complain, "If the police had been doing their job, this never would have happened."

An important starting point for building a positive relationship with young people is to help them understand the difference between a police officer's responsibilities on the job and his role as a community resident. A law enforcement officer has the same feelings as anyone else, as well as a family, a home, and a difficult job to perform.

It's also important for officers to understand that while they may be victims of negative public perceptions, youth also are victims of negative attitudes and stereotypes by adults.

Developing a Positive Relationship With Youth

The following pointers can help you develop or cement a rapport with young people:

- Talk *with* young people; don't patronize.
- Be prepared to have your commitment, reliability, and sincerity tested.
- Tell the truth.
- Be yourself — don't try to be a peer.
- Be sure your conversations with young people are relevant to their experiences.
- Present a balanced picture of the job of a police officer.
- Be patient. Learning takes time.
- Avoid stereotypes and accept each person as an individual.
- Listen to and be receptive to a young person's ideas and concerns.
- Encourage youth to ask questions, but don't feel that you have to know all the answers. Admit it if you don't know an answer, and tell the questioner you'll get back to them. Be sure to follow through.

Understanding the Police Officer's Job

The following are some important points to make with young people. Someone who joins the police force promises to uphold the law and to protect and serve the people by:

- preventing crime;
- patrolling the streets and helping people in trouble;
- helping to find lost children, pets, and property;
- investigating crimes;
- catching criminals;
- writing reports about daily activities;
- answering calls from people who need help;
- providing first aid to people who are hurt; and
- helping people to settle arguments peacefully.

Your community has entrusted its police force with the authority to maintain safety, protect residents, support laws, and arrest people who break laws or endanger residents. In order for police officers to do their jobs, they must have the respect and cooperation of everyone in the community.

Police officers have jobs that are important, difficult, and sometimes dangerous. In order to help them do their best, all police officers must attend classes where they are taught about laws, how to use different kinds of equipment, and how to handle difficult situations.

Police officers aren't perfect. They make mistakes just like everyone else. Many people expect police officers to always be able to prevent crimes, but there are many more criminal opportunities than there are police officers.

There are several things that people can do to help police officers keep communities safe:

- Practice personal crime prevention strategies.
- Work with others in the community to reduce causes of crime.
- Cooperate with police officers.
- Report crimes and suspicious activity.

Rules and Laws

Rules are guidelines for acceptable behavior made by persons in authority such as parents, teachers, group leaders, or the school principal. Other people may be able to take part in making them, too. Rules can serve large or small groups of people.

Laws are public rules that apply to all people living in a certain area, such as a town, city, county, state, or nation. Laws determine what conduct is allowable, helping people to live together in an orderly manner. Laws are made by elected officials in governments at local, state, and federal levels. There are several different kinds of laws:

- **Some laws require certain behavior.** Examples include the requirement that children attend school until they reach a certain age or that employers must pay their workers at least a minimum wage.

- **Some laws prohibit certain behavior.** Examples include those that say you can't drive faster than the posted speed limit, you can't steal or vandalize someone's property, or you can't beat someone up.

- **Some laws give status or rights.** For instance, a law says that people 18 years of age and older have the right to vote, that persons over a certain age have the right to obtain a driver's license or to run for public office.

- **Some laws resolve disputes.** Examples include laws that define the terms of a contract when two people disagree about it, that determine the rightful owner of property when the title is questioned, or that define rights to money and property.

- **Some laws allocate responsibility and authority within the government.** For example, the Constitution, the supreme law of the United States, says that the U.S. Congress has the right to pass laws. State and local laws may give a police officer the right to arrest people. The health department may be given the right and duty to inspect public food services, to be sure cleanliness and good food handling rules are obeyed.

People obey laws for a variety of reasons, including:

- They agree with the values that the law supports.
- They believe that obeying the law is good for individuals and society.
- They are afraid of the legal consequences (penalties) of breaking the law.
- They are afraid that other people will find out that they have broken the law.

Messages For Parents

- Be sure your children understand why there are rules in the form of laws, and that all communities have them. Explain the rules that govern your family.

- Help children understand how laws are made under our form of government, and the role of the criminal justice system, including police, in helping us keep these laws.

- Set a good example. Children imitate adults, especially parents, in their thoughts and actions. Don't badmouth police or show disrespect for the law.

- Don't use the threat of a police officer or the threat of going to jail to coerce a child into behaving.

- Remember, police don't make the laws; they only enforce them.

- Help children separate the fantasy of television and movie police from real police duties.

Sample Materials and Activities

What a Police Officer Does at Work

Directions: Try to find the words listed below. The words are twisted all kinds of ways — horizontal, vertical and backwards. All of the words tell what a police officer does at work.

Find: Help People, Direct Traffic, First Add, Catch Criminals, Write Reports, Lost Pets, Settle Argument

A	H	C	O	L	O	S	T	P	E	T	S
B	E	O	D	P	C	D	O	C	T	M	P
F	L	D	T	E	A	I	S	A	B	A	N
G	P	P	E	C	T	R	E	R	M	D	R
T	P	D	I	K	C	E	T	G	S	C	A
B	E	M	F	D	H	C	T	U	T	M	T
Q	O	T	I	C	C	T	L	M	R	A	H
S	P	C	R	V	R	T	E	E	O	E	S
V	L	O	S	M	I	R	N	N	P	H	A
W	E	D	T	D	M	A	D	T	E	T	I
M	Z	T	A	P	I	F	C	S	R	N	S
P	M	U	I	W	N	F	K	V	E	L	E
C	N	W	D	K	A	I	M	T	T	W	B
T	T	V	K	R	L	C	H	V	I	H	I
Z	D	T	I	E	S	J	K	D	R	V	Y
X	C	B	S	M	B	A	B	T	W	E	H

Rules and Laws — Who Needs Them?

Objective:
To understand why rules are important.

Time:
15 to 20 minutes.

Materials:
Chalkboard or flip chart.

All communities have rules and laws that keep the residents safe. Ask the children to name some rules. Then ask them for examples of what could happen if the rules are broken. What are the penalties, who could get hurt?

Rule	If It's Broken ...	
	Penalties	Who Gets Hurt

Suggestions

- **traffic rules:** stopping at red lights, having a driver's license, driving on the correct side of the road;

- **school rules:** walking — not running — in the halls, leaving the building when there is a fire drill, raising your hand when you want to be called on in class; and

- **family rules:** calling your parent at work when you get home from school, not using the stove when there's no one to help you, not letting anyone into the house when your parents aren't home.

Resources

State and Local Contacts

Police Athletic Leagues
Boy Scouts
Boys & Girls Clubs
Local police departments
Local Fraternal Order of Police chapter
State police departments

National Contacts

Fraternal Order of Police
National Legislative Office
309 Massachusetts Avenue, NE
Washington, DC 20002
202-547-8189

Seeks professional advancement of policemen. Conducts seminars and compiles statistics. Publications cover law enforcement topics, law enforcement equipment, etc.

International Association of Chiefs of Police
515 North Washington Street
Alexandria, VA 22314-2357
703-836-6767

Membership organization of law enforcement executives that develops policy, offers advocacy and training, and publishes information on the full range of policing issues.

Police Executive Research Forum
1120 Connecticut Avenue, NW
Suite 930
Washington, DC 20036
202-466-7820

A national membership organization of progressive police executives from the largest city, county, and state law enforcement agencies. PERF is dedicated to improving policing and advancing professionalism through research and involvement in public policy debate. It provides an extensive number of publications on a wide range of law enforcement topics.

Publications

Center for Civic Education. *Foundations of Democracy, Elementary Level.* 1996. Available from the Center for Civic Education, 818-591-9321.

Constitutional Rights Foundation. *Police Patrol.* 1991. Available from CRF, 213-487-5590.

Traffic Responsibility

Grades K–6

Traffic is one of the few "daily life" areas in which younger children learn that obeying the law routinely can protect them. Respect for the law and a sound prevention attitude can begin here. Many young people are injured each year in traffic-related accidents that could have been prevented if they had understood and practiced the rules and laws of traffic safety. This chapter will help you to help young people become responsible pedestrians, cyclists, and car passengers. You will be able to teach children ages five to 12 to:

- understand pedestrian laws and safety tips;
- know the importance of traffic laws for bicycle and safety tips;
- know the importance of seat belt use; and
- explain why these rules help keep them safe.

Educating young people — as pedestrians, passengers, or drivers of unmotorized vehicles — to understand the importance of obeying traffic rules and laws will not only increase their chances of avoiding accidents, but may also positively influence their own future behavior and actions by their friends and families.

Pedestrian Responsibility

Every year, approximately 957 child pedestrians are killed in traffic accidents in the United States. Many of these accidents could have been prevented if the children had known and practiced pedestrian safety. While adults usually recognize the dangers of carelessness around auto traffic, children are generally more impulsive and less aware of these dangers. According to the National Highway Traffic Safety Administration (NHTSA):

- Most young children are injured near their home or on their own street.
- Most accidents happen between 3:00 and 5:00 p.m.
- Most accidents occur in fair, warm weather.
- Twice as many boys are injured as girls.

Effective pedestrian education program should:

- focus on the ways children usually behave around traffic;
- teach skills rather than information because children learn by doing;
- use realistic settings for practice sessions; and
- reinforce positive behaviors.

Pedestrian Safety Rules

Many pedestrian accidents can be prevented by obeying these rules — which are laws in many states:

- **Walk on the sidewalk.** If there is no sidewalk, walk facing traffic and keep as far to the left side of the roadway as possible.

- **Cross at the intersection.** Drivers expect pedestrians at crosswalks, not in the middle of the block. At traffic signals with pedestrian signals, wait until the signal says "WALK." If the signal starts to flash "DON'T WALK" while you're in the street, keep walking. Don't run because you might stumble and fall. At corners without pedestrian signals, wait until the traffic signal facing you is green; look left, then right, then left, then over your shoulder for cars turning right on red; then cross when it is safe.

- **Stop.** Always stop at the curb or edge of the road to look for cars before stepping into the street.

- **Look.** Always look in both directions before crossing the street. Look left-right-left for approaching traffic. Continue to look until you've crossed the street safely. If you can't see the traffic because of parked cars (or something else), move carefully to a spot where you can see and an approaching driver can see you.

- **Walk, don't run.** Walking gives you time to look for cars and gives drivers time to see you, too.

Myths and Facts About Pedestrian Responsibility

NHTSA has compiled a list of some common myths children believe about pedestrian safety:

Myth: A green light means it's safe to cross.

Fact: A green light means you have permission to stop and check for cars. Look left-right-left. If you see no vehicles, cross the street but keep looking as you cross. Be alert for vehicles turning right on red.

Myth: You are safe in a crosswalk.

Fact: You may cross at a crosswalk, but you must stop at the curb before crossing. Look left-right-left for cars. When the way is clear, cross but keep looking.

Myth: If you see the driver, the driver sees you.

Fact: The driver may not see you. Because of their size, children are sometimes harder to see than adults. Make certain that the driver sees you and stops before you cross in front of the car. Try to make eye contact with the driver.

Myth: The driver will stop if you are in a crosswalk or at a green light.

Fact: The driver is supposed to stop, but he or she might fail to do so. The driver may not see you because his view is blocked. He may drive through a traffic light illegally or turn without looking for pedestrians.

Myth: Wearing white at night makes you visible to drivers.

Fact: White or light clothes are better than dark, but even if you are wearing bright white clothes, drivers can have a hard time seeing you at night. It is safest to wear reflective clothing, carry a lighted flashlight, and walk facing traffic.

Bicycle Responsibility

Many bicyclists are young, inexperienced, and unfamiliar with the laws and rules for bicycling.

Inexperience and lack of knowledge lead to hundreds of deaths and thousands of accidents each year:

- Seven hundred and sixty-one bicyclists were killed in 1996 in collisions between bicycles and motor vehicles on roadways.

- An additional 59,000 were injured in traffic crashes.

- Head injuries are the most serious type of injury suffered by bicyclists and the most common — and preventable — cause of fatal injury. Wearing a bicycle helmet can reduce head injuries by 85 percent.

Young people account for a high percentage of bicycle deaths and injuries. About one-third of the deaths and two-thirds of the injuries involve children under the age of 15. Many deaths and injuries can be prevented through education and training.

According to the American Automobile Association's (AAA) Traffic Safety Department, bicycle accidents involving youth occur most frequently when a bicyclist:

- enters the roadway from a driveway, alley, or mid-block location without first stopping and looking for motor vehicles;

- enters an intersection without obeying traffic signs or signals;

- swerves left into the path of a car suddenly and without warning; or

- performs an unsafe or unexpected behavior, such as riding against the flow of traffic or riding double.

Bicycling Rules

- **Always wear a helmet.** Every cyclist should wear an approved safety helmet when riding. In many places, it is the law. Helmets should fit snugly but comfortably with a chin strap and buckles that stay securely fastened. The Snell Memorial Foundation and the American National Standards Institute have established safety standards for helmets.

- **Keep your bike in good condition.** Be sure the mechanical parts of your bike work well and that there are reflectors on both the front and back. It's also wise to have a bell or horn on the handlebars to alert pedestrians that you are approaching.

- **Under nine years of age, don't ride in the street.** Experts advise that most children under the age of nine aren't skilled enough to respond properly to traffic situations they may encounter on the street. For them, riding in the street is dangerous and should be forbidden.

- **Ride on the right side of the street.** Move with the flow of traffic.

- **Stop and check.** Come to a complete stop and look for traffic before entering a street from a driveway, parking lot, or sidewalk.

- **Obey traffic signs, signals, and pavement markings.** If a bicyclist must ride on the street, he or she must obey traffic laws that apply to motor vehicle operators.

- **Give cars and pedestrians the right-of-way.** It's an act of courtesy, and it's safer, too. This concept must be explained to most children in grades K-6.

- **Keep both hands on the handlebars.** Carry packages or books in a basket, carrier, or backpack.

- **Watch for car doors opening into the roadway or driveway.**

- **Ride in single file.** Bicyclists should always ride in single file on the right side of the roadway.

- **Use hand signals to let drivers know what you are going to do.**

- **Don't ride double.** A bicyclist has trouble balancing and steering a bicycle if he has a passenger on board.

- **Never hitch a ride on a truck or other vehicle.**

Preventing Theft

Thousands of bicycles are stolen each year. Most are stolen from home, but they can be stolen from parks, schools, stores, and libraries. People can help prevent bicycle theft or recover a stolen bicycle by following these rules:

- **Register your bicycle.** Check to see if your local police have a registration program. At a minimum, record the serial number and keep it in a safe place together with a photograph of your bike.

- **Lock your bicycle whenever you leave it.** Most bikes that are stolen weren't locked. Use a high quality "U" lock or a padlock and case-hardened chain. Put the chain through the front wheel, the frame, and then around a post or bike rack. Be sure your bike is fastened to something solidly anchored, so that it can't just be lifted off and carried away.

- **Don't leave your bicycle outside where it can be seen.** Keep it locked out of sight in a garage, a secure hallway, or a basement.

Responsible Use of Tricycles and Other Riding Toys

Tricycles, Bigwheels™, and other riding toys can cause serious injury or even death if used improperly. When talking with young children, keep the rules clear and simple. Young children are less likely to obey complex or unclear rules. Obeying the following rules recommended by the AAA and other child safety experts will help keep young riders safe:

- **Ride on the sidewalk, in your yard, or at the playground.** Stay out of the street!
- **Do not go so fast that you cannot turn or stop.**
- **Don't wear loose-fitting clothes, such as baggy shirts or jeans.** Your clothes could get caught in the wheels of your toy.
- **When you ride on the sidewalk, watch out for people who are walking.**
- **When you come to an intersection or a driveway, get off your tricycle and walk it to the other side.** Drivers who are backing out of driveways can't always see you, even if you can see the driver.

Skateboarding Wisely

Skateboarding can be an enjoyable form of recreation for young people as long as they follow safety rules. The most common injuries to skateboarders are stress fractures. Experienced skateboarders and skateboard manufacturers add that a number of accidents also occur when riders attempt to maneuver skateboards through traffic or parking lots. In a number of communities, skateboarding in certain areas is forbidden by law.

Skateboarders are strongly encouraged to skate in areas that are specifically designated for the sport. If there is no such area, skateboarders and their parents should petition their local government to create one. Remember these additional safety tips:

- **Good protective equipment is critical for skateboarding.** Riders should wear hard, plastic-shell safety helmets and leather gloves. Knee and elbow pads are also strongly recommended in order to avoid serious and painful cuts, scrapes, and bruises.
- **Know your own ability.** If you think a trick on your skateboard might be too difficult, don't try it! Progress slowly and practice until you have enough experience to safely perform a trick.
- **Know your own equipment.** Always check your skateboard for any problems (for example, loose wheels) before riding it. Taking your skateboard to a sport shop for service will help keep you safe and help your skateboard last longer.
- If there are no skateboard designated areas in your town, remember to stay on sidewalks and out of streets and parking lots. If you ride on sidewalks, slow down at each driveway and check for cars backing out.
- **Show consideration for walkers.** Ride your skateboard in areas that are not crowded with walkers or joggers.

Roller Skating Responsibility

Roller skating has been a recreational and fitness sport for more than 100 years. Recently, the advent of in-line skating has renewed the popularity of roller skating.

The use of roller skates in streets and parking lots can result in injury if the rider is inexperienced. Skates that are not properly maintained can malfunction.

The National Safety Council and the Roller Skating Rink Operators Association recommend the following safety tips:

- **When shopping for skates, make safety and comfort important considerations.** For proper ankle support, test the plastic of the boot on your roller skate: If you can squeeze it, the material is not strong enough to give you reliable support. Take socks with you to ensure a proper fit.

- **When skating outdoors, always wear protective equipment.** Elbow and knee pads, light gloves, helmets, and wrist guard's are recommended. In the event that you fall, safety equipment can reduce your risks of injury.

- **Skating while wearing headphones is dangerous.** The headphones can keep you from hearing other skaters, cars, cyclists, or runners approaching from behind or the side.

- **Be conscious of others.** Skaters, pedestrians, joggers, and bicyclists frequently use the same areas. When skating backwards, avoid collisions with other people.

- **Skate on the right-hand side of sidewalks, bike paths, and trails.** Pass on the left, after yelling "passing on the left." Pass only when it is safe and there is enough room between you and the person you want to pass.

- **Don't skate in the street.** When you are crossing a street, look left-right-left and cross when it is safe to do so. Remember that you must obey all traffic regulations.

Buckling Up Is the Law

Many children forget to buckle their seat belts when they ride in a car, even though they know they should. Parents and other adults have a strong influence on children's attitudes and behavior about the importance of buckling up every time they ride in a car. According to the U.S. Department of Transportation:

- Seat belts can reduce the risk of fatal and serious injury to front seat passengers by 45-50 percent.

- Unrestrained vehicle occupants suffered more reported injuries than those who were using seat belts.

- Less than 1 percent of passenger car occupants reported as restrained were thrown out of the vehicle, while 17.3 percent of the unrestrained occupants were ejected. Seven out of ten of those ejected were killed.

Seat belts save lives and reduce injuries for the following reasons:

- They keep people from being thrown around inside the car if the car stops suddenly or crashes.

- They keep occupants from being thrown out of the car in a crash.

- They keep the driver in better control of the car.

Children may offer a number of excuses for not using safety restraints. These can be rebutted with facts:

Excuse: My parents don't wear seat belts.

Fact: Everyone should wear a seat belt. Just because someone else isn't being safe doesn't mean that you shouldn't be. Buckling up is smart, and it's the law in most states.

Excuse: We're not going on a long trip.

Fact: Most crashes happen close to home.

Excuse: Seat belts can trap you in a vehicle.

Fact: Most people are injured or killed by getting thrown out of the car through the windshield or the door. Seat belts help keep the people inside the car from getting knocked unconscious or badly hurt by hitting their heads. People who wear seat belts are more likely to be able to rescue themselves in nearly every kind of crash, including when the car catches on fire or goes into the water.

Excuse: Seat belts are uncomfortable.

Fact: The people who make cars try hard to make sure that they're as comfortable as possible. Wearing a seat belt may be inconvenient, but it is always more comfortable than recovering from cuts, bruises, internal injuries, and broken bones from a car crash.

Excuse: Seat belts will wrinkle my clothes.

Fact: Seat belts may wrinkle your clothes, but a few wrinkles are better than stitches or broken bones.

Messages For Parents

- Parents need to decide on the values, limits, and guidelines they want to impress upon their children when discussing traffic responsibility. You are probably your child's most significant role model for traffic responsibility.

- You need to be sure your behavior demonstrates you believe in obeying the law — practice good pedestrian behavior, use safety belts, wear helmets where appropriate, and don't drive while impaired.

- Work with the children to rehearse and anticipate their concerns concerning traffic responsibility.

    — establish guidelines and think through ramifications of those guidelines;
    — role-play different scenarios to reinforce learning and build judgment; and
    — establish rules concerning transport of your child by others.

- Inspect bikes, tricycles, roller skates, etc. frequently for signs that repairs are needed or that equipment is worn out.

- Set clear limits for where your children may walk and ride.

- Recognize that, in general, limits for unsupervised travel should be adjusted as the child grows old.

- Insist that every child (and adult) in your car use proper safety restraints (seat belt or car seat).

- Help your child understand that obeying the traffic laws as a pedestrian is good training for becoming a driver some day.

- Draw parallels between good car driving habits and good bicycling/tricycling, etc., habits.

Sample Materials and Activities

Observing Road Signs

Objective:
To help children understand the importance of road signs.

Time:
Ten minutes.

Materials:
Pen or pencil and "Being Safe With Signs" sheet. (See sample materials.)

Understanding road signs is very important. Below these pictures of road signs are questions and beneath the questions are answers for you to choose from. Read each question and provide the best answer. Remember some answers are used more than once.

Laws and the Crazy Elephant

Objective:
To demonstrate how rules contribute to the safety of children and the community.

Time:
15 minutes.

Materials:
Photocopied sheets of "Laws and the Crazy Elephant" worksheet. (See sample materials.)

Audience:
Grades 2-4.

Discussion questions:
- What laws did Elliot break?
- Should Elliot be punished? How?
- What are some of the things that might have happened because Elliot disobeyed the law?
- Do you think Elliot learned why laws should be obeyed?

Being Safe With Signs

Fill in the blanks with the answers provided. Some answers are used more than once.

In these situations, you are either riding your bike or walking. . .

1. You have ridden up to #4. This sign tells you that you cannot make a _____.
2. You have ridden up to #1. You must _____.
3. You have walked up to #3. This sign tells you to _____ near the _____.
4. You are walking and see #9. This warns you of a _____ _____. You must _____, look and _____.
5. You see sign #5. It means NO _____ allowed. You must take another _____.
6. You have come to a traffic signal showing #6. You may _____.
7. You come to triangular sign with a red border. This is a sign and is # _____. You must yield _____ of _____ to the other _____.
8. You see sign #10. You should watch for traffic entering your path from the _____.
9. You are riding along and come to a one way street. This is sign # _____ and means DO NOT ____.
10. You are looking for a place to cross the street other than a corner. You may cross if you see # _____ which means crossing.

ANSWERS:
cross, walk, traffic, turn, yield, right, school, stop, listen, #8, enter, railroad, bicycles, #7, crossing, route, #2, pedestrian, way

Laws And The Crazy Elephant

There was once this crazy elephant named Elliot. He acted crazy because he did things without thinking.

When Elliot's birthday came, he got a brand new bike. He was very proud of this new bike and wanted to show it off. His mother said, "Now Elliot, you must let your father show you how to ride and teach you bike laws." Elliot really wanted everyone to see his new bike so when his mother went to the store, he decided to ride it to town. As he got close to town he noticed all the cars were headed straight toward him. He heard someone yelling, "Get over you dummy. You're on the wrong side of the road." Elliot kept on going. A little later he saw a red light hanging above him, and he pedaled right underneath it. He heard horns honking and people shouting, but he kept on going.

As Elliot rode into town, he saw his friend Jumbo. He hollered, "Hey, Jumbo, want a ride?" So Jumbo jumped on the handlebars. Elliot could not control the bicycle very well, and the cars started honking again. He decided it would be safer to ride on the sidewalk. Suddenly, he saw a trash can right in his path, and he turned to miss it. He ran right into a lady elephant and knocked her down. Elliot decided maybe he had to learn bike rules after all.

Resources

State and Local Contacts

Department of Motor Vehicles
State Highway Safety Office

National Contacts

American Automobile Association
Foundation for Traffic Safety
1440 New York Avenue, NW
Suite 201
Washington, DC 20005
202-638-5944

Provides books, films, and classroom curricula on traffic safety. Materials are designed to be used with several age groups. Topics include bicycle safety, alcohol-impaired driving, school bus safety, and pedestrian safety.

National Highway Traffic Safety Administration
US Department of Transportation
400 7th Street, SW
Washington, DC 20592
202-366-0123

Compiles statistics on traffic fatalities and distributes educational books and pamphlets to the public at little or no cost. Stickers, posters, and buttons that promote general traffic safety messages are available.

National Safety Council
Customer Service Department
PO Box 558
Itasca, IL 60143
800-621-7619

Promotes personal safety. The Council's free catalog lists low-cost pamphlets, booklets, posters, and displays on drinking and driving, safety restraints, and pedestrian safety.

Publications

American Automobile Association, Traffic Safety Department. *Bike Basics: A Guide to Safe Bicycling for Ages 10-15.* 1997. Available from your local AAA chapter.

American Automobile Association: Traffic Safety Department. *Traffic Safety Teacher's Guide for K-3.* 1997. Available from your local AAA chapter.

Alcohol and Other Drug Use Prevention

Grades K–6

A large number of children use alcohol and other drugs. Of particular concern for those working with children ages five to 11 are the so-called gateway drugs: alcohol, tobacco, and marijuana. Use of these drugs can be a precursor to involvement with other drugs.

To be truly effective, drug prevention education must be ongoing. Your one-time classroom presentation will help, but you need to work in partnership with other important members of the community — teachers, youth leaders, other young people, and parents — to ensure that clear, consistent messages are delivered over and over.

Age-appropriate lessons for children in each elementary grade build on and reinforce basic anti-drug messages. Materials, activities, and other resources are included to enable you to tailor your presentation to your community.

After reading this chapter, you will be able to teach children ages five to eight to:

- know that some drugs can help when they are sick but that, at other times, drugs are harmful; and
- know at least two reasons why they should not use alcohol, tobacco, or other illegal drugs.

Additionally, you will be able to teach children ages nine to 11 to:

- identify at least three ways that the use of alcohol and other drugs damages their bodies; and
- learn to make responsible choices about using alcohol and other drugs.

This chapter also includes a section on resisting peer pressure that is appropriate for children ages five to 11. There are tips on what a young child should do if he knows someone who is illegally using drugs or alcohol or finds drug paraphernalia. Finally, there are suggestions for involving young children in constructive activities in the community. When young people have a stake in community-building, they are less likely to become involved in activities that are destructive, such as drug use.

Youthful Substance Abuse

Problems with youthful substance use are significant:
- Every day 3,000 children begin smoking regularly.
- The younger an individual starts drinking and the greater the intensity and frequency, the greater the risk of using other drugs.
- By sixth grade, nearly 2 percent of children have used marijuana.

What Children Think About Alcohol and Other Drugs

Although every community is different, national surveys suggest that most children by age 11:
- know that marijuana, cocaine, and alcohol are drugs;
- think that beer, wine, distilled spirits, and wine coolers are relatively harmless;
- believe that fitting in with peers is the main reason some children use alcohol or other drugs;
- experience peer pressure to use drugs and alcohol as early as fourth grade;
- undergo a change in attitude toward alcohol and other drugs, from negative to more positive, as they mature;
- become skeptical of parents and teachers as reliable sources of drug information as they grow older; and
- think that talking about drug-related problems can be effective in preventing the use of alcohol and other drugs.

Risk Factors

No one can predict with certainty who will use drugs, but studies have identified factors that increase the likelihood that some young people will use alcohol and other drugs. These include:
- friends or siblings who smoke, drink, or use other drugs;
- adults in the home who abuse substances;
- a history in the biological family of substance abuse;
- family history of criminal or other antisocial behavior;
- a family environment lacking consistent direction or discipline;
- absence of strong anti-drug role models;
- poverty;
- a feeling of being at odds with or alienated from the family;
- poor academic performance, boredom, or a lack of connection at school;
- early antisocial behavior; and
- early experimentation with illicit substances.

The presence of any one of these risk factors doesn't guarantee that a young person will turn to alcohol or other drugs. There are many examples of resilient young people who beat the odds. However, as the number of risk factors increases, so does the probability of drug use.

Why Some People Use Drugs

The reasons people say they have for using alcohol or other drugs are varied. Young people using alcohol and other drugs cite emotional, physical, social, or intellectual reasons. A decision to use drugs can also be influenced by a young person's environment.

Emotional Reasons
- to feel more grown up;
- to feel more self-confident;
- to escape problems;
- to reduce stress and anxiety;
- to take a risk; or
- to assert independence.

Physical Reasons
- to feel relaxed;
- to stop pain;
- to feel good; or
- to increase energy or endurance.

Social Reasons

- to be accepted or admired by peers;
- to "loosen up";
- to overcome shyness; or
- to escape loneliness.

Intellectual Reasons

- to reduce boredom;
- to satisfy curiosity; or
- to improve attention span.

Environmental Influences

- movies, songs, ads, etc. that endorse substance use;
- stores that sell drug paraphernalia;
- easy availability of alcohol and other drugs; or
- family members and friends who use drugs.

Understanding the Five- to Eight-Year-Old

Children five to eight years old begin to learn how to cooperate and get along with others. Although their families are still very important to them, they are starting to develop their own identity apart from the family. Their world is expanding to include the opinions and influences of others around them, such as teachers, scout leaders, older siblings, and friends.

As these children learn more about their family environment and the world outside their household, they need to:

- learn about the difference between therapeutic medicines taken with adult approval (aspirin, prescription medicines, cough syrups) and substances that are dangerous or illegal, such as alcohol;
- know that drugs and other chemicals can cause harm;
- know how to call 911 (or the emergency number in their area) when someone has consumed something harmful (See the "Self-Protection" chapter); and
- know how to say no when someone wants them to take medicine or other drugs without their parent's OK.

Drugs That Heal and Drugs That Harm

A young child can be confused about a message on television. It may say, "Take two of our little yellow pills and you will feel good again." Sometimes it is difficult for a youngster to distinguish between the medicine for a stomach ache or an allergy and the uppers or downers that the 15-year-old boy across the street offered last weekend.

This distinction can be made for children ages five to eight by including alcohol, tobacco, and illicit drugs in the category with other things that should be avoided.

Young children know that some things are bad for them. They know that they shouldn't touch something that is very hot, such as the stove. They know that they shouldn't cross the street without looking both ways. They know that they shouldn't put dirty things in their mouths. Likewise, they must also learn that using alcohol, tobacco, and illicit drugs can be harmful to their bodies and their minds.

A young child isn't particularly impressed by the long-term effects of the use of alcohol or other drugs. Rather, he or she should be taught short-term or immediate negatives, such as:

- Alcohol can make you throw up, and too much alcohol at once can kill you.
- Smoking tastes bad, makes you smell bad, and turns your teeth yellow.
- Taking pills without your parent's or doctor's permission can make you very sick and can kill you.
- Using alcohol, tobacco, or other drugs is a crime and could get you into a lot of trouble.

Understanding the Nine- to 11-Year-Old

Children ages nine to 11 begin to accept more responsibility for their own behavior. They more strongly develop an identity as individuals apart from their family, and peer influence becomes stronger.

Children at this age usually know the difference between drugs they take when they are sick and drugs that are harmful and illegal. They may be responsible for taking their own medicines, such as aspirin, cough syrup, or allergy pills.

As part of the growing-up process, children ages nine to 11 are likely to try new behaviors and test information they've been given. They may be asking themselves such questions as:

- What is smoking like?
- How does drinking alcohol make you feel?
- Why can't I smoke and drink now?
- What does it mean when someone is an alcoholic?
- My brother smokes pot and says there isn't anything wrong with it. What should I do?

For this age group, it's important that they:
- learn how to make responsible decisions about their behavior;
- learn to cope with negative peer pressure;
- feel comfortable standing up for themselves and what they feel is right; and
- know where they can go if they have a problem.

Resisting Peer Pressure

Learning the facts about drug use and its consequences is only a start. It's also important that young people learn how to make healthy decisions and resist pressures from friends and classmates to experiment. Here are five steps to saying no intelligently when someone offers alcohol or other drugs:

- Understand what is happening. Someone is asking you to use something that is illegal and will harm your body and mind. You have a serious choice to make.
- Make a mental list of reasons why you should say no, such as:
  — It's illegal.
  — It's bad for you — it can make you sick or kill you.
  — You could get caught and be punished by your parents, the school, or the juvenile justice system.
  — You could lose your other friends.
- Say no! It takes courage to stand up for what you feel is right. You don't have to give a reason if you don't want to. Here are some ways to say no:
  — "No, I really don't want to."
  — "No thanks, it's against the law."
  — "No, I don't want to mess up my body."
  — "No, I'm not into chemicals."
- Offer another choice. Use this step if the person who is pressuring you is a friend that you want to keep. Choose an activity that is legal and will be fun for both of you:
  — "No, thanks. Let's play basketball instead."
  — "I don't do that. Do you want to go bike riding with me?"
- If your friend doesn't respect your "no," you should walk away and find friends who don't use drugs.

Understanding the Effects of Alcohol and Other Drug Use

Children ages nine to 11 have a better understanding of the negative effects of using alcohol, tobacco, and other drugs. They can be taught that:

Alcohol
- puts brain tissue to sleep;
- can make you nauseated or dizzy;
- slows reaction time;
- affects judgment; and
- is addictive.

Tobacco
- causes lung, throat, and other cancer;
- causes other respiratory illnesses;
- causes heart disease; and
- is highly addictive and difficult to quit.

Marijuana

- builds up in the brain;
- attacks the immune system, which can make you vulnerable to serious illness;
- affects memory function; and
- affects judgment and coordination.

"I Saw Someone Using Drugs. What Should I Do?"

A presenter on drug prevention should be ready to answer this question from a young audience member: "What should I do if I see someone who is smoking pot? Or … a kid drinking beer? Or … a neighbor sharing pills with my brother?"

There are two types of situations you might face when you are presenting information on drug prevention. The first might be in the form of a disclosure: "My brother (or sister or friend) is doing drugs. What should I do?"

This sort of disclosure can be difficult to handle if you are not prepared. It is important to listen to the young person and let him or her know that it's OK that you have been told. It is also important to know your agency's policies on disclosure.

The second type of question is less difficult to handle: An audience member might have seen a syringe in a public place and not known what to do about it. Suggest these guidelines for young people to remember if they see someone drinking alcohol or doing drugs, or if they find drug paraphernalia:

- Tell a trusted adult (such as a parent, a school teacher, a police officer, a counselor, or a minister) immediately.
- Don't get involved with the drinker or drug user. Tell an adult and let him or her help the person.
- Don't touch any drug paraphernalia that you find. Tell an adult and let him or her take care of it.

Community-Building Alternatives to Drug Use

In many communities, young children — even as young as five or six — are actively engaged in community-building activities that are changing attitudes toward the use of alcohol and other drugs. These youngsters are channeling their energies and efforts into making their neighborhoods and schools healthy, drug-free places. They are cleaning up parks and playgrounds on Saturday mornings, performing puppet shows for neighborhood children, marching in anti-drug and anti-alcohol rallies, monitoring younger children, or helping elderly neighborhood residents with outdoor chores.

These neighborhoods are acknowledging young people as responsible citizens who can contribute to the well-being of the entire community. This benefits both the community and the young people:

- The residents benefit from the creative and constructive energies of the young people.
- The young people benefit by feeling needed and valued. A young person who feels valued is less likely to turn to alcohol and other drugs. He or she will make an effective partner in a community effort to prevent the use of alcohol and other drugs.

Other Alternatives to Drug Use

There are other healthy and legal alternatives to meet a young person's physical, emotional, intellectual, and social needs. For example:

- **Physical alternatives.** To satisfy physical needs and to relax, try:
    — basketball or other team sports;
    — tennis;
    — body-building;
    — dancing;
    — swimming; or
    — walking.

- **Emotional alternatives.** To satisfy emotional needs, try:
  — talking with a friend or counselor about your problems;
  — keeping a diary; or
  — volunteering your time in your neighborhood.

- **Intellectual alternatives.** To stimulate your mind, try:
  — drawing pictures;
  — writing poems or stories;
  — composing music;
  — learning to play a musical instrument; or
  — starting a new hobby.

- **Social alternatives.** To get involved in positive, healthy social activities, try:
  — spending time with friends who are drug-free;
  — joining a youth organization; or
  — starting your own group to work on a cause that is important to you.

Messages for Parents

- Start to talk with your child about alcohol and other drugs when he or she is young. Give accurate information and answer questions with facts. Explain that drug use is wrong, harmful, and unlawful, and reinforce this messages.
- Listen carefully to your child.
- Help your child feel good about himself or herself.
- Help your child develop strong values.
- Encourage self-discipline by giving your child daily responsibilities, and expect your child to be accountable.
- Be a good example to your children; don't use illegal drugs. If you choose to drink or smoke, do so only in moderation.
- Help your child learn to counter negative peer pressure. Encourage your child to stand up for what is right.
- Make family policies that help your child say "no."
- Encourage healthy, creative activities that help your child develop lifelong skills.
- Know where your children are, whom they are with, and what they are doing at all times.
- Be selective about your children's viewing of television and movies that portray or suggest drug use as acceptable.
- Team up with other parents to establish and support a drug-free climate in your neighborhood.
- Support school administrators who are tough on drugs, and encourage prevention education.
- Monitor your children's status, performance, and behavior in school.
- If you suspect that your child has a problem with alcohol or other drugs, speak to your doctor or a trained school counselor

Sample Materials and Activities

To Be What You Want To Be, Be Drug-Free

Objective:
To inform children of the advantages of being drug free.

Time:
5 minutes.

Materials:
Pen, pencil, or crayon; "To Be What You Want To Be, Be Drug-Free" handout. (See sample materials.)

Distribute the "To Be What You Want To Be, Be Drug-Free" handout to the class. Ask them to put themselves in the picture by drawing what they want to be. Discuss how drugs could hurt your chance of being what you want to be.

Learning About Medicine

Objective:
To teach children that there are some people from whom it is OK to take medicines, and that there are certain people from whom they should not take medicine.

Time:
15 minutes.

Materials:
Pen, pencil, or crayon; "Circle the People Who Can Give You Medicine and X Out the Ones Who Can't!" handout. (See sample materials.)

Distribute the "Circle the People Who Can Give You Medicine and X Out the Ones Who Can't!" handout to the class. The class should be instructed to circle the people who can give you medicine and X out the ones who can't. Discuss all the pictures after finishing the exercise. Ask the children how they can tell that it's OK to take medicine from someone.

Seek and Find: Fun Things To Do With Friends and Family

Objective:
To teach children fun things to do with friends and family.

Time:
20 minutes.

Materials:
Pen or pencil; "Seek and Find" handout. (See sample materials.)

Ask the students to complete the "Seek and Find" handout. Have them think up other fun things to do and make their own seek and find, as an extra activity.

Alcohol and Other Drug Abuse Prevention • Grades K-6

NAME: _____

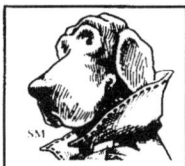

CIRCLE THE PEOPLE WHO CAN GIVE YOU MEDICINE AND X OUT THE ONES WHO CAN'T!

YOUR DOCTOR

YOUR FRIEND

YOUR MOTHER

YOUR GRANDMOTHER

A STRANGER

NOTE FOR TEACHER AND PARENT: The message of this game is that there are some people from whom it is OK to take medicines, and there are some people from whom you should not take things. Before giving this sheet to your children, have a discussion on this subject and then give the activity to them to reinforce the message.

Alcohol and Other Drug Abuse Prevention • Grades K-6

Seek & Find

These words and phrases are in the puzzle, but they are written up, down, sideways, backwards and diagonally. Can you find them?

ACTIVITIES	DRUGFREE	CRIME DOG
CLUBS	USERS ARE LOSERS	FAMILY
WINNERS	SPORTS	MCGRUFF
HOBBIES	SAY NO TO DRUGS	FUN
COOL	TAKE A BITE OUT OF CRIME	FRIENDS

```
S T A E B X Y N O P S E I T I V I T C A
T A Z K G B F O T K E L L A T E H A L B
P K Y Q A L V U I M D S X R O I C O R J
T E A N E W A T N O F D Y Z B M L W O Z
Z A V H O S E R K Z P N B A E S U Y T N
F B B U Q T S A L M L E N T N C B T N H
O I L H J D O G C R I I A I U E S E S B
B T L R W A T D N E K R R L O P U R E G
D E S I T M C G R U F F U G O F E D T E
K O B C E O J Y T U I U N R G S W A H R
M U R M S F H N A N G C T E O R L J I E
B T G A L A O W P B T S S L G E S A R S
W O C R I M E D O G E W E H E L N W O E
C F T E N I S E H I H R B L S U T L S E
N C D L H L E O S O A G E E R F G U R D
H R A T B Y C M W S I F C O A I R A E D
U I S C O V I F R A M N L O O C M I N G
T M O U R M L E P N A T B M N A D O N E
L E N P T E S L A T R E N A K C U D I S
D X Y Z T U M T O H O B B I E S P C W P
```

Resources

State and Local Contacts

Alateen
Alcoholics Anonymous
Boys & Girls Clubs
Boy Scouts, Girl Scouts
Campfire, Inc.
Junior League
Local Alcohol and Drug Abuse Commissions
Local and State Education Departments
Local and State Health Departments
Regional Drug Enforcement Administration Office,
 Demand Reduction Coordinator
Regional Federal Bureau of Investigation Office,
 Drug Demand Reduction Coordinator

National Contacts

American Council for Drug Education
164 West 74th Street
New York, NY 10034
800-488-DRUG

Educates the public on the dangers of alcohol and drug use. Develops educational media campaigns and publishes anti-drug materials.

National Congress of Parents and Teachers
330 North Wabash Avenue, Suite 2100
Chicago, IL 60611-3690
312-670-6782

Designs kits and brochures on drugs and related issues for local chapters. Focuses on positive alternatives to drug use.

National Council on Alcoholism
12 West 21st Street
Seventh Floor
New York, NY 10010
212-206-6770

Nonprofit organization combating alcoholism, other drug addictions, and related problems. Provides drug prevention and education materials, public information and policy advocacy, and medical and scientific information.

National Crime Prevention Council
See "General Resources" section.

National Institute on Drug Abuse
U.S. Department of Health and Human Services
Parklawn Building, Room 10A39
5600 Fishers Lane
Rockville, MD 20857
301-443-1124

Produces a national directory of drug abuse and alcoholism treatment programs, as well as leaflets and drug abuse statistics. Sponsors research, model programs, and technical assistance for drug use prevention programs nationwide. Publishes a nationwide listing of training opportunities.

Office for Substance Abuse Prevention
National Clearinghouse on Alcohol and Drug Information (NCADI)

See "General Resources" section.

Publications

American Council for Drug Education. *Building Drug Free Schools.* 1986. Available from the Council, 800-488-DRUG.

National Crime Prevention Council. *McGruff's Elementary Drug Prevention Activity Book.* 1992. Available from NCPC, 202-466-6272.

U.S. Department of Education. *Learning to Live Drug-Free: A Curriculum Model for Prevention.* 1990. Available from NCADI, 800-729-6686.

U.S. Department of Education. *What Works: Schools Without Drugs.* 1987. Available from NCADI, 800-729-6686.

U.S. Department of Health and Human Services, Public Health Service, Alcohol, Drug Abuse, and Mental Health Administration, Office of Substance Abuse Prevention. *10 Steps to Help Your Child Say "No": A Leader's Guide.* 1988. Available from NCADI, 800-729-6686.

U.S. Department of Health and Human Services, Public Health Service, Alcohol, Drug Abuse, and Mental Health Administration, Office of Substance Abuse Prevention. *The Fact Is ... You Can Prevent Alcohol and Other Drug Problems Among Elementary School Children.* 1988. Available from NCADI, 202-729-6686.

Conflict Management

Grades K–6

Violence continues to be a problem in communities of all sizes throughout the United States. In an effort to stem this tide, more people are recommending that conflict management training become a mandatory class in schools. Until that time comes, small pockets of practitioners are introducing techniques to children to help them effectively manage conflicts in everyday life. The thought of conflict makes most adults uneasy, but it is amazing to see young children effectively using "I feel" messages and assisting their elders to better manage conflict in their lives. This chapter will introduce you to a variety of techniques that are successful with children. Please refer to the "Conflict Management Grades 7-12" chapter for additional information and resources.

Using the information in this chapter, you will be able to teach children ages five to 11:

- the causes of conflict;
- a variety of methods to handle a conflict; and
- constructive methods of expressing anger and frustration.

Causes of Conflict

We often tend to find ourselves working, playing, learning, and living in an atmosphere that creates inappropriately expressed emotions. Lack of communication and conflict management skills helps create a climate that favors violence through:

Competitive atmosphere: People feel they must work against one another instead of with each other.

Poor communication: An inability to appropriately communicate feelings and needs or to deal constructively with disagreement frequently moves a person to react to stress in a violent manner.

Inappropriate expression of emotion: As frustration and anger increase, people choose inappropriate, aggressive methods of expressing their emotions. This can range from totally repressing their concern to reaching for a weapon.

Lack of conflict management skills: In many cases, a person is able to see no alternative to violence. Recent research indicates that young people who have conflict management skills are less inclined to resort to violence.

Methods of Managing Conflicts

Many conflict management techniques can be practiced by even young children. The following is a sampler of techniques that are usually helpful:

- **Reflective listening.** "Active listening" is another term for this technique. (See information in "Conflict Management Grades 7-12" chapter.) This is a skill that contributes to successful conflict management rather than a technique for managing conflict. It allows the parties to clarify their perceptions before identifying the problem and choosing appropriate solutions.

- **Smoothing.** This method simply means choosing not to focus on the conflict at this time, for any or all of a variety of reasons. "Smoothing" is another term for conflict avoidance. You may choose smoothing when it is not the right time or you do not have time to focus on the conflict. Needs and feelings must be considered when attempting to smooth over a conflict. Children need to know that things do not always have to be settled immediately — especially because waiting a few minutes enables people to talk more calmly.

- **Storytelling.** This method helps the parties to distance themselves from the conflict. You begin the story with "Once upon a time," then describe events (but not people) that led to conflicts. When you reach the point of the conflict, stop and ask for suggestions in the story and conclude the tale. Ask the parties in conflict if the solutions are helpful and will assist them with future conflict.

- **Time Out.** This method can be used to get the parties to work out their own solutions. Instruct participants that you are going to put them in a quiet place for three to five minutes, where they will have an opportunity to work out their problems without your assistance. At the end of the allotted time, see where they are in the process. If the problem has been addressed, praise them and their solution. If it is unresolved, assist them in the process.

- **Fight Fair Method.** This is a method that you can introduce as an activity and teach as a technique. It is based on the Bach and Wyden's Fight Fair Method:
    — State the facts as calmly as possible. Refer only to the present situation, not the past or the future.
    — Express how you feel. Talk about your feelings without making negative remarks about the other person.
    — Find out what you can do about the situation. Try and think of a solution that will satisfy all participants.

- **Mediation.** This method utilizes a third party to help the disputing parties to identify their problems and generate options. Children as young as elementary-school age have been successful as mediators or conflict managers. The mediator establishes ground rules that include an opportunity for each person to tell his story without interruption, stating the problem and telling what happened during the event; generating possible solutions; and choosing the appropriate solution (or if the problem no longer exists, asking the young people to brainstorm alternative methods of handling the conflict).

- **Stopping fights.** This usually requires third-party intervention. First, you must stop the fight and get tempers cooled, then work out the situation. Methods of defusing the situation could include establishing a cooling-off corner, getting the participants to practice deep breathing exercises, or having the parties sit silently for a few moments in order to settle down.

Messages For Parents

- You are your child's most important role model. The child learns from what you do in handling disputes and disagreements far more than from what you say about how to handle them.

- Don't threaten children with the police to break up an argument. Law enforcement officers should not be regarded as the bogeyman threat in conflict resolution.

- Learn about anger management and conflict resolution techniques so you can help your child use them effectively.
- Support and reward your child for using non-violent ways to settle disputes. Don't allow other adults or children to suggest that your child is a sissy or wimp for using non-violent methods.
- Get help — counseling, advice, therapy — if you are resorting to violence yourself. Free or low-cost counseling is available almost everywhere. If nothing else, talk to an understanding friend or to a religious leader.
- Help your child learn to be aware of and critique violence on TV shows and in movies, videos, books, and magazines. Monitor children's TV and movie watching.
- Find out if your child's school or a group in your neighborhood has a conflict resolution or mediation program — either one providing training or one offering help in settling disputes or one doing both. If there's no program, start one!
- Don't allow name-calling or other taunting. Teach children to respect the feelings and sensitivities of others.
- Help children learn to "fight fair" when they disagree.
- Check in your local library for books or magazine articles on how to help children manage conflict without using violence.

Sample Materials and Activities

Elementary Conflict Management Process

Introduction and Ground Rules

1. Introduce yourselves.
2. Get agreement to these five rules:
   — Face the person looking at you.
   — Do not interrupt the other person; each person will get a chance to talk.
   — Do not call each other names or put them down.
   — Be honest.
   — Agree to work to solve the problem.

Defining the Problem

3. Decide who is going to talk first.
4. Ask Person #1 what happened — repeat what you heard him or her say. Ask Person #2 how he or she feels because of what happened and why.
5. Ask Person #2 what happened — repeat what you heard him or her say. Ask Person #2 how he or she feel because of what happened and why.

Generating Solutions

6. Ask Person #1 what he or she can do to resolve the part(s) of the problem for which he or she is responsible.
7. Get agreement from Person #2.
8. Ask Person #2 what he or she can do to resolve the part(s) of the problem for which he or she is responsible.
9. Get agreement from Person #1.
10. Ask each person what he or she could do differently if the problem happened again.
11. Ask them is the problem solved.
12. Ask parties to tell their friends that the conflict has been solved, so that rumors will not spread.
13. Write up an agreement and have everyone sign it and receive a copy.
14. Congratulations!

The Lorax

Objective:
To define conflict and talk about ways of resolving the conflict in a win-win manner.

Time:
20 to 30 minutes.

Materials:
The Lorax, by Dr. Seuss. Random House, 1971.

Through storytelling, you can assist children to define conflict and talk about successful resolution methods.

Read aloud *The Lorax* by Dr. Seuss. (You may want to consult with the teacher or the youth division of the public library for storytelling tips for the age group you are working with.) This is an excellent story since it involves a conflict between two strong opponents.

After reading the story, ask the children to define the conflict. Get their opinions on ways that the problem could be solved (a) without conflict and (b) in a win-win manner.

If time is available, you may want to ask some of the children to role-play the story and work out the characters' differences.

The Bug Board

Objective:
To identify things that make you angry.

Time:
30 minutes.

Materials:
Crayons and drawing paper.

Discuss feeling bugged — that is, annoyed and angry. Have children draw and label a picture of something that bugs them. (Remember that younger children may need to dictate labels to you. Check in advance with the teacher about their writing skill level.)

Have the children show their pictures to each other and discuss them. Then post them on the bulletin board. This becomes the bug board. Use the situations on the board for the students to explore in discussion.

- What do you do when someone or something bugs you?
- What else could you do?
- Do two or more of you get bugged by the same thing? If yes, how could you help each other get rid of the bugs?
- What could you easily do to stop bugging someone?

Feelings

Objective:
To identify the four basic feeling groups and understand that having feelings and expressing them is OK.

Time:
20 to 45 minutes.

Materials:
Paper plates, crayons, markers, yarn, popsicle sticks.

Discuss the four basic feelings groups with the class:

- glad/happy;
- mad/angry;
- sad/unhappy; and
- scared/afraid.

Talk about each feeling and ask the students if they have ever felt that way. Ask them to make facial expressions to show different emotions. Have the students make masks for each of the four feeling groups using the paper plates, crayons, markers, yarn, and popsicle sticks. After they have finished making their masks, make up and act out a story that includes each of the four feeling groups.

Talk with the students about some of the things people do when they are happy, sad, angry, or scared. Explain that everyone has these feelings and they are all okay. Talk about the difference between safe and unsafe ways to show your feelings. For example:

- Safe:
  — talking;
  — laughing;
  — crying;
  — having a quiet time; and
  — reading.

- Unsafe:
  — yelling or shouting;
  — calling names;
  — teasing;
  — hitting, pinching, or kicking; and
  — running away.

Resources

State and Local Contacts

State law-related education office
State and local Bar Associations
Department of Health
Department of Education

National Contacts

American Bar Association
Standing Committee on Dispute Resolution
740 15th Street, NW, Ninth Floor
Washington, DC 20005
202-662-1000

The ABA Standing Committee on Dispute Resolution, established in 1978, sponsors over 400 dispute resolution programs nationwide. It also provides many other services, including a clearinghouse for information on conflict mediation. The ABA also has a program that encourages law offices to adopt local high schools and assist them in implementing conflict mediation programs.

Community Board Program
1540 Market Street, Suite 490
San Francisco, CA 94102
415-552-1250

One of the largest conflict mediation organizations in the country, Community Boards works to foster mediation programs in schools, universities, businesses, and any other place where conflict may arise. They provide curriculum training and assist in starting conflict mediation programs.

Iowa Peace Institute
917 Tenth Avenue
PO Box 480
Grinell, IA 50112
515-236-4880

Provides periodic training opportunities throughout the year and advises in developing training programs that meet the needs of a particular school.

National Coalition Building Institute
1835 K Street, NW, Suite 715
Washington, DC 20006
202-785-9400

NCBI is a national organization committed to building coalitions and reducing prejudice in a variety of different work places. The organization works with businesses, universities, schools, and any other groups that have coalition potential. NCBI sponsors three institutes every year to educate the public about conflict mediation and prejudice reduction.

National Institute for Dispute Resolution
1726 M Street, NW
Washington, DC 20006
202-466-4764

A private, nonprofit, grant making and technical assistance organization that facilitates the synthesis of ideas drawn from practitioners and research in dispute resolution and translates them into improvements in the field. Publications, including a periodic newsletter, are available.

Street Law, Inc.

See "General Resources" section

Community Relations Service
U.S. Department of Justice
600 E Street, NW, Suite 2000
Washington, DC 20530
202-305-2935

This division of the Justice Department was established in 1964 to assist communities experiencing racial strife. Today, the organization works in communities all around the country, mediating disputes that have arisen as a result of racial strife.

Publications

Community Board Programs. *Classroom Conflict Resolution: Training for Elementary Schools.* 1987. Available from Community Board, 415-552-1250.

Community Board Program. *Conflict Managers Training Manual for Grades 3-6.* 1986. Available from Community Board.

View NIDR's catalog on www.nidr.org for dispute resolution publications.

Gangs

Grades 4–6

Gangs — often bringing fear, drug activity, community destruction, and random shootings — have become a serious problem in many communities, including small cities and towns that once were thought to be immune.

Gangs offer some children a way to escape problems at home, but gang membership creates serious and sometimes life-threatening problems on the street. The gang may serve as surrogate family, friend, and protector, but gang members live violent lives, characterized by turf wars, drug traffic, and slain friends.

Children in elementary school are targets for gang recruitment. Parents, teachers, law enforcement, and community leaders need to work together to educate preteens about gangs, provide alternatives to gang activities, and ensure that children feel wanted and secure in their family environment.

This chapter focuses on preventing young children from joining gangs. Robert Burgreen, Chief of the San Diego Police Department, says, "If there is one hope, it is to change the young peoples' minds before they get into this type of activity." To offer children realistic alternatives to gangs, the community must address the causes of gang activity. Gang prevention must involve parents, teens, schools, community leaders, and local government agencies.

In this chapter, you will learn to teach children ages nine to 11 to:

- understand why preteens are tempted to become involved with gangs;
- describe the criminal activities and characteristics of gangs;
- identify the negative consequences of gang membership;
- recognize the signs of gang activity in your community; and
- know that there are alternatives to gang membership.

Gangs and Youth

Gangs are organized groups involved in territory protection, criminal activities, violence, and/or drug use and sales. Gangs often use special symbols on their clothing or to mark their territory, and they frequently require a strict code of behavior from their members.

Gangs often function as surrogate families for young people. They offer identity and a sense of belonging, and they attract young people who are not part of a strong family unit. However, gangs do not provide their members a caring and safe environment. Many gangs require their members to steal, fight, or even murder. As gang members, young people run the risk of being arrested by police or being hurt by rival gang members.

According to some experts, the increased attention focused on the gang problem by the media has caused some youth to imitate gang behavior in their own community. The glorification of gangs in some films and music videos contributes to the problem.

Law enforcement officials are encountering second- and third-generation gang members, indicating that gang membership has become a way of life in some areas.

Young gang members arrested for selling drugs or committing other crimes are often subject to lighter penalties than older members, encouraging some gangs to recruit young children — even eight- and nine-year-olds — who can "take the rap" for older members.

Profile of a Preteen Gang Member

Anyone — male or female, wealthy or low-income, from a functional or dysfunctional family — can be recruited to join a gang. Experts, however, have identified high-risk characteristics that can contribute to a youth being vulnerable to gang membership. Gang members more often:

- are male, although girls are also recruited;
- have other family members or friends involved with gangs;
- have seen excessive use of alcohol or other drugs in the home;
- live with a single parent, grandparents, other relative, or foster parents;
- have poor academic performance;
- are known for fighting and general aggressiveness in early adolescence, or have chronic delinquency problems;
- experience poor living conditions or poverty; and
- have experienced social deprivation or isolation.

Of course, the existence of one or more of these conditions does not guarantee that a young person will join a gang. Identifying risk factors helps a community understand which youth may be more vulnerable to gang recruitment than others, and enables the community to be more effective in implementing anti-gang programs.

Why Preteens Join Gangs

In many neighborhoods, the adolescent social environment draws younger children into gangs. Street gangs breed in areas where social and economic conditions and meager job opportunities offer young people a bleak future. After-school and recreational activities aren't available, causing youths to turn to gangs for social activities, excitement, and "something to do."

A young person who turns to gang membership may be motivated by some or all of these needs:

- **Surrogate family:** Young people join gangs to receive the attention, affirmation, and protection they may feel they are lacking at home.
- **Identity or recognition:** Some youth join gangs for status they may feel they are lacking if they are unemployed or performing poorly at school. If young people don't see themselves as the smart ones, the leaders, or the star athletes, they join groups where they feel they can excel.
- **Family history:** Many gang members carry on a family tradition established by their fathers, grandfathers, uncles, cousins, or brothers, whom they see as role models.
- **Protection:** Some youth join gangs to protect themselves. They may be directly threatened or feel

threatened; they may feel alienated from the police and other authorities. They rely on fellow gang members to help protect them from attacks by outsiders seeking revenge — or paybacks — for harm caused by third parties.

- **Intimidation:** Some young people feel pressure from friends to join a gang. Some actually feel threatened to join by other gang members.
- **Money:** Gang members can share profits from drug trafficking and other illegal activities. To a teen, money is often translated into social status. A teenage girl in Detroit remarked, "If a guy ain't got no crew [gang], he probably ain't got no cash. Guys with no paper don't interest us."

Gang Criminal Activities

Members of gangs are frequently arrested for burglary, attempted murder, or possession of firearms. Members are also known to engage in drug trafficking and extortion of small businesses and individuals. In many large cities, drug trafficking has allowed gangs to expand into the suburbs and outlying areas.

Vandalism is the crime very frequently committed by gang members. Although often viewed as a victimless crime, vandalism is destructive to communities and their residents. It creates a sense of fear and isolation among residents while damaging a neighborhood's sense of pride. The gang may see vandalism not as a criminal or malicious act but as marking of its territory.

Gangs seek recruits to carry drugs and weapons and carry out risky assignments, such as robberies or drug sales. The prime source for gang member recruitment is public schools.

Signs of Gangs

Gang members frequently use graffiti, special clothes or emblems, hand signals, and tattoos to signify membership and to communicate their gang affiliation to others. Each gang has its own signals, signs, colors, jewelry, and costumes that serve to identify gang members and promote group solidarity.

- It is very important to gang members that their symbols be protected from insults by rivals. Street gangs are humiliated by having their symbols degraded by others. A gang's emblem or identifying sign drawn upside down by a rival gang member can set off a gang war.
- Many gangs select special colors to identify their members. Gang members (or others) can be murdered for wearing the wrong color in the wrong neighborhood.
- Gangs vandalize buildings and public property by marking their territory with special symbols.
- Some gang members wear tattoos that identify the wearer as a member of a particular gang. The tattoo can include the gang's name, initials, or symbols.
- Gangs use hand signals — "throw signs" — to communicate gang affiliations or to challenge rival gangs. These signals or signs are made by forming letters or numbers with the hands and fingers, depicting the gang symbol or initials.

While many gangs consist of relatively informal small bands of young people, some are highly organized and use state-of-the-art communication equipment, including police radio frequency monitoring devices.

Consequences of Gang Membership

When youngsters seek membership in a gang, they often focus on the companionship and excitement they feel the gang can offer. Many children don't understand that their decision to join gang can also result in many negative short-term and long-term consequences, such as:

- being at risk of being beaten, knifed, or shot at by rival gang members;
- facing bodily injury in violent gang initiation rites;
- placing their family and friends at risk of being threatened or harmed;
- being forced to commit crimes;
- arrest and time in jail; and
- facing pressure to use or sell alcohol and other drugs.

Keeping Children From Joining Gangs

Experts agree that younger children will be less likely to join a street gang if:

- they are educated about the dangers of gang membership, especially violence;
- they have positive teenage role models;
- they are involved in healthy activities; and
- their parents teach them that joining a gang is wrong and why.

Preteens must be encouraged to become involved with sports programs, hobbies, youth clubs, after-school activities, church programs, and community-building projects, such as neighborhood cleanup activities. When presenting information about the dangers of joining a gang, have with you a list of community organizations and programs that offer positive alternatives to gangs membership, including:

- Boys & Girls Clubs, Scouts, or other youth group;
- programs offered in neighborhood parks;
- programs offered at libraries;
- sports programs, such as swimming, basketball, football, or soccer;
- community service projects; and
- hobby clubs, such as performing, model airplanes, hiking, or chess.

Ask the young people to generate their own list first, but be ready to prompt them with programs or ideas that are actually feasible or available in their area.

Messages for Parents

- Young children need to recognize and obey family rules. Set rules that are clear, fair, consistent, and enforceable.
- Some children join gangs because they are not involved in other activities. Encourage your child to join a sports team, learn to play a musical instrument, join a youth club, or play with other children who have developed positive interests and hobbies.
- Be sure to tell and show your child that you love him or her.
- Tell your child that it is wrong to join a gang.
- Discuss with your child why gangs aren't as attractive as they may appear. Find out what, if anything, your child finds attractive about gangs. Try to ask questions and conduct dialog instead of lecturing.
- Know where your child is, and with whom, at all times.
- Be aware of the level of drug and gang activity in the neighborhood. Warn your child about the dangers of using alcohol or other drugs, or associating with people who sell or use drugs.
- Know your children's friends.
- Talk to other parents or community residents about problems in the community. Form an action team to rid the community of drugs and gangs. You can:

    — Remove graffiti in your neighborhood;
    — Organize a residents' patrol;
    — Encourage after-school activities;
    — Help organize a class to teach parenting skills;
    — Find out if your child's school has gang awareness classes and if not, help start them;
    — Volunteer to take neighborhood children to the park;
    — Work with community organizations or agencies to educate parents about preventing gang membership.

Sample Materials and Activities

No One Can Enter Main Street

Objective:
To demonstrate the effects of gang activity on a community.

Time:
Five to ten minutes.

Materials:
None.

Throughout the history of gangs in America, members, young and old, have battled over protecting their territory, or so-called turf. To many, the turf is worth killing or dying for. Often, gangs will delineate their specific territory and forbid others to enter it. Unfortunately, the consequences of this can be demoralizing and/or deadly for residents and casual passers-by. This lesson attempts to focus students on what turf wars mean and how they affect others.

First, choose a street in the community that everyone will be familiar with (for the purpose of this lesson, we will call it Main Street). Begin by telling students that Main Street is closed today and forever. Why? Tell them that a new gang, the Crowns, has taken over Main Street and proclaimed it as their turf. Unless you are a gang member or friend of the Crowns, you can't walk on the street. If you do, you will be teased and harassed and physically ejected.

Engage the students in a discussion about the Crowns taking over Main Street. Is it fair to everyone else? How would you feel if you lived on Main Street? Do you think fewer people will use Main Street? What if you have to walk along Main Street to get to school or if your parents have to travel it to get to work?

Resources

State and Local Contacts

Juvenile division, city police department
Superintendent's office, Department of Education
Child Protective Services, Department of Human Services
State Department of Education
Juvenile Court
State or county youth authority
Boys & Girls Clubs

National Contacts

Community Youth Gang Services
544 West 53rd Street
Los Angeles, CA 90059
213-291-4538

A nonprofit, community-based organization that has developed a variety of strategies and programs to deter youth from gang membership and related crimes. Prevention programs for youth include the Career Paths curriculum for fourth and fifth graders, which focuses on self-esteem and addresses the motivations for joining gangs, and the Star Kids program, which focuses on developing mentoring programs.

Gang Intervention Program
2201 North Martin Luther King Jr. Drive
Milwaukee, WI 53212
414-265-8925

Operating in partnership with four other local agencies, this program offers young people alternative activities and counseling that fosters positive behavior and life styles.

Juvenile Justice Clearinghouse

See "General Resources" section.

National School Safety Center

See "General Resources" section.

Publications

Bing, Leon. *Do or Die.* 1991. New York: Harper and Collins.

Bryant, Dan. *Communitywide Responses Crucial for Dealing with Youth Gangs.* Department of Justice, Office of Justice Programs, Office of Juvenile Justice and Delinquency Prevention. 1989. Available from NCJRS, 800-851-3420.

California Office of Criminal Justice Planning. *Project Yes: Anti-Drug and Gang Violence Prevention Project.* 1997. Available from the Orange County Department of Education, 714-966-4000.

National Crime Prevention Council. *Tools to Involve Parents in Gang Prevention.* 1992. Available from NCPC, 202-466-6272.

National School Safety Center. *Gangs In Schools: Breaking Up Is Hard to Do.* 1993. Available from NSSC, 805-373-9977.

Spergel, Irving and Ronald Chance. *National Youth Gang Suppression and Intervention Program.* Department of Justice, Office of Justice Programs, Office of Juvenile Justice and Delinquency Prevention. 1991. Available from NCJRS, 800-851-3420.

Property Crime and Vandalism

Grades 4–8

Property crime is the most common type of crime committed in the United States and accounts for 74 percent of crimes reported to the police. Teens are the most frequent victims of crimes of theft and the most common vandalism offenders. Almost everyone will be the victim of personal theft at least once, with about seven of every eight persons being victimized three or more times. Most property crimes can be prevented using common sense and simple crime prevention strategies.

Millions of dollars are spent each year repairing the physical damage caused by vandalism. The costs of psychological damage experienced by the victim and the impact of vandalism on the community as a whole are inestimable.

This chapter will enable you to teach young people ages nine to 13:

- the definition of property crime, including vandalism;
- causes and costs of property crimes including vandalism;
- the impact of property crimes including vandalism on young people and the community;
- strategies for preventing vandalism and property crimes; and
- how to report a crime.

The "Resources Section" lists a variety of materials, activities, and organizations that can help you develop a presentation tailored to the needs of particular communities.

What Is Property?

Property is anything that is owned or can be owned. It includes houses, cars, bicycles, sweaters, school books, televisions, and stereos. It also includes intellectual property such as computer programs, the words to a song, a short story, or a video game. Property falls into two categories:

- **Real property:** is land and items attached to it, such as houses and sheds.
- **Personal property:** is all property that can be moved, such as cars, clothing, books, stereos, jewelry, and appliances.

Property Crime

Property crime is "taking (or damaging) property without force or threat of force against the individual." Property crimes can include:

- **Arson:** Setting fire to a structure with the intent to damage or destroy it. It can be someone else's property or the property of the owner who sets the fire to collect insurance.
- **Burglary:** Unlawful entry into a structure, usually (but not necessarily) accompanied by theft. The entry may be by force (such as picking a lock, breaking a window, or slashing a screen) or without force such as through an unlocked door). Burglary includes illegal entry into a garage, shed, or any other structure on the premises.
- **Larceny:** Taking without permission someone else's property with intent to keep it. Shoplifting is a particular kind of larceny that involves stealing goods from a store or market. Pocket picking and purse snatching are also forms of larceny. Taking property by mistake or borrowing it with intent to return it isn't larceny.
- **Motor vehicle theft:** The theft or attempted theft of a motor vehicle.
- **Receiving stolen property:** The purchase or acceptance of property by someone who knows or has good reason to know that it was stolen.
- **Vandalism:** The willful destruction of or damage to the property of another.

Myths and Facts About Property Crimes

Myth: Property crime doesn't really hurt anyone because insurance will cover the costs.

Fact: Many people don't have insurance policies to cover replacement costs for their stolen items. Those who do have insurance still pay for property crimes because most policies have deductibles and limitations. Insurance premiums increase when thefts go up. Victims of property crimes also suffer emotional costs, and no insurance policies cover those.

Myth: Property crime isn't violent.

Fact: Sometimes property crimes become violent crimes in which people are injured. For example, a burglar who has entered a house whose owners are away on vacation, surprised by a neighbor who comes by to pick up the mail, uses a gun to protect himself.

Myth: Stolen items can always be replaced.

Fact: Although some items can be replaced, photo albums, family heirlooms, and other items that have sentimental value are irreplaceable. Moreover, many people without insurance or on limited budgets suffer personal hardship because of a theft the criminal thought was "harmless."

Myth: Stores aren't really hurt by shoplifting.

Fact: The costs of stolen merchandise and increased security to prevent shoplifting are passed on to all customers through higher prices for goods. Stores also pass on the costs of security guards, video cameras, one-way mirrors, magnetic tags or strips attached to clothing and other merchandise, the machines to neutralize them when merchandise is paid for, and special detection devices at exits.

Myth: People can't really protect themselves against property crimes.

Fact: Most property crimes can be prevented if people work together and follow basic prevention guidelines. Crime prevention doesn't have to involve elaborate security devices. People can often protect their property with little expense and a lot of common sense.

Myth: Vandalism doesn't really hurt anyone.

Fact: Everyone pays a high price for vandalism. There are direct costs when our own property is damaged and indirect costs when our tax dollars must be spent on repairs to public property. We also pay through lost tax revenues, decreased property values, and reduced quality of life when our neighborhoods begin to deteriorate.

What is Vandalism?

The word "vandalism" comes from the name of fifth century warriors, the Vandals, who destroyed property and terrorized the Roman Empire. Today we use their name to describe anyone who destroys public or private property. Common examples of vandalism include:

- breaking windows in buildings or cars;
- knocking out street lights;
- painting or writing on walls;
- stealing street signs;
- slashing automobile tires;
- breaking car antennas;
- knocking over trash cans and mail boxes;
- sticking chewing gum onto furniture;
- carving initials on desks;
- defacing library books and textbooks; and
- littering.

Most vandalism is opportunistic. Researchers have estimated that as much as 75 percent of all vandalism is aided by characteristics of the setting and can be reduced by better design and planning, such as the strategic placement of outside lighting, well-planned landscaping, and the installation of fences, gates, or security systems. The costs of safer design can be significant, but they can be a sound investment in crime prevention.

Dealing with vandalism is expensive. For example:

- The annual costs of vandalism in the United States are estimated at $5 billion in addition to the costs of a degraded environment and increased fear among residents. Consider also the value of the life of a child killed by an automobile because someone removed a stop sign. Consider that money spent to repair the damage caused by vandalism can't purchase new playground equipment, plant shrubbery, buy new textbooks, or be used to pay for other improvements to our neighborhoods.
- The annual cost of replacements and repairs as a result of school crimes, including vandalism, is more than $200 million.
- One in four schools is subject to vandalism monthly.
- Each incident of school vandalism costs an average of $81. In one urban school district, a broken classroom window cost $315 to replace; a vandalized basketball standard cost $500. One estimate for graffiti removal from doors and walls was $3,400 for cleaning and painting.
- Vandalism is the most frequently occurring rural property crime.

Who is the Vandal?

The majority of vandals are young people, but there is no typical vandal. He or she might be the smartest kid at school or the dropout, from the biggest home on the block or the smallest, a fourth grader or a sophomore. Most vandals damage property for one or more of three reasons: boredom, anger, or revenge.

Many acts of vandalism are committed by people who are trying to show defiance for rules, laws, and authority. Most property is vandalized by youth in groups, often as a result of negative peer pressure. These groups are predominantly male, but girls have become increasingly involved in acts of vandalism.

Who Are the Victims of Vandalism?

Many young people think that vandalism is just mischief and has no real victim, either because insurance will cover the costs or because it's public property that "nobody owns." "Victimless crime" is a term that refers to illegal acts that do not specifically harm an individual. People who are the victims of vandalism feel anger, fear, and outrage when their private property or nearby public property is deliberately defaced or destroyed. Vandalism also inflicts enormous costs for property repair, cleanup, and replacement.

Jammed public telephones, missing stop signs, closed public restrooms, false fire alarms, and broken windows and street lights affect everyone. Sometimes it's a question of inconvenience; other times it could mean the difference between life and death. Consider the call to 911 that couldn't be made to report a heart attack because the public phone had been vandalized.

Vandalism Costs

Dallas, Texas:
Authorities are still searching for vandals who killed several cattle with high-powered rifles. Sheriffs investigators said that someone shot four animals valued at $4,500. No attempt was made to use the animals for food. It appeared that whoever did it was just using the animals for target practice.

St. Paul, Minnesota:
A teenager accused of planning a $2 million train wreck in February pleaded guilty in federal court to charges of criminal mischief. He faces up to 20 years in prison. Two hundred new automobiles, headed for West Coast auto dealers, were on board cars of the freight train that was wrecked.

Salt Lake City, Utah:
A nature trail that gives blind people a chance to enjoy a half-mile stroll in the woods was closed after vandals cut the guide ropes, destroyed Braille signs, and placed logs in the trail to make the blind hikers stumble and fall.

Prince George's, Maryland:
Several youths were arrested for throwing large rocks from a highway overpass onto passing cars. Several windshields were broken, and one person was seriously injured and permanently disabled.

Peoria, Illinois:
A railroad employee was blinded in one eye when a youth threw a rock through the window of a passing caboose. The employee, sitting inside the car, was hit in the eye by glass from the shattered window.

Duluth, Minnesota:
Three youths were arrested after dumping a drum of chemicals from a factory into a lake. Hundreds of fish were killed.

Preventing Vandalism

Vandalism can be prevented. Consider the three Es of vandalism prevention:

- **Eradication:** Clean it up as soon as it happens.
- **Education:** Pass the word that vandalism is a crime.
- **Enforcement:** If you see someone committing vandalism, report it to the police, school authorities, or someone who can do something about it.

Other Property Crimes

"Invisible" property crimes cause disruption to a service or break a law that protects intellectual property. These crimes include:

- violating a copyright by making a copy of something — a videotape or a library book — without the author's permission;
- "phone phreaking" by setting up a computer program that tricks the phone system and steals long-distance phone service;
- using a computer to look through (without permission) or steal information someone else collected;
- infecting a computer with a virus to destroy data; and
- making unauthorized copies of copyrighted software programs. These crimes steal ideas and services that have real value. Prices must be increased to cover losses, so once again, everyone suffers.

Youth Can Help Prevent Property Crime

Many property crimes can be prevented by using common sense. Here are some crime prevention tips to think about:

At Home

- Never put your name and address on your key ring. It's an open invitation to burglars.
- Always keep your keys with you. Never hide them outside your home.
- Be sure all outside doors have deadbolt locks with at least a one-inch throw.
- Use window locks on all first floor or garden level windows.
- When you leave your home, or are at home alone, be sure to keep your doors and windows locked.

- Light-up or eliminate places someone might hide: trees, shrubbery, stairwells, alleys, hallways, and porches.
- Keep a light on when you're not at home, and ask a neighbor to watch the house when you're away on vacation.
- Keep your bike and sports equipment inside your home when you're not using them.
- Avoid meeting a burglar face-to-face. Property crimes can turn into violent crimes.

At School

- Keep your locker locked. Don't keep money or anything valuable in your locker, especially overnight, through the weekend, or over holidays.
- If possible, use a good key lock on your locker instead of a combination.
- Lock your bike in an area that is in public view. Use a case-hardened chain or cable and lock, winding the cable through the frame and both wheels and then around the bike rack, or a special U-shaped lock. Taking the front wheel off also helps to discourage theft.

In the Car

Be sure to help the driver to remember to:

- Park in well-lighted areas.
- Never leave keys in the car.
- Always lock the car, even if it's in the driveway.
- Never leave the motor running when no one is in the car.
- Never leave valuables in plain view when leaving the car, even if it's locked. Put them in the trunk or out of sight. When possible, put them in the trunk before you arrive at your destination so that people don't see you hiding your valuables.

Out and About

- Keep your money and other valuables from public view. Flashing them invites theft.
- Don't leave your purse or wallet on the counter while you're looking at something in a store.
- Don't dangle or swing your purse or backpack by the straps. Carry it close to you, especially in crowded places and streets.
- Keep your wallet securely in a side or front pocket instead of a back pocket.
- Be wary of someone who tries to sell you something that sounds too good to be true.

With Friends

- Encourage your friends to be good neighbors. When you're going to and from school, watch for strangers or suspicious activities. Tell your parents and the police about anything unusual. Don't tell a stranger that a neighbor is not at home or lives alone.
- If your school has a serious problem with theft and vandalism, get together with friends and do something! School pride and test scores go up when crime declines. Many schools have reduced crime by involving students in patrols and creating an anonymous reporting system. A student court can help reduce crime problems and decide the punishment for classmates caught stealing or vandalizing. Students themselves often plan and organize successful programs that make their schools safer. Talk to your local police or sheriffs' department to find out how.

Messages For Parents

- Understand that when young people are victimized by vandalism, it is as serious as other forms of victimization. Do not dismiss your child's feelings lightly.
- Make it plain that you don't want your child to put his or her life on the line in order to protect property.
- Teach your children by example as well as instruction, by not taking or defacing property.
- The respect and care you give your own neighborhood sends a message that this community is a solid and clean neighborhood. Part of successful crime resistance is keeping things clean.
- Demonstrate there is no such thing as victimless crimes. Vandalism and graffiti have costs.
- You may be financially responsible for the acts of your child.
- Tell your children that the members of this family do not steal, burglarize, do graffiti, or vandalize.

Property Crime and Vandalism • Grade 4-8

Sample Materials and Activities

What a Dump!

Objective:
To identify consequences of vandalism and community prevention strategies.

Time:
20 minutes.

Materials:
"What A Dump!" handout. (See sample materials.)

Discussion

- How do you think these things ended up in the river?
- What impact do you think they have on the environment?
- What do you think should happen to the people who dumped these things in the river?
- What do you think the community could do to prevent this dumping from happening?

Vandalism Costs

Objective:
To identify the costs of vandalism.

Time:
20 minutes.

Materials:
"Vandalism Costs" examples (see text).

Distribute the handout. Assign small groups of students to study each incident and report back to the class on the following discussion questions:

- "Vandalism is a victimless crime because no one is hurt by acts of vandalism." Discuss this statement with respect to the incident you studied.
- What were the financial and/or emotional costs to the victims?
- What were the costs to the public?
- What were the costs to the vandals?

What Would You Do If ...?

Objective:
To identify the effect of peer pressure on criminal behavior and the personal costs of vandalism.

Time:
Ten minutes per scenario.

Materials:
Index cards with scenarios.

This role-play activity will help group members discuss peer pressure and the personal costs of vandalism. They will have the opportunity to practice decision-making skills and identify alternative ways to handle situations and feelings that often lead to vandalism.

Prepare individual cards with the following scenarios:

1. You are at the park with several of your friends. A classmate comes up with a can of spray paint and tries to encourage you to come with him to spray paint someone's name on the side of the school building. Some of your friends want to go. You know it's wrong and are afraid that you'll be caught. Some of your friends start giving you a hard time. What do you say? What do you do?

2. You see some of your classmates taking down a stop sign at the corner. Do you think what they are doing could hurt someone? What would you say to them? Would you report them to the police? Why or why not?

3. You are riding your bike with a group of friends. The leader starts riding through someone's garden. How do you think the owner will feel? What would you do?

4. You are walking past a vacant house with some friends. One of them picks up a rock and throws it through a window. What would you do?

Break into small groups and let each group pick a scenario card. Give them a few minutes to decide on roles and prepare to act out their scenario in front of the other groups. After each small group finishes their role-play, discuss the outcome and solicit other solutions.

DESTROYING SOMEONE ELSE'S PROPERTY ISN'T FUNNY. IT'S VANDALISM AND IT'S A CRIME.

Crime Prevention tips from:

National Crime Prevention Council
1700 K Street, NW
Second Floor
Washington, DC 20006

and

LOOK OUT FOR YOURSELF, YOUR FRIENDS, YOUR COMMUNITY, AND HELP ME...

TAKE A BITE OUT OF CRIME®

McGruff

HERE ARE A FEW IDEAS TO START YOU THINKING...

Clean graffiti off walls in schools, libraries, and other public facilities. Make it a class project in which everyone gets a grade credit for working. Ask local businesses to donate supplies.

Write articles for the school newspaper on how the juvenile court treats vandalism. In most areas, teenagers caught vandalizing property are placed in restitution programs: they must pay for the damage in money or community service. Parents may be financially liable for any damage caused by their children.

Start a hotline to report vandalism in cooperation with police and school officials.

Clean up a park, vacant lot, or school campus. Plant trees, bushes, and flowers.

Paint murals for school walls or on fences to keep them from being vandalized.

Have a carnival or bake sale to raise money to repair damage done by vandals.

Conduct an anti-vandalism poster contest.

Reward the school in a region which reduced vandalism the most.

Interview owners of vandalized property and individuals responsible for park and school maintenance. Ask about their opinions on vandalism and ideas for solutions.

A social studies class could conduct a survey of your school's climate. Low morale and lack of pride provide fertile grounds for vandalism.

Please share this brochure with a friend.

VANDALISM

HOW WOULD YOU FEEL IF SOMEONE...

Wrote obscene words on your bathroom walls?

Kicked your radio or tape deck and broke it?

Smashed a window in your home?

And then said it was just a joke.

Destroying someone else's property isn't funny. It's vandalism and it's a crime.

ASK YOURSELF

How many places do you pass daily that have been vandalized in some way, like graffiti on buildings, broken windows, missing traffic signs?

How many times in one day do you see vandalism in your school - obscenities and racial insults scrawled on restroom walls; ripped pages in textbooks; damaged sports equipment; a pay telephone that doesn't work, even in an emergency?

Maybe you've heard that vandalism is just mischief and doesn't really hurt anyone. That's not true.

In one urban school district, a broken classroom window costs around $315 to replace; a vandalized basketball standard costs around $500; graffiti removal from doors and walls can run $3,400 for cleaning and painting! And that means less money - or no money - for new books, band uniforms, sports equipment, and student activities.

A homeowner has to replace the broken window, the torn-out flower beds, or the knocked-down mailbox.

The town and its taxpayers (your parents) have to pay the costs of replacing damaged swings, basketball hoops, and street lights.

Vandalism isn't a joke. It's an outrage.

How many stories have you read in the newspaper or seen on television about vandalism - an elderly person's greenhouse destroyed, swastikas on a synagogue, students breaking into a school and destroying a teacher's classroom?

Real people - maybe a neighbor, a parent, or a friend - feel angry, sad, and frightened when something of theirs is deliberately destroyed for no apparent reason.

Property that is vandalized makes the neighborhood look bad and encourages more destruction.

Because vandalism has become so commonplace, adults in schools and communities sometimes have given up. But this attitude sends a "we don't care and there's nothing we can do" message that allows the destruction to continue.

It doesn't have to be this way. You and your friends can help make places where you live and go to school places to be proud of. Community involvement and community pride are the answers to preventing vandalism.

TAKE ACTION TODAY!

BY YOURSELF.

Don't destroy or deface someone else's property or places that everyone uses. Think how you would feel if you were the victim. Report any acts of vandalism to the school administration or the police. Quick repairs and cleanups discourage further damage.

WITH YOUR FRIENDS.

Get your class, student council, law related-education or government class, 4-H group, or club to start an anti-vandalism campaign.

First, collect the facts about vandalism and its costs in your school and community. Meet with school officials, the local police, or sheriff's office for information.

Second, educate adults - teachers, parents, local officials - about the problem. Spread the word: Vandalism costs!

Third, plan a project that will have immediate results. Launch it with an event to attract media attention, like a press conference, a school assembly, a balloon launch, or a banquet.

Money spent on cleaning up vandalism is money not spent on something you *really* want.

Property Crime and Vandalism • Grade 4-8

What A Dump!

The following list appeared in the *Washington Post Magazine*. If you doubt the continuing need to keep America clean and beautiful, consider what a team from the Interstate Commission on the Potomac River Basin found in a one-day walk of a 164-foot stretch of an Anacostia River tributary:

1 trash dumpster
1 compressed air tank
1 hot-water heater
1 metal cart
1 roll of fencing
1 piece of wire mesh
1 lawn mower
1 washtub
1 aluminum downspout
1 storm drainpipe
1 artificial Christmas tree
1 plastic bucket
1 piece of packing foam
1 stereo cassette system
1 telephone
1 hazard light
1 stuffed panda bear
2 tricycles
2 electric fans
2 guardrails
2 refrigerators
2 air conditioners
2 shopping carts
2 office chairs
2 foam sheets
2 metal trays
3 railroad ties
3 garden hoses
4 wooden pallets
6 metal grates
7 55-gallon drums
7 rugs
15 plastic trays
16 plastic bags
18 wire cable bundles
43 bottles
58 beverage cans
61 tires
64 major auto parts
79 foam cups

Resources

State and Local Contacts

Department of Highways and Streets
Insurance expert
Public transit company
Parks and Recreation Department
School system security director
School system physical maintenance personnel

National Contacts

Harbor Area Gang Alternatives Program
680 West 9th Street
San Pedro, CA 90731
310-519-7233

A nonprofit organization created in response to the increasing number of gang violence incidents in Northern California. One of the organization's many programs is a Graffiti Abatement Program that involves community residents and youth working together to remove graffiti.

National Crime Prevention Council

See "General Resources" section.

Philadelphia Anti-Graffiti Hotline
1401 John F. Kennedy Boulevard
Room 680
Philadelphia, PA 19102-1683
215-685-9901

Selected as one of the nation's Points of Light, this program works to remove and prevent vandalism in the Philadelphia area. Program volunteers paint murals and run art clinics to train youth.

Publications

Teens, Crime, and the Community. 1992. Available from NCPC, 202-466-6272.

Personal Protection Against Crime
Grades 7–12

Young people ages 12 to 19 are more frequent targets of violent crime than any other age group in the United States. An important part of working with teens in crime prevention is teaching them to recognize crime, its effects on individual victims and communities, and its costs — physical, financial, and emotional.

This chapter will help you teach teens ages 12 to 19 to:

- define the term "crime" and recognize different types of crime;
- understand their risks of becoming crime victims;
- identify where crimes against teenagers are most likely to occur;
- understand the effects of crime on individuals and communities;
- identify victims' rights and learn how victims' assistance groups can help;
- identify ways that teens can protect themselves against crime;
- learn how to report a crime; and
- learn how to help friends who are crime victims.

What Is Crime?

Crime is breaking the law. Laws are rules and regulations that reflect the values of society and are made by federal, state, and local legislative bodies.

Crime can also be defined as behaviors and acts for which society provides a penalty. Federal, state, and local legislative and judicial bodies determine penalties for people who do things that are illegal or fail to do things that are legally required.

Crimes can involve violence against a person or taking or damaging property. Violent crimes against people include:

- **Assault:** an attempt or threat to physically attack a person or an unlawful physical contact inflicted by one person upon another without consent;
- **Homicide:** intentionally causing the death of another person without legal justification;
- **Robbery:** taking or attempting to take another person's property by force or by threat of force; and

- **Rape:** sexual intercourse by force or without consent.

Crimes against property include those in which property is damaged, destroyed, or stolen without direct confrontation with the victim. Property crimes include:

- **Arson:** damaging or destroying property by fire or explosion without the owner's consent, or an attempt to do so;
- **Burglary:** unlawful entry into a building or other fixed structure with or without the use of force, with the intent of taking something;
- **Extortion:** use of threats to obtain the property of another, commonly called "blackmail";
- **Forgery:** falsely creating or altering a document with intent to defraud, such as signing someone else's name to a check;
- **Larceny:** taking, or trying to take, another person's property, other than a motor vehicle, without permission but without the use of force or threat;
- **Motor vehicle theft:** taking, or trying to take, another person's motor vehicle without permission;
- **Receiving stolen property:** receiving or buying property that is known or believed to be stolen;
- **Robbery:** taking property from a person's immediate possession by force or threat of force; and
- **Vandalism:** willful destruction of or damage to the property of another person.

Teenage Crime Victims

According to a 1995 report on teenage victims published by the U.S. Department of Justice, teens are more likely to become victims of violent crimes (including rape, robbery, and assault) and crimes of theft than older persons. In 1995, about a third of all victims of violent crimes were ages 12 to 19.

The Effects of Crime

All crimes have harmful consequences to the victim and to the community. The victim may suffer primary injuries (arising directly from the crime) or secondary injuries (caused by other people).

Primary Injuries

Primary injuries are a direct result of the crime and may be physical, financial, or emotional. Examples of primary injuries include:

- **physical injuries:** generally those which are obvious and visible, including:
  — cuts, bruises, broken bones, and other wounds; and
  — damaged or destroyed property.
- **financial injuries:** seldom readily apparent, but often economically devastating, including:
  — medical expenses;
  — lost money, or lost or destroyed property;
  — legal fees;
  — lost income from having to take time off from work to recover from the crime, to cooperate with police investigations, to attend legal meetings, or to attend court proceedings;
  — costs of transportation, lodging, meals, child care, and other expenses for attending legal meetings and court proceedings; and
  — lost job or career because of a crime-related physical or emotional injury.
- **emotional injuries:** crime victims may suffer emotional costs that are both severe and long-lasting. Emotional costs are often the most significant harm victims endure, although they also may not be apparent. Examples of emotional injuries include:
  — a victim of assault becomes distrustful of strangers;
  — a victim of robbery is afraid to be home alone;
  — a rape victim is avoided by her family and friends; and
  — a burglary victim loses priceless family heirlooms that can never be replaced.

Secondary Injuries

The victim's secondary injuries are a result of the crime and are not caused by the assailant, but by other people, systems, and agencies. Friends may send subtle messages that the victim could have done more to avoid the crime, or they may withdraw from the victim, unsure of what to say or do. Even family members may become impatient when victims take a long time to get over their trauma. Sometimes police investigations or court processes upset victims because they seem to be getting less fair treatment than the accused, or because they see no progress being made by authorities.

How Victims Respond

It is hard to tell how long it will take a victim to recover from a crime, but there are certain stages that most victims experience on their way to recovery. The feelings and thoughts in each of these stages are normal and healthy. Some victims may stay in one stage for hours or days, others for months. A victim stuck in one stage for a long period of time may need professional counseling.

- **Shock/denial:** Immediately after the crime, the victim feels out of control and can't believe what happened. The victim may refuse to talk about what happened and may become confused or disoriented.
- **Anger:** The victim realizes what has happened and may become very angry at the assailant, at someone close to them who they felt should have protected them, or even at the world for allowing bad things to happen.
- **Powerlessness:** The criminal took control of the victim's life; if the crime was reported to police, the criminal justice system may seem to have taken control; and at times it may seem that the victim's feelings are taking over.
- **Guilt:** The victim thinks about the crime scene and asks such questions as "What did I do wrong?," "What could I have done differently?," "Could I have prevented the crime?," "What would have happened if I had … ?"
- **Depression:** The victim may continue to feel fear, anxiety, and vulnerability and have difficulty resuming regular activities.
- **Acceptance:** As time passes, victims begin to focus more on day-to-day living and accept how their lives have been affected by the crime. Their problems may not have gone away, but they feel they are regaining control of their lives.

The Effects of Crime on the Community

Crime hurts communities in many ways. Here are just a few examples:

- People become fearful and distrusting.
- Public spaces are surrendered to criminals.
- Prices of goods and services increase to cover the costs of increased security and stolen items.
- Taxes increase to support the increased costs of police, jails, and courts.
- Businesses close or relocate.
- Property values decline in areas where many crimes occur.
- Insurance costs increase.
- The strength and spirit of the community is damaged as neighbors become more isolated from each other.

Help For Victims

As of January 1995:

- There are more than 10,000 victim service programs in the United States.
- Forty-eight states have enacted some form of crime victims' "Bill of Rights" that offers protection for victims.

Most larger communities have at least one program to assist victims. Some provide services to all crime victims, and others focus on victims of specific crimes such as rape, spouse abuse, drunk driving, or child abuse. Many programs have staff available 24 hours a day to provide services at no cost or on a sliding fee scale.

Victims' Rights

Many state laws were inspired by the following list of victims' rights, first published by the National Organization for Victim Assistance in 1980:

- Victims and witnesses have a right to be treated with dignity and compassion.

- Victims and witnesses have a right to protection from intimidation and harm.
- Victims and witnesses have a right to be informed about the criminal justice system.
- Victims and witnesses have a right to counsel.
- Victims and witnesses have a right to receive compensation for damages.
- Victims and witnesses have a right to preservation of property and employment.
- Victims and witnesses have a right to due process in criminal court proceedings.

How Teens Can Reduce Teen Victimization

It's always smart to think prevention. Many crimes can be prevented when individuals practice commonsense personal safety procedures.

The crime prevention Golden Rule for teens is:

- Know how to avoid danger and be alert to your surroundings, and help others do the same.

You and your friends can do a lot to help each other be safe. Common sense doesn't have to rob you of fun — it can keep you from being robbed or worse.

Here are tips to help teens reduce chances of becoming crime victims while out in the community, using public transportation, or in someone else's home.

On the Street

- Travel with a friend or in a group. Travel during daylight hours whenever possible.
- Always let someone responsible know where you're going and what time you'll be back.
- Never accept a ride from a stranger. Don't hitchhike, and don't pick up hitchhikers.
- Travel familiar, busy, and well-lighted routes. Avoid taking shortcuts through deserted, poorly lighted areas, especially at night.
- Keep your money and other valuables out of sight. Flashing them invites theft. Carry only the money you need that day and always have enough change for a phone call.
- Never have your name and address on your key ring.
- Lock your bike in an area that is in public view. Use a case-hardened chain or cable and lock, winding the cable through the frame and both wheels and then around the bike rack or pole, or use a special U-shaped lock.

On Public Transportation

- Be alert when waiting for a bus or subway. Avoid waiting alone at night.
- Have your fare ready to avoid the need to open your purse or wallet in view of others
- Sit near the driver or conductor, especially during non-rush hours. Avoid sitting near the exit door where you could invite an attacker to "hit and run."

In the Car

- Keep your car locked while parked and while driving.
- Keep valuables in the car out of sight, preferably in the trunk.
- Park in well-lighted areas.
- Have your keys in your hand, ready to unlock your car as you approach it.
- Be alert to suspicious persons near your car. Check the front and back seats and floors before entering the car.

At Home or While Babysitting at Someone Else's Home

- Always keep doors and windows locked, whether you are at home or leaving the house for even a brief period.
- Never let a stranger into the house, even if he or she says it's an emergency. If necessary, offer to phone for help while the stranger waits outside.
- Never indicate to anyone calling on the telephone or knocking on the door that you are home alone.
- Know where all the exits and telephones are.

How To Report a Crime

Teens who see or experience a crime should remember to do the following:

- Call the police immediately!
- Try to stay calm. It is important to report crimes to the police, even though seeing or experiencing crime can be upsetting.
- Tell the police who you are, where you are, and what happened.
- If anyone is hurt, ask for an ambulance.
- When the police arrive, tell them exactly what you saw. As quickly as possible, write down what you remember.
- Try to describe the scene of the crime. How many suspects were there? Did they say anything? If the crime was robbery, did they take anything?
- Tell the police what the suspect looked like: age, sex, race, height, weight, clothing, facial features, etc. Was a car or other vehicle involved? If so, try to remember the make, model, color, license plate number, and which direction it was going when the suspect drove away. If possible, write down the license number.
- You may be asked to make a complaint or testify in court. Remember that if you don't help the police, the criminal might victimize someone else.
- The police may ask you to attend a lineup or look through photo albums to try to identify the suspect. Do your best.

Always report a crime. If you don't report it, the police can't help you, and someone else might become a victim.

How To Help a Friend Who Is a Crime Victim

If a friend is a crime victim, here are things you can do:

- **Just be there:**
  — Let your friend know you care and that you will be glad to listen or talk, whether it's about the crime or some other subject. Your caring shows in your presence.
  — Offer to be with your friend the first time he or she goes out after the crime. Some victims feel very vulnerable and may be afraid of going out alone.
  — If the victim wants to revisit the crime scene, offer to go along.
  — Anniversary dates of the crime are often very important to victims and a time when they spend a lot of time thinking about the crime. You may want to call or send a card to say you're thinking about your friend.

- **Listen:**
  — Let your friend know that you're sorry the crime happened and that you blame the criminal, not your friend.
  — Let your friend talk through how he or she feels about the crime. A crime victim may want to repeat the story over and over again one day and not even want to mention it the next.
  — Be prepared for your friend to have confused and intense emotions about the event and about his or her treatment by the police, hospital personnel, and others.
  — Avoid telling the victim you "understand" or "know" how she or he feels — unless you've been a victim of the same or similar crime yourself. Even then, don't assume similar reactions.

- **Fix up:**
  — Help your friend by offering to repair broken locks, torn screens, bike or car damage, torn clothing, or other visible results of the crime, or to replace school books or meet other needs like these.

- **Lend a hand:**
  — Offer to go with your friend to follow-up doctor's visits, or babysit younger siblings for free so a parent can go with him or her.
  — Offer to cook a special meal for your friend's family.
  — Be in court to provide moral support when your friend must testify.

- Help with the red tape of getting new licenses, IDs, school books, or other things that may have been stolen or damaged.
- Help with day-to-day chores that your friend may not be ready to cope with, such as preparing meals, watching children, or keeping up with school assignments.

■ **Refer your friend to someone who can help:**

- Know what special victim assistance resources are available in your community. Is free counseling available? Will special compensation programs help pay for losses? Is there a hotline?
- Let your friend know that it's all right to seek trained help.

Community Crime Prevention Strategies

Crime in the community can be reduced through five important strategies that everyone can do:

■ Educate the community about crime. Hold assemblies or workshops in your school or neighborhood. Plan a crime prevention week for your community. Talk about crime safety tips with older people who live in your neighborhood.

■ Take away the opportunities for crime to be committed. Follow safe commonsense procedures when playing outside, staying at home, driving your car, and riding public transportation. Be there for your friends when they need someone to walk home with.

■ Set a good example for younger kids, friends, family, and neighbors. If the residents in your community see that you are reducing your chances of becoming a victim, they will learn from your good example. Help others learn the rules for safe behavior.

■ Report crimes and help the police make the criminal responsible for his or her acts. Your willingness to report the crime may keep the criminal from victimizing someone else.

■ Build community support and cooperation in organizing crime prevention efforts. Work in partnership with civic groups, PTAs, church groups, youth clubs, or victims' groups to develop programs and projects that address the causes of crime in your community. If there are no projects you can join, talk to some friends and helpful adults about starting one.

If You're Confronted

Despite a community's best efforts, not all crimes will be prevented. If you are confronted by a criminal, remember the following things:

■ Don't panic. Try to stay calm.

■ If approached by someone who demands your valuables, give them up. The criminal may have a weapon. Your belongings can be replaced — you can't.

■ Don't make sudden moves — the offender is probably as nervous as you are.

■ Remember details of the crime, such as a detailed physical description of the suspect(s), weapon, and method of leaving the scene (by car, on foot).

■ Immediately report the crime to the police or sheriff's department. Without a report, the police have no legal right to pursue an alleged criminal. Although they're most often victimized, teens are much less likely than adults to report crimes to the police.

Messages For Parents

- Teens are the nation's most frequently victimized age group.
- Establish rules and penalties for breaking those rules. Make sure the penalty is clear in advance. Don't punish retroactively by creating new rules.
- Engage your child in discussions of risks, consequences, and prevention strategies. Help them enhance judgment-making skills.
- Be sensitive to ramifications of new situations that occur as the child matures — situations that may require different prevention behaviors and decisions.
- Work with children about what can happen when they go onto unfamiliar turf. Teach them how to practice sensible behaviors that avoid sparking incidents.
- Conflict management skills will stand any child in good stead, and may even keep a child alive. Take the time to teach, practice, and model these skills.
- Help your child understand why, how, and what to report as a crime.
- What young people wear today can make them more vulnerable to crime. Understand the expensive athletic shoes, starter jackets, and jewelry could place a child in danger.
- Teach your child not to carry any more cash than absolutely necessary.
- Take time with your child to identify appropriate places in the community where they could seek help. Role-play scenarios to reinforce where they can go for help.
- Create an atmosphere where an older child can feel safe in admitting a victimization. Be careful not to blame the crime victim.

Sample Materials and Activities

Are You a Good Witness?

Objective:
To assist participants to identify key information needed to be an effective witness.

Time:
15 to 30 minutes.

Materials:
"Are You a Good Witness" handout. (See sample materials.)

Pretend you are a witness. Carefully study the crime scene picture for thirty seconds.

Divide participants into two groups. Give the "Are You a Good Witness" handout to one group with instructions to keep it face down. The other group will be police officers and will receive a blank police report form. Advise witnesses they will soon be observing a crime. They are to attempt to remember everything in order to report the incident to the police. Ask them to turn over their sheets and give them 30 seconds to observe. During that 30 seconds, create a disturbance or distraction. For example, have another adult come in upset or angry and engage you in a loud discussion, or drop a box of paper clips on the floor or knock over a glass of water onto the (tile) floor. Now, call the police to interview the witnesses. Have different officers report their findings. After all of the information has been gathered, review the scene. Finally, discuss what factors are important to being a good witness.

Personal Protection Against Crime • Grades 7-12

Are You A Good Witness?

Pretend you are a witness. Study this crime scene carefully for one minute. Now, turn the page and write down all the details you can remember to tell the police.

Copyright Oct. 1985 by the Young Lawyers Section of the Bar Association of the District of Columbia.

Personal Protection Against Crime • Grades 7-12

What Do You Know About Teens as Crime Victims?

Test Your Knowledge

1. In which age category are persons most likely to be victims of crime?

   A. Elderly (65 and over)
   B. Middle-aged group (35-49 years old)
   C. Teenagers (12-19 years old)

2. If you were 12 years old, what were the chances, based on crime rates of that time, that you would be a victim of violent crime during your lifetime?

   A. 1 in 2 (50%)
   B. 5 in 6 (83%)
   C. 2 in 3 (66%)

3. Are teenage males or females more likely to be victims of violent crime?

   A. Males
   B. Females
   C. Males and females are victimized equally

4. For the three violent crimes of rape, robbery, and assault, are teens more likely or less likely to be victimized by persons they know than are adults?

   A. Teens are less frequently victimized by persons they know than are adults.
   B. Teens are more frequently victimized by persons they know than are adults.
   C. Teens are victimized by persons they know at about the same rate as adults.

5. Of the violent crimes of homicide, rape, robbery, and assault, which is the most likely to be committed by a stranger?

   A. Homicide
   B. Rape
   C. Robbery
   D. Assault

6. Of the violent crimes of homicide, rape, robbery, and assault, which is the most likely to be committed by someone the victim knows?

   A. Homicide
   B. Rape
   C. Robbery
   D. Assault

7. What are the two leading causes of injury-related death among people under 20?

   A. Suicides and homicides
   B. Motor vehicle crashes and homicides
   C. Motor vehicle crashes and suicides

8. What fraction of rape victims are teenagers?

   A. One-tenth
   B. One-third
   C. One-half

9. Which of the following age groups are least likely to report a crime?

   A. Elderly (65 and older)
   B. Teenagers (12-19 years old)
   C. Middle-aged group (35-49 years old)

10. What portion of violent crimes against teens occur on the street or in a park or playground?

    A. 1 of 3 (33%)
    B. 1 of 8 (12%)
    C. 1 of 2 (50%)

A Teaching Guide for Law Enforcement and Others

Personal Protection Against Crime • Grades 7-12

Answers to "Test Your Knowledge"

1. C. Teenagers are crimes most frequent target. Teens are victims of violent crime and crimes of theft at about twice the rate of the adult population age 20 and older.

Source: *Criminal Victimization in the United States*, 1992, U.S. Department of Justice

2. B. Someone 12 years old has a 5 in 6 (83 percent) chance of being a victim of a violent crime during his or her lifetime. And 50 percent of all victims will be victims more than once.

Source: *Lifetime Likelihood of Victimization*, Bureau of Justice Statistics, U.S. Department of Justice, March 1987

3. A. Similar to the adult population, male teenagers had higher violent and theft crime rates than did female teens.

Source: *Teenage Victims: A National Crime Survey Report*, May 1991

4. B. Teenagers are more likely to be victimized by people they know than are adults. The proportion of violent crime victims whose offenders are known to them in some way (casual or close acquaintances, friends, relatives) is 37 percent for adults, 44 percent for older teenagers (16-19), and 59 percent for younger teenagers (12-15).

Source: *Criminal Victimization in the United States*, 1994

5. C. Robbery is the violent crime most likely to be committed by a stranger. In 1994, more than 78 percent of robberies (against all victims, not just teens) were by strangers, compared with 36 percent of rapes and 53 percent of assaults. Males are more likely to be victims of all types of violent crime (with the exception of rape) by strangers than females — 86 percent of robberies by strangers, compared to 64 percent for females.

Source: *Criminal Victimization in the United States*, 1994

6. A. Homicide is the violent crime in which the victim is most likely to know the offender in some way. According to the Uniform Crime Report for 1995 (this report contains only the crime that is reported to the police, not the unreported), almost half of the murder victims in 1995 were related to (11 percent) or acquainted with (34 percent) their assailants. Among all female murder victims in 1994, 26 percent were slain by husbands or boyfriends. Three percent of the male victims were killed by wives or girlfriends. Arguments resulted in 27 percent of the murders in 1995.

7. B. According to the National Center for Health Statistics, injury was the leading cause of death for youth below age 20 in 1991. Homicide was second only to motor vehicle crashes as the leading cause of fatal injuries. Two in five injury deaths of these youth in 1991 were the result of motor vehicle collisions. More than one in five injury deaths resulted from homicide.

Source: National Center for Health Statistics, U.S. Department of Health and Human Services, 1991

8. B. Women ages 16-24 were three times more likely to be raped than other women. The average annual rate of completed and attempted rape from 1973 to 1987 for women ages 12-15 was 2.3 per 1,000; for women ages 16-19, 4.8 per 1,000; and for women ages 20-24, 4.1 per 1,000.

Source: Bureau of Justice Statistics

9. B. Teenagers are the age group least likely to report crime. Crimes against teenagers are less likely to be reported to the police than crimes against adults. Among teenagers, crimes against younger teens are less likely to be reported than crimes against older teens.

Source: *Criminal Victimization in the United States*, 1994

10. A. Almost one-fourth (25.8 percent) of violent crimes against teens occur on the street or in the park or playground. An additional 13 percent occur at school. Teenagers were most likely to experience crimes of theft in a school building or on school property.

Source: *Criminal Victimization in the United States*, 1994

Resources

State and Local Contacts

Attorney General's Office
Victim advocate or victim assistance staff of the
 State Crime Victim Compensation Board
Local victim assistance specialist
Local Prosecutor's Office
State Victim Assistance Office

National Contacts

American Bar Association Criminal Justice Section
740 15th Street, NW
Ninth Floor
Washington, DC 20005
202-662-1000

The ABA committee on victimization develops a victim-related policy and researches selected victims' issues. Provides information on victims' rights legislation and legal issues concerning victims.

National Association of Crime Victims
Compensation Boards
PO Box 16003
Alexandria, VA 22302
703-370-2996

A membership organization of states with crime victim compensation boards. Offers information about victim compensation and can make references to local agencies.

National Organization for Victim Assistance
1757 Park Road, NW
Washington, DC 20010
202-232-6682

NOVA works to achieve recognition and implementation of victim's rights and services. Provides training, technical assistance, and direct services to crime victims. Maintains an information clearinghouse on issues relating to victimization.

National Victim Center
2111 Wilson Boulevard
Suite 300
Arlington, VA 22201
703-276-2880

A national resource organization established in 1985 to help victims of violent crime, organizations, and others concerned with victims' rights and criminal justice issues. Many organizations and individuals benefit from the Center's programs and services, which include information and referral, research, library resource education, and technical assistance.

Office for Victims of Crime
Office of Justice Programs
U.S. Department of Justice
810 7th Street, NW
Washington, DC 20531
202-307-5983

Federal office for addressing the needs of crime victims. Recommends system reforms for improving victim treatment and provides national leadership by administering grants. Supports training, forums, publications, and task forces that help improve their response to crime.

Publications

National Crime Prevention Council and Street Law, Inc. *Teens, Crime, and the Community.* 1997. Available from NCPC, 202-466-6272.

Sexual Assault and Acquaintance Rape Protection

Grades 7–12

One rape occurs every 1.3 minutes in the United States. It is estimated that one out of four females will be a victim of sexual assault in her lifetime. Adolescents and young adults are particularly vulnerable.

Some people think that rapists are sex-starved men who jump out of the bushes, grab an attractive female, and drag her away. The reality is very different:

- Most rapes occur at the victim's home, or the home of a friend, relative, or neighbor.
- Sixty-two percent of those rapes are committed by someone that the victim knows — often a friend, neighbor, boyfriend, or casual acquaintance.
- Girls and women of all ages and physical appearances are victims.

Only 16 percent of rape victims report the crime to the police. Rape is a very personal violation, and the victim's feelings of shame and guilt often cause him or her to keep the crime a secret. Many victims know the attacker, which can inhibit them from both reporting the crime and seeking the help they need.

This chapter will assist you in dispelling common myths about rape, particularly acquaintance rape, and provide a variety of strategies that young people can use to reduce their chances of becoming victims. Because many people are unsure about what they can or should do or say, this chapter also includes tips for helping a friend who has been raped.

After reading this chapter, you will be able to teach teens ages 12 to 18 to:

- define sexual assault;
- recognize that rape includes both acquaintance rape and stranger rape;
- identify factors that can cause them to be more vulnerable to rape;
- identify ways to make themselves less vulnerable to rape; and
- know what to do if they or their friends are victims.

Sexual Assault

Sexual assault is defined as any sexual activity that is against a person's will. The force may be physical threat or attack, or it may be psychological or emotional pressure, coercion, or manipulation. There are many acts that can be included in this definition of sexual assault:

- rape, which is sometimes specially characterized, although these characterizations are not always well defined — for example:
  - stranger rape;
  - acquaintance rape;
  - date rape;
  - forced sodomy or oral sex;
  - marital rape;
  - gang rape; and
  - incest;
- indecent exposure;
- obscene phone calls;
- voyeurism; and
- sexual abuse of children.

This section will focus on rape, although much of the information presented is relevant to other forms of sexual assault.

Rape

Historically, the word rape comes from the Latin word rapere, which means to steal, seize, or carry away. Today, the primary definition of rape is sexual intercourse against the will of the victim. The legal definition of sexual intercourse varies from state to state. You should be familiar with the definition in your jurisdiction.

Rape can happen to anyone regardless of age, sex, race, or social background. No one is immune from the risk, but adolescent girls and young women have the highest risk of being raped. Many people feel uncomfortable talking about rape, but dramatic statistics demand that the problem be addressed:

- One rape occurs every 1.3 minutes in the U.S.
- Conservative estimates state that one out of 12 females will be a victim of sexual assault in her lifetime.
- Over half of all attempted rapes occur in or near the home of the victim, and more than 62 percent of those rapes are committed by someone the victim knows — often a friend, neighbor, boyfriend, or casual acquaintance.

Rape is a crime that people often keep secret. Only 16 percent of rape victims report the crime to the police, partly because until recently rape has been a taboo subject. Society's understanding of rape has been clouded by misinformation and myths. A 1994 publication, *The Social Organization of Sexuality: Sexual Practices in the United States,* stated that:

- twenty-two percent of the women surveyed said they had been forced to do sexual things against their will; but
- only three percent of men ever admit to forcing themselves on women.

Experts on rape report:

- Three of five men and two of five women surveyed said they believed that "women provoke rape by their appearance or behavior."
- Three out of four women blame themselves for being raped.
- Sixty percent of male college students admit that they would rape a woman if they could get away with it.

Myths and Facts About Sexual Assault

A good place to start in preventing rape is to clarify the misinformation and present the facts. Here are some common myths and the facts:

Myth: A sexual assault must involve intercourse in order to be reported to the police as a crime.

Pact: Sexual assault includes any forced sexual activity and does not require intercourse to be classified as a crime.

Myth: Rape is a sexual act, and women who are raped have "asked for it" by flirting, wearing provocative clothing, walking in certain ways, or being in certain places.

Pact: Rape is an act of violence, not of passion. The rapist has a need to control, overpower, or humiliate his victim. Victims don't invite or cause rape. No one has the right to force another person to participate in sex, for any reason.

Myth: A rapist is a sex-starved adult man who is suddenly overcome with uncontrollable passion at the sight of an attractive woman.

Pact: Rape is a crime of violence. Many adult rapists in prison report that they committed their first crime at 14, the age of the average high school freshman. Also, many rapists were involved in a sexual relationship with a wife or girlfriend at the time of the crime.

Myth: Most rapes are committed by strangers.

Pact: Most rapes are committed by someone the victim knows. It could be a relative, a neighbor, a boyfriend, an ex-lover, a friend of a friend, or a person the victim has seen at the bus stop or grocery store.

Myth: Rape is an impulsive, uncontrollable act.

Pact: Most rapes have a strong element of premeditation. With acquaintance rape, the use of alcohol and other drugs is often involved and may impair judgment, but there is no evidence that use of alcohol or drugs prevents a rapist from controlling himself.

Myth: Only attractive women are victims of sexual assault.

Pact: Rapists do not look for victims who are physically attractive or provocatively dressed. Instead they tend to look for situations where the victim is vulnerable. Infants, young children, boys, and men are also victims.

Myth: A person cannot be raped by someone with whom he or she has previously had sex.

Pact: Rape is any sexual intercourse that is against a person's will. The force may be physical, psychological, or emotional. Regardless of whether the parties had previously engaged in consensual sex, if one party refuses or resists and is forced, the other party has committed rape.

Myth: If a man spends money on a woman on a date, she owes him sex.

Pact: No one owes sex as a payment to anyone.

Myth: If a woman agrees to kiss or pet, that means that she is willing to have intercourse.

Pact: Everyone has the right to set limits on sexual activity. A person's "no" should be respected under any circumstances.

Myth: A husband cannot rape his wife.

Pact: Many states recognize marital rape as a violent crime.

Rape can happen to anyone. Consider the stories of the following victims:

- Tracie is a successful lawyer. She lives in an apartment building with a security system and a guard posted in the lobby. She was raped by an attacker posing as a delivery man.
- Carmen was driving home from her aunt's house. When she stopped at a traffic light, a man jumped in her car, forced her to drive to a deserted area, and raped her.
- Tonya was driving home from a movie with the boy she had been dating for six months. Instead of driving her home, he pulled into an office building parking lot, locked her door, and, despite her resistance, raped her.
- Rachel is a 67-year-old grandmother. One night she awoke to find a stranger in her bedroom. The intruder raped and beat her.
- Trevor had been helping a neighbor with work around his house for several months. One afternoon the neighbor caught him smoking marijuana behind

the garage. The neighbor told Trevor that if he came into the house "to do some extra work," he wouldn't tell his parents about the marijuana. Trevor followed him into the bedroom, where he was raped.

- Mary was babysitting for a couple she had known for several years. One night when the husband was driving her home after babysitting, he parked the car behind an abandoned building and raped her. He told her that if she ever told anyone he would "get her."

Acquaintance Rape

An acquaintance rape victim could be your classmate, best friend, sister, brother, cousin, or grandmother. Acquaintance rape is a rape committed by someone the victim knows. It may be a casual friend or a boyfriend. It has been estimated that over 50 percent of all rapes are acquaintance rapes. Girls and young women are the most frequent victims.

Victims often find that acquaintance rape is more difficult to talk about than stranger rape and is less frequently reported to the police. It may be that the victim:

- doesn't realize that the act was rape, especially if the victim knew or dated the rapist before the rape occurred;
- feels that he or she could have prevented it from happening;
- experiences confusion, guilt, and loss of trust in both other people and his or her own judgment;
- fears that no one will believe the incident; and
- fears retaliation from the rapist or the rapist's family and friends.

Teens are especially vulnerable to acquaintance rape for a number of reasons:

- Many teens don't understand what constitutes rape or why it happens.
- Many teens feel pressured by their peers to be sexually active and to ignore their feelings against having sex.
- They may lack accurate knowledge and understanding of sexuality and of issues relating to sexual relationships.
- They may be more trusting than the typical adult.
- They may fail to report the crime because the rape occurred when they were somewhere they weren't supposed to be or doing something they weren't supposed to be doing.
- They may lack the self-esteem and self-confidence to articulate clear limits on their sexual activities.

Facts About Rapists

People who rape can be young, old, rich, poor, handsome, plain, students, professionals, people on welfare, and of any race, creed, or color. Rapists don't wear signs advertising their criminal intent; there is no simple guide that can accurately predict who may or may not rape if given the opportunity:

- Most rapists are seen as "normal" by people they know.
- Most rapists don't look or act differently than anyone else.
- Age, appearance, social class, and race are not indicators of a person's potential to rape.

Reducing Your Risks

Statistics show that it is very difficult to generalize about the victim or the rapist, but there are three basic strategies that can reduce your chances of becoming a victim:

- Understand the facts about rape.
- Avoid situations that increase your risk.
- Listen to your instincts.

Since most rapes are committed by someone the victim knows, there are special things to consider when dating:

- Know your date. If you don't know him well, stay in public places and with other people.
- Be especially careful with anyone who always wants to have his way, is manipulative, doesn't respect your feelings, or seems to have a short fuse.

- Let a parent or responsible friend know where you're going, with whom, and how long you expect to be gone. Let your date know that there is someone else who knows that you're together and that you're expected home.

- Don't be in a hurry to get physically involved, and don't let anyone talk you into being "swept away." Let a relationship develop slowly at a speed that lets you keep control.

- If you feel uncomfortable, trust your instincts and get out of the situation immediately.

- Let your date know clearly and firmly what your limits are. These limits may change over time or with different people.

- Be clear about your feelings. Don't depend on your date to try to figure out what you are comfortable with.

- Make sure what you say and the way you say it are consistent.

- Be assertive. Act immediately if something happens that makes you feel uncomfortable. If you've been assertive and it doesn't work, it's OK to be blunt or rude. Don't worry about the other person's feelings.

- Be prepared to find your own transportation home. Always take along change for a phone call and (if possible) enough money to pay for a taxi.

- Remember that many acquaintance rapes are linked to the use of alcohol or other drugs by one or both parties. These drugs reduce your ability to think clearly and make good decisions.

Here are some additional tips that can help you reduce your chances of becoming a victim:

At Home

- Be sure your windows and doors have sturdy, reliable locks and use them.

- Keep entrances well-lighted.

- Don't let any stranger or anyone you don't trust or feel comfortable with come into your house when you're alone.

- If someone comes to your door to make an emergency phone call, offer to make the call yourself while he or she waits outside.

On Foot

- Walk with a group or at least one other person at night, if at all possible.

- Avoid areas where there aren't many people.

- Be alert to your surroundings. Stay away from dark doorways, bushes, and alleys. Stay in well-lighted areas.

In the Car

- Keep your car in good condition and keep the gas tank at least half full.

- Park in well-lighted areas and lock the doors, even if you'll be gone only a short time.

- Check the rear and front seats and floors for intruders before getting into the car.

- Drive with all the doors locked.

- Never pick up hitchhikers.

- If you have a flat tire, drive on it until you reach a safe, well-lighted place in a well-traveled area.

- If your car breaks down, put the hood up, turn your emergency flashers on, and use warning triangles or flares if you have them. If someone stops to help you, keep your doors locked and don't get out of the car. Roll down the window slightly (if necessary) and ask the person to call the police or your tow service for you.

- If you see another motorist in trouble, help by going to the nearest phone and calling the police for assistance.

- Be cautious if you park in an underground or enclosed parking garage. Park near your exit point but away from possible places of concealment.

If Rape Happens

No victim asks to be raped, wants to be raped, or deserves to be raped. If you're victimized you should:

- Go to a safe place, such as your home or a trusted friend's home.

- Call the police immediately.

- The police will want to collect evidence, so don't brush your teeth, gargle, bathe, shower, or douche. Save the clothing you were wearing and don't disturb anything at the crime site.

- Call a friend or family member to be with you for emotional support, and call your local rape crisis center, listed in the phone book under "Rape." They can help you understand that the rape wasn't your fault and usually have rape victim companions who will go with you to the police station and/or hospital. They can explain the procedures to you and provide support.

- Go to the hospital emergency room for a medical examination and for evidence collection. Even if you decide not to report the rape, it's important to see a doctor immediately. He or she will be able to estimate your chances of getting pregnant and can test you for sexually transmitted diseases, including AIDS.

- Find someone, such as a trained counselor, to talk with about the rape. Your local rape crisis center will have specially trained counselors and advocates who are familiar with what you're going through.

Effects of Rape on the Survivor

In addition to physical injuries, victims of rape can suffer from sexually transmitted diseases (such as AIDS), pregnancy, judgmental reactions from their friends and family, and serious emotional trauma. Rape victims typically go through several stages of recovery:

- shock/denial;
- anger/rage;
- powerlessness;
- guilt;
- depression; and
- acceptance.

These recovery stages are explained in detail in the "Personal Protection" chapter.

Helping a Friend Who Has Been Raped

Because they don't know what to say or do when a friend has been raped, people often don't do anything at all or may unintentionally hurt rather than help. There are several things teens can do to provide practical and emotional support. Don't assume that a male friend can handle being a victim better that a female friend. All victims need support.

- **Be there:**
  — Let your friend know you care and that you will be glad to listen or talk, whether it's about the rape or some other subject. Your caring shows in your presence.
  — Offer to be with your friend the first time he or she goes out after the rape. Most victims feel very vulnerable and may be afraid of going out alone.
  — If your friend wants to revisit the rape scene, offer to go along.
  — Anniversary dates of the rape are often very sensitive times for victims, when they spend a lot of time thinking about the rape. You may want to call your friend to see how she or he is doing.

- **Listen:**
  — Don't judge your friend. Express your sorrow that the rape happened and explain that you blame the rapist, not your friend.
  — Let your friend talk through how he or she feels about being raped.
  — Be prepared for your friend to have confused and intense emotions about the event and about his or her treatment by the police, hospital personnel, and others.
  — Avoid telling the victim you "understand" or "know" how they feel, unless you've been a victim of the same crime.
  — Don't tell anyone else about the rape, unless your friend says it's OK.

- **Fix up:**
  — After the police say it's OK, help your friend

by offering to repair broken locks, torn screens, torn clothing, or other damage of the crime.

- **Lend a hand:**
  — Offer to go with your friend for doctors' visits, or babysit younger siblings for free so a parent can go along.
  — Offer to cook a meal for your friend's family or help with other chores.
  — Be in court when your friend must testify, to provide moral support.
  — Help with day-to-day chores that your friend may not be ready to cope with, such as watching children or keeping up with school assignments.

- **Refer your friend to someone who can help.**
  — Know what rape victim assistance resources are available in your community. Is free counseling available? Is there a hotline?
  — Let your friend know that it's all right to seek trained help.

Messages For Parents

- Be acutely aware that both young men and women need to be educated concerning prevention of rape.
- Rape is an act of violence and not an act of lust. It is not invited by the victim.
- Both young men and women need to realize that it is acceptable to refuse to engage in sexual intercourse.
- Help your child clarify his or her ideas about male/female relationships. If a young person is clear about the qualities of relationships and the position he or she wants to sustain about sex, it can be easier to effectively communicate and set limits.
- When possible both male and female role models should help the young person discuss male/female relationships and how to minimize mixed messages. Most people agree that men and women communicate differently.

- Saying no means the young person may not feel popular. Work with him or her to understand popularity. The child should not feel that saying yes to sex is necessary in order to gain popularity.
- Insist on knowing who your child is going out with, where they are going, and when they expect to return.
- Alcohol and drugs use increase the risk of rape because they dull self-protective instincts. Parents also need to be aware that many young people believe that if a young woman is drunk she deserves to be raped. Parents may want to work on modifying this attitude if their child holds it.
- Make sure you have rehearsed with the young women in your family methods of leaving uncomfortable situations. Also, encourage them to travel with change for a phone call and bus or cab fare.
- Young women need to understand the various settings in which they can be vulnerable. Work to help them understand the different risks.
- Review your home's security. Is it designed to deter rape?
- It is important for a victim to report a rape, receive immediate medical attention, and participate in counseling. Encourage follow-up medical testing for pregnancy, AIDS, and other conditions.

Sexual Assault and Acquaintance Rape Prevention • Grades 7-12

Sample Materials and Activities

Dater's Bill of Rights

- I have the right to refuse a date without feeling guilty.

- I can ask for a date without feeling rejected or inadequate if the answer is no.

- I do not have to act macho.

- I may choose not to act seductively.

- If I don't want physical closeness, I have the right to say so.

- I have the right to start a relationship slowly, to say, "I want to know you better before I become involved."

- I have the right to be myself without changing to suit others.

- I have the right to change a relationship when my feelings change. I can say, "We used to be close, but I want something else now."

- If I am told a relationship is changing, I have the right not to blame or change myself to keep it going.

- I have the right to an equal relationship with my partner.

- I have the right not to dominate or to be dominated.

- I have the right to act one way with one person and a different way with someone else.

- I have the right to change my goals whenever I want to.

Sexual Assault and Acquaintance Rape Prevention • Grades 7-12

Stereotypes

Objective:
To identify stereotypes about rape in our society.

Time:
15 minutes to one hour.

Materials:
Bowl, basket or bag, and index cards.

Put the following stereotypes on index cards or slips of paper and put them into a bag or box. Divide the class into two groups, designating one group to support the stereotype and the other to refute it. Alternating groups, have one member pick a stereotype card and read it aloud. Facilitate the interaction between the groups.

- Men and women can never be just friends.
- Woman expect men to spend a lot of money on dates, to buy the privilege of having sex.
- Men have to be strong and able to protect themselves, and a man who is raped is weak.
- It's OK for a man to have sex if he's turned on.
- If there is no weapon or physical abuse, it isn't rape.
- Women may say no to sex, but they really mean yes.
- Overconfident, powerful, or teasing women need to be put in their place by being forced to have sex.
- If a man is dating a woman, he has to have sex with her.
- It's wrong for a woman to be firm and assertive.
- Women should have sex, even if they're uncomfortable about it.
- A man isn't a "real" man if he starts a sexual encounter and doesn't complete it, even if he has changed his mind.

Reducing Your Risk

Objective:
To identify high-risk actions that could make you more vulnerable to a sexual assault.

Time:
20 minutes.

Materials:
Copies of scenarios.

The scenarios present two different discussion options. One is diagnostic: What is the risk-taking or unwise behavior? The other is projective: What would the students do to alter or avoid the behavior? Each scenario can be discussed from both perspectives, or several can be discussed from one perspective.

1. Catherine is an 18-year-old student at the local high school. Two nights a week, Catherine practices basketball in the school gym. She is careful to watch for suspicious people entering the gym, but she feels safe because the school is crowded at this time of night, with evening adult classes in session. After practicing, Catherine walks to her car in the lot. She parks in her usual spot towards the back of the parking lot. She usually does not have time to move her car before practicing, so she just leaves it in the back corner.

2. After her shift is over at her part-time job at the mall, Maria often calls her mom to pick her up. When her mom is not available, Maria takes the bus. She usually waits at the bus stop with her co-worker, Ron, who takes a different bus. When she gets on the bus, there are usually only five or six other riders. Maria generally sits in the back of the bus, and sometimes falls asleep during the 20-minute ride.

3. Leslie is invited to a high school graduation party at Bob's house. Since Bob's parents are out of town, he serves alcohol. Leslie drinks several glasses of wine and ends up feeling tipsy by the end of the evening. She stumbles when she walks, but she feels generally in control. Since Leslie lives only a half-mile away, she decides to walk home alone. A guy from another school, John, offers her a ride home. John seems like a nice guy, but she

A Teaching Guide for Law Enforcement and Others

does not recognize him nor do her friends.

4. As a waitress at the diner, Sally, an 18-year-old high school senior, is on her feet all evening. At the end of each shift, Sally stays late with her manager to count the cash. Each time, he offers to escort her across the parking lot to her car. Sally always politely refuses, telling him that she can take care of herself. As she leaves the diner, she notices four guys from a nearby school who appear to be drunk and unruly. When Sally walks by, they taunt and threaten her.

5. Mike, a high school senior, is out on the town with two older guys from the local college, Gene and Jeff. While cruising the neighborhood streets, Mike consumes a quarter of a bottle of whiskey. When he wakes up in the morning, he is in a strange bed, and his clothes are on the floor. He cannot remember the events of the previous evening. He feels sick and confused.

What Would You Do ...

Objective:
To help students apply their knowledge of how to prevent sexual assault.

Time:
20 minutes.

Materials:
Copies of scenarios.

This exercise can be conducted as a discussion or as role-playing. Ask students to suggest more than one completion. Have them discuss decisions, feelings of both parties, next steps, consequences, and prevention strategies.

1. Beth and John are on their first date. Near the end of the evening, John drives to a secluded spot and turns off the car. Beth becomes nervous.

2. Tunney and James are alone at Tunney's home. They have been dating for six months and have never had sex. James tries to convince her to have intercourse, but Tunney refuses. They begin to argue. Tunney is sure that her boyfriend will not resort to violence, but she feels emotionally pressured.

3. Jody is at a party on a Saturday night. Although she is having a good time, she feels uneasy about a guy who is constantly following her around. He does not speak to her, but he watches her the entire evening.

4. Raymond and Kathy are making out on the couch at his house, and his parents are out for the evening. He begins to take Kathy's shirt off, and she tells him to stop. He does not say anything but does not stop, either.

TEEN DATING VIOLENCE

Crime Prevention Tips from
National Crime Prevention Council
1700 K Street, NW, Second Floor
Washington, DC 20006-3817
www.weprevent.org

and

The National Citizens' Crime Prevention Campaign, sponsored by the Crime Prevention Coalition of America, is substantially funded by the Bureau of Justice Assistance, Office of Justice Programs, U.S. Department of Justice.

Distribution made possible in part by a grant from **ADT** Security Services, Inc.

- Encourage them to confide in a trusted adult. Talk to a trusted adult if you believe the situation is getting worse. Offer to go with them for help.

- Never put yourself in a dangerous situation with the victim's partner. Don't be a mediator.

- Call the police if you witness an assault. Tell an adult – a school principle, parent, guidance counselor.

WHAT YOU CAN DO

- Start a peer education program on teen dating violence.

- Ask your school library to purchase books about living without violence and the cycle of domestic violence.

- Create bulletin boards in the school cafeteria or classroom to raise awareness.

- Perform a play about teen dating violence.

ARE YOU GOING OUT WITH SOMEONE WHO...

- Is jealous and possessive, won't let you have friends, checks up on you, won't accept breaking up?

- Tries to control you by being very bossy, giving orders, making all the decisions, not taking your opinions seriously?

- Puts you down in front of friends, tells you that you would be nothing without him or her?

- Scares you? Makes you worry about reactions to things you say or do? Threatens you? Uses or owns weapons?

- Is violent? Has a history of fighting, loses temper quickly, brags about mistreating others? Grabs, pushes, shoves, or hits you?

- Pressures you for sex or is forceful or scary about sex? Gets too serious about the relationship too fast?

- Abuses alcohol or other drugs and pressures you to take them?

- Has a history of failed relationships?

- and blames the other person for all the problems?

- Makes your family and friends uneasy and concerned for your safety?

If you answered yes to any of these questions you could be the victim of dating abuse. Dating violence or abuse affects one in ten teen couples. Abuse isn't just hitting. It's yelling, threatening, name-calling, saying I'll kill myself if you leave me, obsessive phone calling, and extreme possessiveness.

- Do not meet your partner alone. Do not let him or her in your home or car when you are alone.

- Avoid being alone at school, your job, on the way to and from places.

- Tell someone where you are going and when you plan to be back.

- Plan and rehearse what you would do if your partner became abusive.

HOW TO BE A FRIEND TO A VICTIM OF TEEN DATING VIOLENCE

Most teens talk to other teens about their problems. If a friend tells you he or she is being victimized, here are some suggestions on how you can help.

- If you notice a friend is in an abusive relationship, don't ignore signs of abuse. Talk to your friend.

- Express your concerns. Tell your friend you're worried. Support, don't judge.

- Point out your friend's strengths – many people in abusive relationships are no longer capable of seeing their own abilities and gifts.

WHAT IF YOUR PARTNER IS ABUSING YOU AND YOU WANT OUT?

- Tell your parents, a friend, a counselor, a clergyman, or someone else whom you trust and who can help. The more isolated you are from friends and family, the more control the abuser has over you.

- Alert the school counselor or security officer.

- Keep a daily log of the abuse.

RAPE

Rape is About Power, Control, and Anger . . .

Surviving Rape

- Report rape or any sexual assault to the police or rape crisis center. The sooner you tell, the greater the chances the rapist will be caught.

- Preserve all physical evidence. Don't shower, bathe, change clothes, douche, or throw any clothing away until the police or rape counselor say it's okay.

- Go to a hospital emergency room or your own doctor for medical care immediately.

- Don't go alone. Ask a friend or family member to go with you or call a rape crisis center or school counselor.

- Get counseling to help deal with feelings of anger, helplessness, fear, and shame caused by rape. It helps to talk to someone about the rape, whether it happened last night, last week, or years ago.

- Remember, rape is not your fault. Do not accept blame for being an innocent victim.

If Someone You Know Has Been Raped

- Believe her or him.
- Don't blame the victim.
- Offer support, patience, and compassion to help the rape victim work through the crisis, heal, and emerge a survivor.

Take a Stand

- Ask a Neighborhood Watch group, school, employer, church, library, or civic group to organize a workshop on preventing rape. Make sure it addresses concerns of both men and women.

- Volunteer at a rape crisis center.

- If you see a TV program or movie that reinforces sexual stereotypes and sends the message that women really like to be raped, protest. Write to the station, the studio, or the sponsors. On the other side, publicly commend the media when they do a great job in depicting the realities of rape.

Crime Prevention Tips from
National Crime Prevention Council
1700 K Street, NW, Second Floor
Washington, DC 20006-3817
www.weprevent.org

and

The National Citizens' Crime Prevention Campaign, sponsored by the Crime Prevention Coalition of America, is substantially funded by the Bureau of Justice Assistance, Office of Justice Programs, U.S. Department of Justice.

Distribution made possible in part by a grant from ADT Security Systems, Inc.

Think about the unthinkable. Don't mask the facts about rape with myths and stereotypes.

THE TRUTH IS...

RAPE is an act of violence. It is an attempt to control and degrade using sex as a weapon.

RAPE can happen to anyone — children, students, wives, mothers, working women, grandmothers, the rich and poor, and boys and men.

RAPISTS can be anyone — classmates, co-workers, a neighbor or delivery person, ugly or attractive, outgoing or shy, often a friend or family member.

RAPISTS rape again and again, until caught.

USE YOUR HEAD

- Be alert! Walk with confidence and purpose.
- Be aware of your surroundings — know who's out there and what's going on.
- Don't let alcohol or other drugs cloud your judgment.
- Trust your instincts. If a situation or place makes you feel uncomfortable or uneasy, leave!

COMMON SENSE INDOORS

- Make sure all doors (don't forget sliding glass doors) and windows have dead bolt locks, and use them! Install a peephole in the door. Keep entrances well-lighted.
- Never open your door to strangers. Offer to make an emergency call while someone waits outside. Check the identification of any sales or service people before letting them in. Don't be embarrassed to phone for verification.
- Be wary of isolated spots — apartment laundry rooms, underground garages, parking lots, offices after business hours. Walk with a friend, co-worker, or security guard, particularly at night.
- Know your neighbors so you have someone to call or go to if you're scared.
- If you come home and see a door or window open, or broken, don't go in. Call the police from a public phone or neighbor's home.

COMMON SENSE OUTDOORS

- Avoid walking or jogging alone, especially at night. Stay in well-traveled, well-lighted areas.
- Wear clothes and shoes that give you freedom of movement.
- Be careful if anyone in a car asks you for directions — if you answer, keep your distance from the car.
- Have your key ready before you reach the door — home, car, or office.
- If you think you're being followed, change direction and head for open stores, restaurants, theaters, or a lighted house.

COMMON SENSE OUTDOORS

- Park in areas that will be well-lighted and well-traveled when you return.
- Always lock your car — when you get in and when you get out.
- Look around your car and in the back seat before you get in.
- If your car breaks down, lift the hood, lock the doors, and turn on flashers. Use a Call Police banner or flares. If someone stops, roll the window down slightly and ask the person to call the police or a tow service.
- Don't hitchhike, ever. Don't pick up a hitchhiker.

WHEN THE UNTHINKABLE HAPPENS

How should you handle a rape attempt? It depends on your physical and emotional state, the situation, the rapist's personality. There are no hard and fast, right or wrong, answers, surviving is the goal.

- Try to escape. Scream. Be rude. Make noise to discourage your attacker from following.
- Talk, stall for time, and assess your options.
- If the rapist has a weapon, you may have no choice but to submit. Do whatever it takes to survive.
- If you decide to fight back, you must be quick and effective. Target the eyes or groin.

Sexual Assault and Acquaintance Rape Prevention • Grades 7-12

DATE RAPE

Rapists aren't always strangers. When someone you know – a date, steady boyfriend, or casual friend – forces you to have sex, it's still rape.

PREVENTING DATE RAPE

As a woman, you can...

- Be careful not to let alcohol or other drugs decrease your ability to take care of yourself and make sensible decisions.
- Trust your gut feelings. If a place or the way your date acts makes you nervous or uneasy, get out.
- Check out a first date or a blind date with friends. Meet in and go to public places. Carry money for a phone call or taxi, or take your own car.
- Don't leave a social event with someone you've just met or don't know well.
- Do not accept beverages from someone you don't know and trust. Always watch your drink and never leave it unattended.

As a man, you can..

- Accept a woman's decision when she says "no." Don't see it as a challenge.
- Ask yourself how sexual stereotypes affect your attitudes and actions toward women.
- Avoid clouding your judgement and understanding of what another person wants by using alcohol and other drugs.
- Realize that forcing a woman to have sex against her will is rape, a violent crime with serious consequences.
- Never be drawn into gang rape.
- Seek counseling or a support group to help you deal with feelings of violence and aggression toward women.

What are "date rape" drugs?

Rohyponol ("roofies," roopies," "circles," "the forget pills") works like a tranquilizer. It causes muscle weakness, fatigue, slurred speech, loss of motor coordination and judgment, and amnesia that lasts up to 24 hours. It looks like an aspirin – small, white, round.

GHB (also known as "liquid X," "salt water," or "scoop") also causes quick sedation. Its effects are drowsiness, nausea, vomiting, headaches, dizziness, coma, and death. Its most common form is a clear liquid although it can also be a white, grainy powder.

Rohypnol and GHB are called the date rape drugs because when they are slipped into someone's drink, a sexual assault can take place without the victim being able to remember what happened.

IF DATE RAPE HAPPENS...

- Get help. Don't isolate yourself, don't feel guilty, and don't try to ignore it. It is a crime and should be reported.
- Get medical attention as soon as possible. Do not shower, wash, douche, or change your clothes. Valuable evidence could be destroyed.
- Get counseling to deal with the emotional trauma.
- If you think you've been assaulted while under the influence of Rohypnol or GHB, seek help immediately, try not to urinate before providing urine samples, and, if possible, collect any glasses from which you drank.

Sexual Assault and Acquaintance Rape Prevention • Grades 7-12

INHALANTS

WHAT PARENTS SHOULD KNOW

We carefully label and safely store many household products that are harmful or fatal if swallowed. But what about the hundreds of products–glue, paint, lighter fluid, fingernail polish, permanent markers, and anything in aerosol cans–that young people can sniff to get a rapid, dangerous "high"? It's easy to buy or find inhalants, and abuse is on the increase.

An inhalant "high" gives a feeling of well-being and reduces inhibitions, much like the effects of alcohol and other sedatives. Larger doses produce laughter and giddiness, feelings of floating, time and space distortions, and hallucinations.

SOME SIGNS OF INHALANT ABUSE

- slow speech
- disorientation
- spots or sores around the mouth
- headaches and nausea
- a general drunken appearance

MAKE NO MISTAKE—INHALANTS CAN BE DEADLY

Some people die from heart failure or suffocation the first time they sniff to get high. Chronic abuse can cause severe, permanent brain damage.

Other side effects include breathing problems, heart palpitations, muscle weakness, abnormalities in liver and kidney function, chromosome damage, loss of appetite and weight, and impaired judgment that can lead to confusion, panic, and violent behavior.

"Sniffing" is frequently a first step to such drugs as crack and heroin.

MARIJUANA

SMOKIN' POT? ASKIN' FOR TROUBLE

It's easy to get...maybe cool to try. Everybody does it.

But it's your decision.

Here's what we do know about marijuana.

- It's a powerful drug that messes with your mind, like alcohol. It makes users clumsy, less coordinated. When you're using, there's short-term memory loss. Marijuana causes accidents on the highway, in workplaces, and around home.

- With these effects of marijuana in mind, you know that this drug won't improve your athletic, academic, or artistic skills. It won't solve any problems either.

- Smoking pot is harder than cigarettes on your lungs. Marijuana smoke has 50 to 70 percent more known carcinogens than tobacco smoke. Inhaling deeply and lack of filters increase the damage

- It's illegal. Depending on where a person is arrested, penalties for possession, use, and dealing in marijuana can be harsh. Convictions carry fines, possible prison sentences, and a criminal record that can bar the subject from federal benefits.

Resources

Local Contacts

Local Rape Crisis Center
County Office on Women
Victim Advocate or victim assistance staffer, District Attorney's Office
Sexual assault or abuse information specialist, Health Department
Sex crimes officer or unit, police department

National Contacts

Center for Women's Policy Studies
1211 Connecticut Avenue, NW
Suite 312
Washington, DC 20036
202-872-1770

The Violence Against Women project of CWPS conducts research on rape and domestic violence. The project defines violence against women as a gender-motivated hate crime and supports local and state efforts to combat this crime. Some resource collections and fact sheets are available.

National Center on Women and Family Law
799 Broadway, Room 402
New York, NY 10003
212-594-1008

Provides information and technical assistance on family law topics, including rape. Publishes a newsletter and distributes rape resource packets.

National Crime Prevention Council
See "General Resources" section.

National Organization for Victim Assistance
1757 Park Road, NW
Washington, DC 20010
202-232-6682

Works to achieve recognition and implementation of victims' rights and services. Provides training and technical assistance and direct services to crime victims; serves as an information clearinghouse on issues relating to victimization.

National Victim Center
2111 Wilson Boulevard
Suite 300
Arlington, VA 22201
703-276-2880

A national resource organization established in 1985 to help victims of violent crime, organizations, and others concerned with victims' rights and criminal justice issues. Programs and services include information and referral, research, library resources, education, and technical assistance.

Rape Treatment Center
Santa Monica Hospital
1250 Sixteenth Street
Santa Monica, CA 90404
310-319-4503

Develops educational/training materials on rape/sexual assault for high school students, including the film *Campus Rape*, and accompanying discussion guide, posters, and print ads. Distributes materials addressing stranger and acquaintance rape, as well as effective prevention strategies.

Publications

Adams, Caren and Jennifer Fay. *Nobody Told Me It Was Rape (A Parent's Guide for Talking With Teenagers About Acquaintance Rape and Sexual Exploitation).* 1984. Santa Cruz, CA: Network Publication.

Brownmiller, Susan. *Against Our Will.* 1986. New York: Bantam Books.

Hughes, Jean O. and Bernice R. Sandler. *Friends Raping Friends.* 1987. Available from Center for Women's Policy Studies.

Porter, Eugene. *Treating the Young Male Victim of Sexual Assault: Issues and Intervention Strategies.* 1986. Syracuse: Safer Society Press.

Warshaw, Robin. *I Never Called It Rape.* 1988. Cambridge: Harper and Row.

Alcohol and Other Drug Use Prevention

Grades 7–12

Teenage drug use continues to be a serious problem in urban, suburban, and rural communities in this country. The use of so-called gateway drugs — alcohol, tobacco, and marijuana — is particularly popular with teens and increases the possibility that the user will try other drugs, such as cocaine and LSD.

However, some communities are discovering that teens can be the solution to the problem of teen drug use. Teen-led anti-drug efforts are changing attitudes in neighborhoods and schools, and young people are investing their time and creative energies to strengthen their communities against drug-related problems.

Information in this chapter will help you teach teens ages 12 to 18:

- what drugs are and how they affect young people;
- how drug use affects a community, including:
    - the economic costs of drug use;
    - links between drugs and crime; and
    - how to report a drug-related crime;

- the personal effects of drug use, including:
    - consequences of driving while impaired by alcohol or other drugs;
    - adverse health effects of regular drug use;
    - drug use and sexually transmitted diseases; and
    - drug use and pregnancy;

- who uses drugs;
- why teens say they use drugs;
- personal and community signs of drug use;
- how to help if a friend is using drugs; and
- how to help make your community drug-free.

What is a Drug?

"Drug" is a shorthand term that includes a wide variety of substances, some of which are legal only for some age groups, such as alcohol and tobacco; some of which are legal only by a doctor's prescription; and some of which are illegal for everyone. Drugs include these legal substances:

- alcohol (legal for those 21 years of age and older) — the drug of choice for most young people;
- tobacco (legal for certain ages, generally 18 and older);
- prescription medicines (legal when properly prescribed for the individual by a physician); and
- over-the-counter cough, cold, sleep, diet, and other medications.

Drugs also include these illegal substances, among others:
- marijuana;
- cocaine and crack;
- inhalants;
- LSD;
- PCP;
- opiates;
- heroin; and
- analog drugs.

Analog drugs, sometimes called "designer drugs," are substances that have been chemically altered to create a variation of an existing illegal or controlled substance. Until the government takes steps to make it illegal, the altered drug can be made, sold, and used legally because it is not chemically identical to the banned substance. Analog drugs are usually more potent than the substance from which they are derived, and their added harmful effects on the human body are unknown.

The use of any drug involves risks. Prescription or over-the-counter medications can be used incorrectly by taking too many, combining them inappropriately, or taking them at the wrong time or in the wrong way. For example, certain cold medicines warn the consumer against driving because the drug can cause drowsiness — ignoring the warning could lead to traffic injuries or fatalities.

Details on a wide variety of drugs, including street names, appearance, packaging, method of use, paraphernalia, and possible effects, are included in the chart on the following page.

Why Teens Need Anti-Drug Education

Teens are most at risk of developing drug use patterns that lead to addiction. The younger the age at first use, the higher the risk that the teen will experiment with other drugs when he or she is older. The following national statistics demonstrate that drug use continues to be a serious problem:

Cigarette Use

- Each day more than 3,000 school children and adolescents smoke their first cigarettes. Young smokers consume more than one billion packs of cigarettes a year.
- One in five high school seniors says he smokes daily.

Alcohol Use

- Alcohol is the drug most often used by young people.
- The average age of first drinking has declined to 15.9 years.
- More than 25 percent of those who drink have binged (five or more drinks in a row) at least once.
- Junior and senior high school students drink one out of three wine coolers sold in the United States.

Marijuana Use

- Between 1994 and 1995, marijuana use among youths aged 12 to 17 increased 37 percent.
- In 1996, one in four high school seniors used marijuana on a past month basis.

Drugs of Abuse: An Overview

The following tables identify characteristics, methods of use, and possible effects of drugs most commonly abused. The street names of these drugs may vary by region and with time.

From Drugs and Youth: An Information Guide for Parents and Educators, California Attorney General's Office

Drug	Drug Group	Street Names	Appearance	Packaging	Method of Use	Paraphernalia	Possible Effects
Alcohol	Depressants	Booze, liquor, beer, wine, product brand names	Liquid	Bottles and cans	Swallowed	Empty bottles, containers, fake IDs	Euphoria, mood swings (may be relaxed or aggressive alternately), impaired judgment, loss of coordination, blurred vision, altered perception, staggered walk. Increased doses may cause dizziness, nausea, and vomiting.
Tobacco	Stimulants	Cigarette, chew, snuff	Dried leaf, varying texture and color	Commercial packaging	Smoked, chewed, inhaled	Matches, lighters	Euphoria, lightheadedness, diminished sense of smell/taste, heart disease, cancer.
Marijuana	Cannabis	Pot, grass, weed, reefer, ganja, Acapulco Gold, joints, smoke	Tobacco-like, dried flowers and leaves on stems, often with seeds	Plastic bags, foil, hand-rolled cigarettes	Smoked in hand-rolled cigarettes or in pipes, or eaten in baked foods	Cigarette papers, roach clips, odd shaped pipes	Low doses may induce restlessness, sense of well-being, and euphoria. Physical signs include red eyes, dry mouth, increased appetite. Higher doses may cause dream-like state, acute sensations (e.g. of smell and sight), and paranoia.
Hashish	Cannabis	Hash or hash oil	Gold, brown, or black gummy substance compressed into cakes	Small chunks or balls wrapped in foil. Oil sold in small vials	Smoked, eaten, or added to cigarettes	Small odd shaped pipes	Same as for marijuana; however, higher doses can result in hallucinations, anxiety, and paranoia.
Cocaine	Stimulants	Coke, blow, white, snow, snort, flake, nose candy, cane	White crystal-like powder or powder chunks	Small foil or paper packets, small clear vials	Inhaled through the nose, injected through the veins or smoked	Straws, razor blades, rolled dollar bills, mirrors, glass pipes, needle & syringe, spoons, belts	Euphoria, increased alertness feelings of confidence and well-being. Can cause dilated pupils, runny nose, and elevated heart rate respiration, and body temperature. Overdose can cause extreme agitation, respiratory failure or death.
Crack Cocaine	Stimulants	Crack, rock, hubba	White to tan pellets or chunks	Small clay vials, clear plastic or glass vials	Smoked in small pipes	Pipes made from glass jars, cardboard cylinders, or glass base pipes	Euphoria, high energy, insomnia, appetite loss, dilated pupils, and elevated heart rate, respiration, and body temperature. Prolonged use may result in irritability, depression, paranoia, convulsions, or death.
Amphetamines	Stimulants	Speed, uppers, pep pills, dexedrine, black beauties, footballs, dexies	Pills, capsules, tablets, or white powder	Pill bottles, plastic bags, or paper packets	Taken orally in pill form, inhaled through the nose, or injected	Hypodermic needles, spoons, belts or tubes to tie off veins; straws and razor blades	Increased alertness, euphoria, appetite loss, increased heart rate, and dilated pupils. Prolonged use may cause blurred vision, dizziness, coordination loss, collapse. Overdose can result in high blood pressure, fever, stroke, or heart failure.
Methamphetamines	Stimulants	Crystal, crystalmeth, speed, methadrine, crank, meth	White to tan powder, capsules	Small foil or paper packets, plastic bags	Injected, taken orally in pill form, or inhaled through the nose	Hypodermic needles, spoons, belts or tubes to tie off veins; straws and razor blades	Same as for amphetamines.
Barbituates	Depressants	Downers, barbs, red devils, blue devils, yellows	Capsules or pills, may be red, blue, yellow or white	Pill bottles, plastic bags, prescription bottles	Taken orally	Pill bottles	Drunken behavior, slurred speech, and disorientation. Overdose can cause dilated pupils, shallow respiration, clammy skin, weak and rapid pulse, coma or death.
Heroin	Opiates	Smack, mud, tar, brown, China white, black tar, Mexican brown	White to brown powder, or black tar-like substance	Small foil or paper packets, toy balloons, cellophane wrappers	Injected into the veins, inhaled through the nose, or smoked	Hypodermic needles, spoons, belts and cotton balls	Euphoria, drowsiness, constricted pupils, nausea, and possible vomiting. Overdose can result in slow and shallow breathing, clammy skin, convulsions, coma, death.
LSD	Hallucinogens	Acid, LSD, microdot, white lightning, blotter acid	Clear liquid, colored pills, or white powder, soaked into paper	Blotter paper squares, gelatin squares, pills in plastic bags, vials, small paper squares	Taken orally or licked off paper	Small vials	Hallucinations, distorted sense of sight, taste, and smell. Dilated pupils, high blood pressure, and fever. "Bad trips" can result in confusion, panic, paranoia, anxiety, loss of control, and psychosis.
PCP	Hallucinogens	Angel dust, super-grass, KJ, rocket fuel, embalming fluid, killerweed, sherms, crystal	Clear liquid, white to brown powder, or a gummy mass	Tablets and capsules or clear liquid applied to marijuana or cigarettes	Taken orally or smoked	Dark cigarettes	Similar to LSD, only with rapid and involuntary eye movement and an exaggerated walk. User may experience extraordinary strength, a sense of invulnerability, and image distortion.
Inhalants	Inhalants	Laughing gas, bullet, poppers, snappers, rush, bolt, locker room	Any substance that emits vapors	Spray cans, glue containers, other household products	Inhaled through the nose	Any product that emits a toxic odor or fumes, cloth rag or plastic bag	Hallucinations, decreased body temperature, lower blood pressure, confusion, psychosis, nausea, sneezing, nosebleeds, fatigue, loss of coordination.

Cocaine Use

- Among twelfth graders in 1996, seven percent had tried cocaine.
- During 1991-1996, lifetime use of cocaine has nearly doubled among eighth graders.

Other Drug Use

- Stimulants are the second-most-commonly used illicit drug among young people.
- LSD was used by 8.8 percent of twelfth graders in 1996.

Know the Drug Problem in Your Community

While national statistics suggest downward trends in the use of alcohol and drugs among teens, individual community and neighborhood problems differ. When giving a presentation on drug prevention, it is critical to present an accurate picture of the situation in your community. Local facts lend credibility and interest to a presentation.

Local facts can be obtained from a variety of sources in addition to those within the police department:

- local junior high and high schools, both public and private. (Check with the school counselor or health professional.)
- neighborhood associations;
- teens themselves;
- drug treatment centers;
- medical professionals; and
- parents.

How Drug Use Affects a Community

Drugs and Crime

Drug-related crime is a problem in neighborhoods of all kinds — large and small, rich and poor, new or well-established, etc. Three-fourths of all robberies and half of all felony assaults committed by young people involve drug users. Drugs are often responsible when innocent bystanders are caught in the crossfire of gang violence and turf battles.

Young drug users sometimes steal to buy alcohol or other drugs. Vandalism and graffiti are often the destructive work of young people who have gotten "high."

One key role teens and others can play in helping drive drugs out of the community is to report crimes. Some communities have anonymous tip lines — police would like to have your name but generally don't require it. To report a crime, it helps if you can provide:

- the name or nickname of the person who is acting suspiciously (dealing drugs, using drugs, giving drugs to younger children);
- a description of the person, including identifying details such as scars, tattoos, and clothing;
- the time of day the person is usually involved with drug-related activities;
- what type(s) of drug the person is involved with;
- the location of the drug activity (including address), such as street corner, car, or apartment;
- if a car is involved, description and license plate number, if possible; and
- how the person operates (for example, the dealer takes the money and someone else goes for and delivers the drugs; the dealer takes the money but an accomplice standing with him gives out the drugs; or the dealer takes the money, goes into an apartment, then comes out with the drugs).

Communities Pay a High Price for Drug Problems

Some of the economic costs of alcohol and other drug use include:

- lost or destroyed property;
- higher costs for security;
- higher insurance costs on property, automobiles, and medical coverage;
- higher taxes to cover increased police services;
- costs for drug treatment and support;
- cost of lost educational opportunities; and
- reduced productivity or lost jobs in the workplace.

Signs That Your Community May Have a Problem

Communities suffer because of drug use. Neighborhoods deteriorate, property values decline, and people live in fear. Common signs of serious community drug problems can include:

- parks with broken bottles, drug paraphernalia, and trash — but no children;
- supposedly vacant, boarded-up buildings — with cars parked out front;
- cars abandoned on the street;
- neighbors who are afraid of being harmed;
- heavy traffic — cars that drive through, stop briefly, or return frequently, even though the drivers don't live in the area;
- broken street lights;
- increased vandalism and graffiti;
- unchaperoned teenage gatherings; and
- increased thefts in the neighborhood.

How Drug Use Affects Teens

A teen who uses alcohol or other drugs is vulnerable to serious physical and emotional harm. His or her health is in jeopardy with every beer, cigarette, or marijuana joint. A drug user is also in danger of such severe emotional damage as becoming depressed, losing friends, or causing family problems.

The physical costs of drug use include:

- **The risk of car crashes:** The use of alcohol and other drugs reduces a person's normal reaction time, thereby increasing chances of accidents for as long as the drug remains in the body. Car crashes are the primary killer of teens.
- **The risk of illness and long-lasting health problems:** Drug use can lead to impaired judgment, loss of coordination, blurred vision, vomiting, restlessness, hallucinations, elevated heart rate, convulsions, high blood pressure, stroke, cancer, and coma. The user even risks death.
- **The risk of addiction:** Users run the risk of psychological and physical addiction. A drug-dependent person substitutes chemicals for personal choice, self-control, and opportunity.
- The risk of arrest and jail.

The emotional costs of drug use include:

- loss of control over one's life;
- guilt;
- anxiety;
- fear of getting caught; and
- alienation from family members and friends who don't use drugs.

Drugs and Sexually Transmitted Diseases

Research shows a link between drugs and sexually transmitted diseases, including AIDS. Drug use impairs judgment. Many substance users who are sexually active use condoms less frequently when they are high. Such unprotected sexual intercourse makes it easier to get sexually transmitted diseases, including AIDS.

Drugs and Pregnancy

As many as 200,000 infants are born each year to mothers who use drugs. Some infants suffer low birth weight or mental and physical damage due to fetal alcohol syndrome. Some are born addicted to drugs and suffer the same painful withdrawal symptoms as an adult. Other babies, born prematurely because of the mother's drug use, die in infancy.

Who Abuses Drugs?

Although anyone can become a drug abuser, studies have identified factors that increase the likelihood that young people will become involved with drugs, including:

- friends or siblings who smoke, drink, or use other drugs;
- adults in the home who abuse substances;
- a biological family history of substance abuse (Research shows that a child born to alcoholic

parents but raised by nonalcoholic foster parents has a greater chance of becoming an abuser than someone without such a genetic link.);

- a family history of criminal or other antisocial behavior;
- a family environment lacking consistent direction or discipline;
- absence of strong anti-drug role models;
- poverty;
- a feeling of being at odds with or alienated from the family;
- poor academic performance, boredom, or lack of connection at school;
- early antisocial behavior; and
- early initial use of illicit substances. If a person tries drugs at an early age, there is a greater chance of serious drug abuse at an older age.

The existence of any of these risk factors doesn't guarantee that a teen will turn to drugs. There are many examples of resilient young people who beat the odds. However, in general, as the number of risk factors increases, so does the probability of substance abuse.

Reasons Teens Give for Using Drugs

Teens give a wide variety of reasons for turning to alcohol and other drugs.

Emotional Reasons

- to feel more grown up;
- to feel better about themselves;
- to feel more self-confident;
- to escape problems;
- to reduce stress and anxiety;
- to take a risk; and
- to assert independence.

Physical Reasons

- to feel relaxed;
- to stop pain;
- to feel good; and
- to increase energy or endurance.

Social Reasons

- to be accepted by peers;
- to be recognized or admired by friends;
- to be a risk-taker;
- to loosen up;
- to overcome shyness; and
- to escape loneliness.

Intellectual Reasons

- to reduce boredom;
- to satisfy curiosity;
- to experiment; and
- to improve attention span.

Environmental Influences

- movies and songs that portray drug use openly and approvingly;
- stores that sell drug paraphernalia;
- easy availability of alcohol and other drugs; and
- family and friends who use drugs.

As discussed previously in this chapter, although some people have a genetic predisposition to drug addiction, most people don't start drug use as full-fledged as addicts. Teens begin to use drugs by experimenting, and no one believes he will get hooked. Not everyone who experiments with drugs becomes a regular or dependent user, but many do.

Signs of Drug Use

Some of the signs of alcohol and other drug use don't appear immediately: They begin slowly and increase over time. Sometimes family and friends close to the user may not notice until the use becomes a serious problem. Some warning signs of teenage drug use include:

- **Physical:**
  — memory lapses;
  — short attention span and difficulty in concentrating;
  — dramatic change in appearance;
  — sleeping more than usual and at irregular times;

— bloodshot eyes;
— dizzy spells;
— persistent coughing;
— possession of large amounts of money and expensive items;
— possession of drug-related paraphernalia, such as pipes, rolling papers, small decongestant bottles, and small butane torches; and
— odor of drugs or smell of incense or other cover-up scents.

- **Emotional:**
  — sudden mood changes;
  — poor judgment;
  — irresponsible behavior;
  — low self-esteem; and
  — depression.

- **Family life:**
  — starts arguments;
  — is hostile when discussing drugs;
  — breaks family rules;
  — is chronically dishonest; and
  — withdraws from the family.

- **School life:**
  — drop in grades;
  — repeated tardiness;
  — frequent absences;
  — assignments not completed;
  — discipline problems; and
  — decreasing interest in extracurricular activities.

- **Social life:**
  — participates in other illegal activities;
  — associates with a different group of friends;
  — changes style of music or dress;
  — identifies with drug use subculture, such as having drug-related magazines, posters, and slogans on clothing; and
  — talks and jokes excessively about drugs.

A teen who exhibits a number of these warning signs needs help. Of course, many of these signs can also indicate other problems that aren't drug-related. Significant changes in appearance, school or job performance, and relationships should always be investigated, regardless of whether drugs may be involved.

How To Help a Friend Who is Using Drugs

There are four very important things a teen can do to help a friend who is using drugs:

- Encourage him or her to talk.
- Listen carefully and caringly.
- Refer your friend to someone who can help.
- Support your friend in the decision to reject alcohol and other drugs.

Encourage your friend to talk about how he or she feels about self, stresses and worries, and how drugs are affecting him or her.

Listen, and don't be judgmental about the personal things your friend may decide to share with you. Explain that you care, and that the two of you will remain friends as he or she works out the problems.

Refer your friend to someone who can help, because the causes of drug use are often complicated, and most people who have drug-related problems need the help and support of a professional. As a friend, you should be familiar with your community's resources. They may include a school counselor, teacher, physician, drug hotline, or substance abuse program. Look in the phone book under "crisis services," "alcohol abuse information and treatment," or "drug abuse information." You can also check community and school bulletin boards and libraries.

Support your friend in deciding to say no to drugs. It's not easy to break a habit, and someone who decides to stop using drugs is going to need all the support possible.

- Try to get your friend involved in activities that don't include drug use, such as sports, working with younger children in the neighborhood, art or music, community service clubs, or camping.
- Help your friend meet new friends who don't use drugs.
- Remind your friend that buying, using, or selling drugs is a crime.

Remember: You can get your friend to talk, you can listen, and you can provide support, but you can't make your friend stop using drugs. That's a decision only the user can make. And sometimes, despite your best efforts to help, your friend won't be ready or willing to quit.

Sometimes, to feel better about themselves, people who aren't ready to admit that they have a problem may try to lure other people into doing what they're doing. If you have friends who try to trick you into their trap of alcohol and other drug use, don't give in to their pressure. Get support for yourself.

Community Building Equals Drug Prevention

One of the most effective methods for preventing problems with teenage use of alcohol and other drugs is to encourage teens to take an active part in shaping the character of the community. Teens are often looked upon as the problem, but many communities have found that they are the solution!

Successful youth-led projects have made a difference in small towns and large cities all over the country. Some examples:

- In the Knox-Gates neighborhood of New York City, teens in COVE (Committee Organized with Visions of Excellence) meet in a basement that serves as a safe zone from alcohol and other drugs. They participate in "dry discos," ice skating, roller skating, and bowling, as well as providing job referrals, a course on survival skills, peer counseling, and tutoring.

- Members of the Natural Helpers Program in Hampton City, Virginia, train to help younger children avoid alcohol and other drugs. They have developed a New Students Program to help youth adjust to new school situations, a Peer Partner Program to help ninth graders get used to high school, an Elementary Project to help younger students prepare for middle school, and an Adopt-A-Class program to help students with learning disabilities. In each program, the Natural Helpers serve as drug-free role models and special friends.

- In a number of U.S. cities, young people in the Youth as Resources program have designed projects to meet the special needs of their communities. The programs include a wide range of students, from former dropouts to Honor Society members, from non-joiners to class leaders. Their projects have included conducting a health fair to distribute literature on the link between intravenous drug use and AIDS, building houses for the elderly, building playgrounds for day care centers, assisting older people with chores, cleaning up littered areas, and teaching young children drug prevention.

Teens who have a stake in their community — and who are valued for their contributions — are more likely to be involved in community-building, not community- and self-destroying behaviors. In order for them to become responsible, caring adults, they need positive opportunities to develop and test their talents. Young people have giant reserves of energy, creative talent, and concern for others. When they invest these in their community, they learn skills, competence, and self-confidence.

Other Alternatives to Drug Use

People use drugs to meet a variety of physical, emotional, intellectual, and social needs — but there are many other healthy and legal alternatives to meet those needs. For example:

- **Physical alternatives.** To satisfy physical needs and to relax, try such activities as:
    — dancing;
    — basketball and other team sports;
    — tennis;
    — body-building;
    — swimming; or
    — walking.

- **Emotional alternatives.** To satisfy emotional needs, try:
    — talking with a friend or counselor about your problems;
    — keeping a diary;
    — expressing your feelings through music or art; or
    — volunteering your time in a community-building project.

- **Intellectual alternatives.** To stimulate your mind, try:
  — writing poems or stories;
  — drawing, painting, and other arts and crafts, or learning to play a musical instrument;
  — starting a new hobby; or
  — learning a new skill, such as cooking or carpentry.

- **Social alternatives.** Get involved in such positive, healthy social activities as:
  — spending time with friends who are drug-free;
  — joining a youth organization;
  — volunteering to work with peers, elders, or children;
  — starting your own group to work on a cause that is important to you; or
  — finding — or creating — places to hang out with people who don't use drugs.

Messages For Parents

- Communicate the fact that you do not find drugs acceptable. Period. Many children say their parents never stated this simple principle. Don't forget to point out that drugs are against the law.

- Utilize "teachable moments" as opposed to a formal sit-down lecture. Look for a variety of opportunities — television news, TV dramas, books, newspapers, local situations. Focus on one point at a time. There will other occasions to focus on other points. Ask you child how he or she would have reacted, what else might have happened.

- Young people indicate they turn to drugs for a variety of reasons:
  — for fun
  — to fit in
  — to take risks
  — out of boredom
  — because of curiosity
  — to get through the day
  — to escape pain in their lives
  — unaware of the effects
  — to do what friends are doing
  — because a role model did it

Talk with your child to identify safe alternative activities, find help for problems, and provide information concerning the effects of drugs.

- Your child will compare your actions with your words. Take a moment think about what kind of message your are sending to your child concerning drug and alcohol use.

- Make sure your child knows you recognize and value his or her special qualities and how important he or she is to you.

- Be tough on the problem and soft on personalities. Arguing about current friends rather than their actions can lead to defensive or defiant reactions.

- Send a clear message to your child concerning the behavior you expect; your trust in your child to live up to your hopes; and the belief that your child, knowing right from wrong, is smart enough to choose to say no to drugs.

Sample Materials and Activities

Alcohol and Drugs: The Consequences You Must Live With

Objective:
To identify the personal effects of drug use.

Time:
20 minutes.

Materials:
Chalkboard.

Begin a class discussion focusing on the consequences of drug use. It is best to begin by asking students for a definition of "consequences." Keep in mind both positive and negative consequences of the use of alcohol and drugs.

After defining the consequences, begin to examine specific drugs — alcohol, marijuana, cocaine, and nicotine. Ask students to list the immediate consequences as well as the long-term consequences. Allow students to list positive consequences as well as negative ones.

After listing the consequences, ask students to create a grid. The grid should be divided into four quadrants — positive short-term, positive long-term, negative short-term, negative long-term. Give students two to three minutes to evaluate the consequences of drug use. Have them list the effects of choosing to use drugs on the grid according to their own evaluations of the likely consequences. Ask students to read their lists after they have completed them. Stress the importance of evaluating your own decision and feelings toward alcohol and drugs. Urge students to think of not only the immediate consequences of their actions but also the long-term consequences.

Negative Short-term	Positive Short-term
Negative Long-term	Positive Short-term

Discussion

- How could you evaluate a decision to choose drugs in light of both the long-term and short-term consequences?
- How does your view of drug use differ depending on whether you take into account short-term or long-term consequences?

Drugs and Your Community

Objective:
To identify the costs of drug use to a community.

Time:
20 minutes.

Materials:
Copies of scenarios.

Divide students into five groups. Give each group a scenario from those listed below. Ask each group to think about the scenario and list its costs to the community. Groups should also focus on the economic, social, and legal questions that may arise.

1. A pregnant woman smokes crack throughout her pregnancy. Her baby is born prematurely and is addicted to cocaine.

2. Your community begins to see drug dealers congregating on the streets in a neighborhood. Cars stop and buy drugs throughout the day and night.

3. As drug sales increase in the community, youth gangs begin to proliferate. Some of the gangs sell drugs, but a majority of them are formed as social clubs and as protection against the few drug gangs.

4. A local teen-run youth center is used by various youth organizations as a place where young people can hang out and plan activities. Recently, though, teens have congregated outside the center at night to drink alcoholic beverages. The city council is concerned and currently is debating whether to close the center because of this development.

DON'T LOSE A FRIEND TO DRUGS

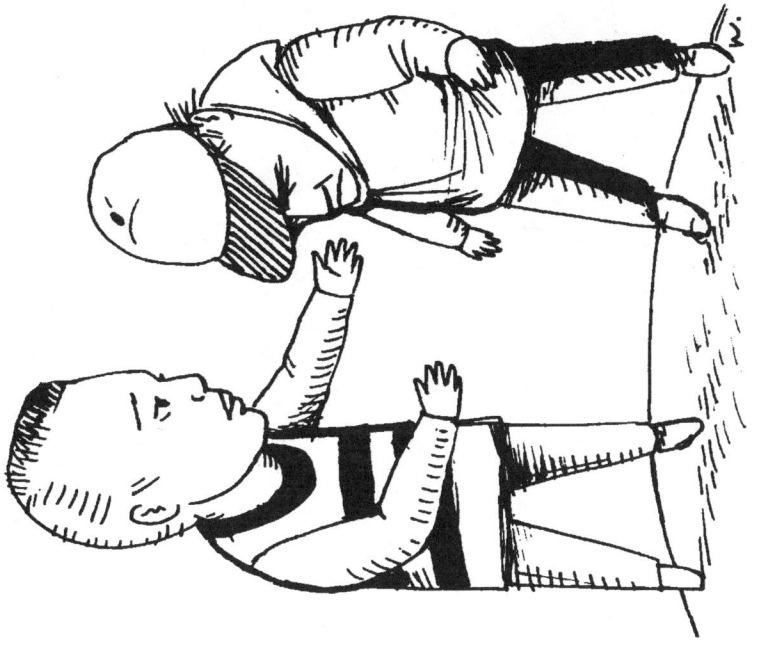

FOR INFORMATION

National Clearinghouse for Alcohol and Drug Information (NCADI)
PO Box 2345
Rockville, MD 20847-2345
800-SAY-NO-TO • 301-468-2600

800-COCAINE
Answers emergency questions about cocaine use.

800-662-HELP
This toll-free, 24-hour hotline can tell you how and where to get help for alcohol and other drug problems.

Crime Prevention Tips from
National Crime Prevention Council
1700 K Street, NW, Second Floor
Washington, DC 20006-3817

and

The National Citizens' Crime Prevention Campaign, sponsored by the Crime Prevention Coalition of America, is substantially funded by the Bureau of Justice Assistance, Office of Justice Programs, U.S. Department of Justice.

TAKE A STAND!

✔ Organize drug-free activities (dances, movies, community service projects, walk-a-thons or marathons, etc.) to raise money for charities.

✔ Use plays, songs, and raps to show younger children the consequences of drug abuse.

✔ Organize an anti-drug rally.

✔ Tell the police, teacher, or parent about drug dealers in your school and community. Many areas have phone numbers to let people report these crimes anonymously.

✔ If your school doesn't have an alcohol or other drug abuse prevention program, start one.

✔ Check recreation centers, youth clubs, libraries, or schools to see if they offer after-school activities — tutoring, sports, study time, craft classes. What about a community improvement project that young people can design and carry out?

Has a friend become moody, short-tempered, and hostile? Does he seem "spaced out"? Is she suddenly failing courses and hanging out with kids you don't trust?

Stop and think about it. Your friend may have an alcohol or other drug problem.

Here are some additional signs of drug or alcohol abuse:

✓ Increased interest in alcohol or other drugs; talking about them, talking about buying them.

✓ Owning drug paraphernalia such as pipes, hypodermic needles, or rolling papers.

✓ Having large amounts of cash or always being low on cash.

✓ Drastic increase or decrease in weight.

✓ Slurred or incoherent speech.

✓ Withdrawal from others, frequent lying, depression, paranoia.

✓ Dropping out of school activities.

If your friend acts this way, it is not a guarantee that he or she has an alcohol or other drug problem. You need to compare behavior now to behavior in the past. But it's better to say something and be wrong than to say nothing, and find out later that you were right to be worried.

HOW TO TALK TO A FRIEND WHO'S IN TROUBLE

✓ Plan ahead what you want to say and how you want to say it.

✓ Pick a quiet and private time to talk.

✓ Don't try to talk about the problem when your friend is drunk or high.

✓ Use a calm voice and don't get into an argument.

✓ Let your friend know that you care.

✓ Ask if there is anything you can do to help. Find out about local hotlines and drug abuse counseling and offer to go with him or her.

✓ Don't expect your friend to like what you're saying. But stick with it — the more people who express concern, the better the chances of your friend getting help.

✓ Remember — it's not your job to get people to stop using drugs. Only they can decide to stop.

✓ Look for help. Talk about the situation with someone who knows about drug abuse and helping abusers.

TAKE CONTROL OF YOUR LIFE AND DECIDE NOT TO USE DRUGS

✓ Skip parties where you know there will be alcohol or other drugs.

✓ Hang out with friends who don't need alcohol or other drugs to have fun.

✓ Get involved in drug-free activities. Ask your friends to join.

✓ Remind friends that buying or possessing illegal drugs is against the law. Penalties for drug-related offenses are harsh, and can include loss of benefits like student loans.

✓ Remind friends that using intravenous drugs places them at risk of getting AIDS.

Alcohol and Other Drug Use Prevention • Grades 7-12

INHALANTS

What Parents Should Know

We carefully label and safely store many household products that are harmful or fatal if swallowed. But what about the hundreds of products — glue, paint, lighter fluid, fingernail polish, permanent markers, and anything in aerosol cans — that young people can sniff to get a rapid, dangerous "high?" It's easy to buy or find inhalants, and abuse is on the increase. In 1994, one in five eighth graders reported using inhalants at least once.

An inhalant "high" gives a feeling of well-being and reduces inhibitions, much like the effects of alcohol and other sedatives. Higher doses produce laughter and giddiness, feelings of floating, time and space distortions, and hallucinations.

Some signs of inhalant abuse:

- slow speech
- disorientation
- spots or sores around the mouth
- headaches and nausea
- a general drunken appearance

Make No Mistake — Inhalants Can Be Deadly

Some people die from heart failure or suffocation the first time they sniff to get high. Chronic abuse can cause severe, permanent brain damage.

Other side effects include breathing problems, heart palpitations, muscle weakness, abnormalities in liver and kidney function, chromosome damage, loss of appetite and weight, impaired judgment that can lead to confusion, panic, and violent behavior.

"Sniffing" is frequently a first step to such drugs as crack and heroin.

MARIJUANA

Common, Dangerous, and Still Illegal

In 1994, three in ten high school seniors said they smoked marijuana at least once. It's the most widely used illicit drug in the United States and tends to be the first illegal drug teens use.

Just because it's common doesn't mean marijuana is safe. In fact, the marijuana used today is far stronger than that available two or three decades ago — and far more dangerous.

Using Marijuana May Cause...

- Memory problems
- Reduced abilities to do things that need concentration and coordination, such as driving a car
- Increased appetite
- Decreased inhibitions
- Bloodshot eyes, dry mouth and throat
- Lower testosterone levels and sperm counts in men
- Increased testosterone in women, which can cause acne and increased facial and body hair
- Paranoia and hallucinations
- Diminished or extinguished sexual pleasure
- Psychological dependence so that over time more of the drug is needed to get the same effect

Marijuana Is Still Illegal.

Depending on where an individual is arrested, penalties for possession, use, and dealing can be harsh. Convicted individuals face fines, possible imprisonment, and a criminal record.

Alcohol and Other Drug Use Prevention • Grades 7-12

HELP IS ONLY A PHONE CALL AWAY

There will be times when you really don't know what to do. Here are some numbers that can answer some questions and help you when you need it

Dial ...
- **AIDS Hotline**
  800-342-AIDS
- **American Council on Alcoholism Helpline**
  800-527-5344
- **Center for Substance Abuse Prevention Treatment Hotline**
  800-662-HELP
- **Children of Alcoholics Foundation**
  800-359-2623
- **Cocaine Hotline**
  800-COCAINE
- **Drug Abuse Information and Treatment Referral Line** 800-821-4357
- **Marijuana Anonymous**
  800-766-6779
- **National Child Abuse Hotline**
  800-4-A-CHILD
- **National Hotline for Missing Children**
  800-843-5678

For ...
- Information and local referrals.
- Referrals to alcohol treatment programs nationwide and educational materials.
- Counseling, referrals in substance abuse emergencies.
- Information and referrals for young and adult children of alcoholics.
- Emergency questions about cocaine use.
- Drug-related information, referrals to local treatment programs and support groups.
- Information and local referrals.
- Information and local referrals.
- Help in locating and recovering missing children.

Check your telephone directory for local helplines.

HOW TO USE: Cut Apart. Use as handouts, bookmarks, newspaper/newsletter articles, or envelope stuffers.

WASTED TRASHED LOADED SMASHED

What Can Alcohol Do For You?

Wreck your car.
Kill yourself or a friend.
Make you act stupid.
Make you vomit.
Tick your parents off.
Do something you'll regret.

Is It Worth It?

Kick the keg off the agenda for the next party. Look for other ways to have fun. Go dancing, rent videos, take a hike, exercise, take up marathon walking or running, read a book, do something for your community—like cleaning up graffiti or tutoring younger kids. There are thousands of alternatives to drinking. The choices are up to you.

Resources

Local Contacts

AlaTeen/Alanon/Alcoholics Anonymous chapters
State/local alcohol and/or drug abuse authority
State/local Department of Education
State/local Department of Mental Health

National Contacts

American Council for Drug Education
164 West 74th Street
New York, NY 10023
800-488-DRUG

Writes and publishes drug education materials, reviews scientific findings, and develops educational media campaigns.

National Council on Alcoholism and Drug Dependence
1511 K Street, NW
Washington, DC 20005
202-737-8122

A referral service for people with substance use problems. Deals with mental health issues and provides direction for support groups.

National Council on Alcoholism and Drug Abuse
8790 Manchester Road
St. Louis, MO 63144
314-962-3456

An alcohol and drug abuse information and reference center. Offers prevention, education, and intervention services for youth and adults.

National Crime Prevention Council

See "General Resources" section.

National Institute on Alcohol Abuse and Alcoholism
6000 Executive Boulevard
Bethesda, MD 20892-7003
301-443-3860

Alcohol abuse research and education agency that sponsors research, model programs, and technical assistance for programs nationwide.

National Institute on Drug Abuse
11426-28 Rockville Pike
Rockville, MD 20852
301-468-2600

A drug abuse research and education agency that sponsors research, model programs, and technical assistance for programs nationwide.

National Parents Resource Institute for Drug Education (PRIDE)
3610 DeKalb Technology Boulevard, Suite 105
Atlanta, GA 30340
800-853-7867

A nonprofit drug information and referral service that provides public speaking activities for any age group.

National Clearinghouse for Alcohol and Drug Abuse Information

See "General Resources" section.

National School Safety Center

See "General Resources" Section.

The Scott Newman Center
6255 Sunset Boulevard
Suite 1906
Los Angeles, CA 90028
800-783-6396 or 213-469-2029

A drug abuse prevention center that provides written and audio-visual material.

Toughlove
PO Box 1069
Doylestown, PA 18901
215-348-7090
800-333-1069

Provides information, surveys, conferences, and training programs on substance abuse. Directs troubled teens to local referral agencies.

Publications

National Crime Prevention Council. *Bringing Up a Drug-Free Generation.* 1995. Available from NCPC, 202-466-6272.

National Crime Prevention Council and Street Law, Inc. *Teens, Crime and the Community.* 1997. Available from NCPC, 202-466-6272.

Motor Vehicle Responsibility

Grades 7–12

Obtaining a driver's license is a major milestone in a young person's life. Driving gives teens a sense of freedom, mobility, and prestige among their peers. Unfortunately, some teens ignore the responsibilities that accompany operating a motor vehicle, breaking laws, committing crimes, and harming — sometimes even killing — themselves or others.

This chapter will provide you with information and tips to reduce a crime that leads to the primary killer of teens — alcohol-related crashes. It also includes information on other driving impairments and on the importance of using seat belts in vehicles. A variety of materials, activities, and resources are provided to enable you to tailor your presentation to your community.

When you have read this chapter, you will be able to teach teens ages 12 to 18 to:

- identify risks associated with driving while impaired;
- identify signs that someone is impaired;
- discuss how the law treats drivers impaired by alcohol or other drugs;
- define the criminal responsibility for drunk or drugged driving;
- identify strategies to reduce impaired driving;
- identify other behaviors that impair driving ability; and
- explain why using seat belts is a good idea.

The Number One Problem

The leading cause of teenage deaths in the United States is motor vehicle crashes. Half of these fatalities involve alcohol, which is illegal for anyone under 21. According to the Surgeon General, while life expectancy has increased for members of other age groups, it has decreased for youth, mainly because of alcohol-impaired driving fatalities.

Inexperience behind the wheel, risk-taking behavior, and frequent night driving combined with alcohol and/or other drugs kill 11 young people each day. Teens are especially at risk because they are affected more readily by alcohol than are adults, their driving skills are relatively new, and their driving performance is likely to deteriorate more rapidly when impaired by alcohol.

Consider these statistics:

- More than two of five deaths of 15- to 19-year-olds are due to motor vehicle crashes. About half of these fatalities occur in alcohol-related crashes.
- In 1996, the number of alcohol-related traffic deaths among youth ages 15 to 20 was 2,315.

No one has reliable national statistics on the additional number of teens who die or are maimed in crashes caused by people who are stoned on drugs other than alcohol, but the problem is so big that states have begun to ban drugged as well as drunken driving.

Although the legal age to purchase or consume alcoholic beverages has been raised to 21 in every state, the 1991 Surgeon General's survey of high school juniors and seniors showed:

- Junior and senior high school students drink 35 percent of all wine coolers sold in the United States and 1.1 billion beers each year.
- Although it is illegal to sell alcoholic beverages to persons under 21, two-thirds of teenagers can walk into a store and buy their own alcohol without showing identification.
- Half of those killed in alcohol-related crashes are not the individuals who were drinking.
- One-third of all teens believe that drinking coffee, taking a cold shower, or getting fresh air will "sober you up."
- Four of five teenagers don't know that a can of beer has the same amount of alcohol as a shot of whiskey. Over half don't know that a can of beer has the same amount of alcohol as a glass of wine
- Though nine of ten teenagers said a person should never drink and drive, almost one third of them had ridden with a friend who had been drinking.

Why Teens Drink

Teens say they drink for a variety of reasons. The list below includes many of the common ones:

Developmental Reasons

- to experiment;
- to feel like an adult;
- to rebel against authority;
- to assert independence; and
- because parents or other adult role models drink.

Social Reasons

- to celebrate a special occasion;
- because it's a family tradition to drink alcoholic beverages with meals; and
- because friends are drinking.

Emotional Reasons

- to feel good;
- to relieve worries or stress; and
- to build courage or overcome shyness.

The Effects of Alcohol on Driving

Alcohol slows down the activity of the brain. It goes directly into the bloodstream and is carried to all parts of the body. Since the brain has a rich blood supply, it is quickly affected. When alcohol reaches the brain, it impairs judgment, vision, and motor skills that are crucial to operating a motor vehicle safely.

Judgment: Good judgment is needed to guide behavior and allow clear thinking and quick, sound decisions. Unimpaired judgment is crucial to safe driving. A driver should be able to answer reliably such questions as:

- Is there time to pass this car before the oncoming car gets too close?
- Should I slow down to make it around this curve?
- What is that in the roadway? Do I have room to stop or go around?
- Will I hit the car in front of me if it stops suddenly?

To drive safely, drivers must be able to accurately judge speed, time, and distance. Judgment is the first thing negatively affected by alcohol.

Vision: Most of the information used to make decisions while driving comes through the eyes. Before the driver is aware of it, alcohol can affect his or her vision in the following ways:

- Visual acuity, the ability to focus and to see sharp, clear images, is reduced by alcohol because it relaxes eye muscles.
- Night vision is half as accurate as day vision for all drivers. Alcohol reduces night vision even more.
- Ability to adjust to and from sudden bright light is affected by alcohol. Unimpaired eyes need seven seconds to recover from headlight glare — at 55 mph, that's almost the length of two football fields. This recovery time is longer when a person has been drinking.
- Peripheral (side) vision helps identify objects to either side while the driver looks ahead, and is particularly important while driving in congested areas, changing lanes, or crossing intersections. A 140-pound person who has had three drinks in two hours will have a 30 percent reduction in peripheral vision.
- Depth perception, the ability to judge how close or far away an object is whether it's moving toward or away from the driver, is also impaired by alcohol. Alcohol causes each eye to receive a slightly different picture instead of the identical pictures needed for accurate depth perception.

Motor skills allow the driver to maneuver a vehicle quickly and accurately, to accomplish such tasks as braking quickly when necessary, and steering skillfully on curves. Alcohol slows reflexes and impairs coordination.

Factors Affecting Level of Impairment

The level of impairment resulting from drinking depends on a number of factors for a given individual:

- amount of alcohol consumed;
- length of time the person has been drinking;
- body weight
- amount and kind of food eaten;
- physical and mental condition; and
- presence of other drugs in the body.

There Is No Quick Way To Sober Up

People try to sober up with a variety of solutions such as cold showers, exercise, coffee, fresh air, and other quick fixes. The results are a clean drunk, a tired drunk, an awake drunk — but still a drunk. Because most of the alcohol consumed oxidizes (is processed by) in the body, time is the only way to regain sobriety. Similarly, the havoc created by other drugs also heals only with the passage of time. In fact, many drugs remain in the body far longer than alcohol. So, either way, there is no quick or easy way to sobriety except not to get drunk or drugged in the first place.

Other Drugs

Alcohol is not the only drug that puts teens at risk on the highway. Other drugs also impair ability to safely operate a motor vehicle. For example:

- **Marijuana:** Research shows that normal levels of driving performance are not regained for at least four to six hours after smoking a single marijuana joint. Marijuana impairs judgment and slows reflexes, reducing the driver's ability to steer well through curves, brake quickly, and maintain proper speed and following distance. The use of alcohol and marijuana together greatly increases the driver's risk of becoming involved in a crash.
- **Tranquilizers and other sedatives:** Studies show that prescribed doses of tranquilizers slow reaction time, interfere with eye-hand coordination, and impair judgment. Some of these drugs accumulate in the body; tranquilizers taken in the evening can even impair driving ability the following morning. Mixing tranquilizers with alcohol can double their effects and be extremely dangerous, even fatal.
- **Stimulants:** Amphetamines, cocaine, phenylpropanolamine, ephedrine, and caffeine (the latter three are often found in cold tablets and cough syrups) stimulate the central nervous system. Repeated use can cause dizziness, visual impairment, loss of concentration, nervousness, and impaired coordination.
- **Over-the-counter drugs:** Cold tablets, cough syrups, and allergy remedies may contain drugs that

are especially dangerous for drivers. It's important that anyone taking any of these drugs read the label carefully before driving. A doctor or pharmacist can explain the effects of over-the-counter drugs.

- **Other drugs:** LSD, PCP, Ecstasy, and other hallucinogens distort judgment and reality, cause confusion and panic, and can produce severe mental problems resulting in violent behavior.

How To Recognize Drunk or Drugged Drivers

If you see the following behaviors, you may be seeing an impaired driver in action:

- driving too fast;
- driving very slowly in the left lane;
- driving over the curb when making a turn;
- drifting into the wrong lane;
- making abrupt or illegal turns;
- weaving or swerving through traffic;
- straddling lane makers or driving over the center line;
- arbitrarily changing speeds from fast to slow or vice versa;
- driving on the wrong side of the street;
- tailgating;
- crossing an intersection on a yellow or red light;
- responding slowly to traffic signals;
- stopping for a green light;
- failing to use turn signals, or using the wrong signal;
- making quick or jerky starts;
- stopping short of, overshooting, or running a stop sign;
- stopping on the roadway for no apparent reason;
- driving with no headlights at night;
- failing to dim high beams for oncoming vehicles; and
- driving with the window down in cold weather.

Encountering an Impaired Driver

If you encounter an impaired driver on the roadway, there are several things to do to help prevent a crash:

- Maintain a safe following distance. Don't attempt to pass; he or she might swerve.
- If you see a driver coming straight toward your car, slow down quickly, move to the right, and stop to avoid a head-on collision, the deadliest type of crash.
- Get the license number of the vehicle and call the police from the nearest phone. Give as much information as possible about the description of vehicle, the driver, and the car's direction.

Consequences of Drunk or Drugged Driving

Arrests, fines, loss of driver's license, time in jail, and high insurance premiums are all painful costs of driving under the influence of alcohol or other drugs. Even these costs pale when compared to the psychological and emotional costs of living with the thought that irresponsible driving has permanently injured or killed a friend or other person. The emotional costs should be obvious. Here are a few of the potential legal and financial consequences of driving under the influence of alcohol or other drugs:

Legal Consequences

Driving under the influence of alcohol or other drugs is a criminal offense. If you drink or use drugs and drive, here's what you can expect to happen to you when you're stopped with probable cause by the police:

- roadside tests for substances;
- arrest and handcuffing;
- trip to jail in the police vehicle;
- booking and check-in at jail;
- reading of express consent laws and other rights;
- Breathalyzer or blood/urine tests;
- formal arrest and summons;
- notification of parent or legal guardian if you are under 18;

- release, jail, or bail;
- formal arraignment;
- alcohol abuse evaluation;
- trial and presuming conviction;
- sentencing — can include jail, alcohol education or treatment, fine, community service, or license suspension or revocation; and
- a permanent record of the offense and conviction.

Being under 21 and using or attempting to use a false ID to purchase alcoholic beverages is also a serious criminal offense and can result in severe penalties including fines and jail sentences.

Financial Consequences

Drunk driving has significant and immediate economic costs. Alcohol-related crashes cost an estimated $45 billion in 1996. This doesn't include legal fees and court costs, public assistance programs, and emergency services. Here are some examples of costs:

- towing vehicle from site of arrest;
- bond;
- attorney fees;
- court fees;
- fine;
- alcohol abuse evaluation;
- alcohol education course;
- lost wages from time spent in court or jail;
- increased insurance premiums or possible cancellation of coverage;
- restitution to victims or their survivors;
- possible loss of job; and
- civil liability to victim or survivors.

Strategies To Reduce Drunk or Drugged Driving

Everyone has a responsibility to help reduce the number of people who drink or take drugs and drive. Individual efforts can significantly reduce the number of deaths and injuries resulting from alcohol- and drug-related crashes. Here are some things that teens can do:

- Don't drink; it's against the law if you're under 21.
- Don't drive if you're impaired. Call home, call a cab, find someone sober to drive you home, or stay where you are until you sober up.
- Don't let friends drink or take other drugs and drive.
- Don't ride or let others ride with a driver who is under the influence of alcohol or other drugs.
- Don't pressure friends to drink or use other drugs.
- Start or join programs that educate teens about the risks of driving under the influence of substances.
- Report impaired drivers.

Seat Belts Really Do Save Lives

Use of seat belts is the law almost everywhere. There's a lot of common sense behind those laws:

- In 1996, 32,317 people died in motor vehicle crashes. More than 9,754 lives could have been saved if all drivers and passengers had worn seat belts.
- Research indicates that use of lap and shoulder seat belts reduces the risk of serious injury or death to front seat occupants by between 40 and 55 percent.
- Young persons ages 15 to 24 constitute 16 percent of the population but 31 percent of traffic fatalities. Fewer than 30 percent of young drivers and their passengers buckle up.
- Safety belts provide the greatest protection against ejection from a vehicle during a crash. Three-fourths of the occupants who are ejected from passenger vehicles during crashes are killed.
- Young males outnumber young females in traffic fatalities by three to one, and they buckle up 30 percent less frequently than their female counterparts. However, the number of young females involved in fatal car crashes is increasing.

There are at least five ways seat belts help prevent or reduce the injuries caused by the crash:

- They prevent the occupant's head and face from striking the dashboard, steering wheel, or windshield.

Motor Vehicle Responsibility • Grades 7-12

- They prevent the driver and passengers from hitting each other.
- They spread the force of the impact across strong parts of the body.
- They help the driver control the vehicle in multiple impacts or in evasive maneuvers.
- They keep vehicle occupants from being ejected.

Why People Don't Use Seat Belts

Despite mandatory seat belt use laws in almost all states, the fatality and injury statistics, and efforts by drivers' education programs, most teens don't take responsibility for their own safety by wearing their seat belt or requiring their friends to wear one. Some common excuses for not using restraints include:

Excuse: Being required to wear a seat belt infringes on my personal freedom.

Fact: Requiring seat belt use in a moving automobile is no more an infringement than requiring it in airplanes, requiring someone to drive on the right side of the road, or requiring someone to obey traffic signals and speed limits. Refusing to wear a seat belt affects everyone through such costs as higher insurance premiums, medical costs, and taxes.

Excuse: It is safer to be thrown clear in a crash than to remain in the vehicle.

Fact: Motorists are four times more likely to be killed or seriously injured if ejected from the vehicle than if they remain inside. A seat belt protects the occupant from the impacts of being ejected through the door or the windshield and striking the ground. People who are ejected are frequently crushed by their own vehicle or another vehicle.

Excuse: Seat belts can trap you in a vehicle.

Fact: Seat belts protect occupants so that they are more likely to be conscious and able to rescue themselves in nearly every kind of crash, including fire or submersions.

Excuse: Seat belts aren't necessary for short, slow, local trips.

Fact: Most crashes, including fatal or severe ones, happen close to home. Even though you may be traveling slowly, the driver who hits you may not.

Excuse: Seat belts will wrinkle my clothes.

Fact: While seat belts may sometimes wrinkle clothes, a few wrinkles are preferable to extensive, restorative plastic surgery.

Messages For Parents

- Help your child understand throughout the teen years that driving is a privilege, not a right, and that it carries responsibilities that must be taken seriously and can be taken away.
- Work with your child to develop a written agreement on responsibilities, rules, and expectations for his or her driving and for use of the family vehicles. Agree in advance on penalties for breaking the rules.
- Reinforce rules of pedestrian safety. Many teen and adult pedestrians are accident victims.
- Talk candidly with your child about the issue of sobriety and driving. Explain your expectations about the child calling home, taking a taxi, or staying over rather than driving drunk (or drugged) or riding with an impaired driver. Remind your child that in addition to other drugs, alcohol is illegal for anyone under 21.
- Be sure your young driver knows how to check the car for roadworthiness (tires, fluids, lights, etc.) and that he or she knows how to summon help safely (including the road service phone and account number if you have one).
- Insist — and be sure your child as driver insists — that all persons in the car use appropriate safety restraints (including seat belts, car seats, etc.).
- Reward good driving habits and practices.
- Remind the young driver that impairment can come from other things other than drugs and alcohol — illness or fatigue can make someone unfit to drive.

Motor Vehicle Responsibility • Grades 7-12

Sample Materials and Activities

Test Your Knowledge

True or False:

1. _____ Mixing different alcoholic drinks makes you more intoxicated.
2. _____ Drinking on an empty stomach makes you more intoxicated.
3. _____ A thin person and a heavy person will have the same blood alcohol concentration after having two drinks in one hour.
4. _____ Foods cooked in alcohol won't make you intoxicated.
5. _____ A can of beer has less alcohol than a gin and tonic.
6. _____ Drinking coffee sobers you up.
7. _____ Taking cold showers sobers you up.
8. _____ A bottled wine cooler is less intoxicating than a typical glass of wine.
9. _____ Parents may be held liable for an accident caused by their teenager while using the family car.
10. _____ Parents may be held liable for an alcohol-related crash that occurs after a party at their house where alcohol was served.
11. _____ Exercise sobers you up.
12. _____ Time sobers you up.

Answers

1. T   5. F   9. T
2. T   6. T   10. T
3. F   7. F   11. F
4. T   8. F   12. T

A Teaching Guide for Law Enforcement and Others

Motor Vehicle Responsibility • Grades 7-12

Decisions, Decisions

Objective:
Identify and practice strategies to reduce drunk or drugged driving.

Time:
10-20 minutes per scenario.

Materials:
Copies of the scenarios.

Many issues influence a person's decisions about drinking and driving. Thinking through choices and practicing making decisions about drinking and driving will help teens use sound judgment when confronted with real-life situations.

Divide the classroom in half and designate one side as Solution A, the other as Solution B. Read the following scenarios requiring a decision. Participants must choose one of the decisions and move to that side of the room. No one can be neutral. Have participants from both sides of the room discuss their decision. Allow time for people to change sides. Have teens who change sides explain their reasons.

1. Sarah has just begun dating Bob. Tonight they went to a party at the home of a friend of Bob's. His friend's parents aren't home, and many people are drinking heavily and smoking marijuana. Sarah's parents told her she must be home by 1 a.m. At 12:30 she finds Bob to remind him and discovers that he is stoned. She asks him if he thinks he can drive OK. He says he's fine. Marijuana improves his driving, he says with a smile. What should Sarah do?

A. She should get in the car with him and hope he gets home safely.
B. She should take his car keys from him and call her parents for a ride home.

2. You've been babysitting, and when the parents return, the father smells strongly of alcohol. He says "I'm ready to take you home." What would you do?

A. I would ask the mother to drive me home.
B. I would call my parents to come and pick me up

3. You're hosting a party and promise your parents that no alcohol or other drugs will be available. Some of your friends show up with six-packs of beer. What would you do?

A. I would ask them to check their six-packs at the door and pick them up on the way out.
B. I would let them drink and then take the empty beer cans to a neighbor's trash can.

Discussion

- What things influenced your decisions?
- If a friend were in this situation and came to you for advice, what would you say to him or her?
- Was your advice to your friend different from your own behavior? Why or why not?

ALCOHOL is NUMBER ONE

For Information

National Clearinghouse for Alcohol and Drug Information (NCADI)
PO Box 2345
Rockville, MD 20852
800-SAY-NO-TO, 301-468-2600
800-662-HELP

This toll-free 24-hour hotline can tell you how and where to get help for alcohol and other drug problems.

Crime Prevention Tips from
National Crime Prevention Council
1700 K Street, NW, Second Floor
Washington, DC 20006-3817

and

The National Citizens' Crime Prevention Campaign, sponsored by the Crime Prevention Coalition of America, is substantially funded by the Bureau of Justice Assistance, Office of Justice Programs, U.S. Department of Justice.

TAKE ACTION

- Make a pledge with your friends that you will help each other avoid alcohol and other drugs.

- If someone you know has an alcohol or other drug problem, encourage them to get help.

- If you belong to any club or other youth group, suggest that its members organize an anti-drinking project.

- Make a presentation to your school's PTA meeting about how teachers and parents can help kids avoid drugs and alcohol.

- Ask for help if someone is pressuring you to try alcohol or other drugs. Talk to someone you trust.

- Organize alcohol-free post-prom and graduation parties.

Alcohol is the number one drug of choice for teenagers.

Alcohol-related car crashes are the number one killer of teenagers in the United States.

Alcohol is the number one drug problem in America.

If you think it can't happen to you, look around. Check your school's yearbooks for the last ten years. How many have been dedicated to a student who was killed in a drunk driving crash?

Ask your friends how many people they know who have had bad things happen to them when they were drinking.

You don't even have to be the one doing the drinking — most teenage passenger deaths are the result of alcohol-impaired teenage drivers.

HOW DOES ALCOHOL AFFECT YOU?

- You see double, speech slurs, you lose your sense of distance.
- Alcohol loosens inhibitions; you make bad judgments that can result in car crashes, unwanted pregnancy, sexually transmitted diseases, or rape.
- A significant proportion of violent crimes and vandalism among and by youth involve alcohol.
- Using alcohol can cost you your freedom. You can be grounded by parents, lose your driver's license, or even end up in jail.

BE AWARE OF ADVERTISING

Take a good look at how the alcohol industry is trying to convince people to use its products.

- Wine coolers are displayed in stores next to fruit drinks. Maybe they don't think you'll notice the difference between a fruit drink and one with alcohol.
- Different brands of beer and other alcoholic beverages are slipped into the movies you watch. They think if you see your favorite actor drinking it, you will too.
- The models on the beer commercials are always young, thin, and beautiful. But alcohol has plenty of calories and little nutritional value. Drinking it will not make you younger or more beautiful.
- Advertisements feature celebrities and sports figures. But drinking will not make you famous or athletic.
- Alcohol advertisers are now trying to be more responsible by telling you not to drink and drive. But drunk driving is not the only way alcohol can affect your life.

Advertisers hope you won't stop and think when you see their ads. Don't be conned. Use your best judgment and learn the facts.

SOME MORE FACTS ABOUT ALCOHOL

- Drinking coffee, taking a cold shower, or breathing fresh air will not sober you up. The only thing that sobers you up is time.
- One beer, one shot of whiskey, and one glass of wine all have the same amount of alcohol. Don't fall for the notion that beer and wine are less intoxicating than hard liquors.
- Only 3-5 percent of alcoholics are what we think of as bums. Most alcoholics are just like the people you know. Anyone can become an alcoholic — young, old, rich, poor, married, single, employed, or out of work.
- The earlier young people start drinking and using drugs, the more likely they are to become addicted.
- Alcohol ages and damages the brain.

Resources

State and Local Contacts
American Automobile Association chapter
State Highway Safety Office
State Department of Motor Vehicles
MADD, SADD chapters

National Contacts
American Automobile Association
Contact your local chapter.

Provides a wide variety of materials, books, films, and curricula on traffic safety and drunk driving. Materials are designed to be used with all age groups. Distributes an excellent pamphlet entitled *You ... Alcohol and Driving.*

Health Education Foundation
200 Virginia Avenue, NW
Suite 502
Washington, DC 20037
202-338-3501

Offers three low-costs publications about drunk driving: *Drunk Driving — What Can I Do, A Plan to Prevent Drunk Driving,* and *The Corporate Task Force on Driving — Seven Steps to Action.*

Insurance Information Institute
110 Williams Street
24th Floor
New York, NY 10038
212-669-9200

Offers information on many topics, including drunk driving. Of special interest is the Institute's publication *Saving Lives,* that serves as a guide for those who want to prevent drunk driving in their community.

Mothers Against Drunk Driving
511 East John Carpenter Highway
Suite 700
Irving, TX 75062
800-438-MADD

Has extensive information on the prevention of alcohol-impaired driving. MADD's mission is to stop drunk driving and to support victims of this violent crime. Publishes an excellent compendium for youth on drunk-driving issues; provides pamphlets, posters, and fact sheets on all facets of drunk driving; and has local chapters around the nation.

National Commission Against Drunk Driving
1900 L Street, NW
Suite 705
Washington, DC 20036
202-452-6004

A private, nonprofit organization established in 1984 as the successor to the Presidential Commission on Drunk Driving. Publications, which are free of charge, include a report on anti-drunk driving strategies entitled *Youthful Driving Without Impairment: A Community Challenge;* and annual *Checklist of State Drunk Driving Countermeasures;* and quarterly newsletters.

National Highway Traffic Safety Administration
U.S. Department of Transportation
400 7th Street, SW
Room 5232
Washington, DC 20590
202-366-9550

Promotes motor vehicle responsibility and compiles statistics on drunk driving and seat belt usage.

National Safety Council
Orders Department
1121 Spring Lake Road
Itasca, IL 60143-3201
800-621-7619

Promotes safety through pamphlets, booklets, posters, and displays on drinking and driving, safety restsraints, and defensive driving techniques.

Students Against Driving Driving
PO Box 800
Marlboro, MA 01752
508-481-3568

Provides assistance to students interested in beginning local chapters. Combats drunk driving by educating students through activities and promotional campaigns that increase awareness.

Publications

American Automobile Association. *You ... Alcohol and Driving.* 1991. Available from your local AAA chapter.

Mothers Against Drunk Driving. *Youth Issues Compendium.* 1991. Available from MADD, 800-GET-MADD.

Cults and Gangs

Grades 7–12

Gangs — bringing drug activity, neighborhood destruction, random shootings, and fear — have become a serious problem in many communities, including smaller cities and towns that once were thought to be immune.

Teens are major targets for gang recruitment. Gangs seem to offer a way to escape problems at home, but gang membership creates serious and sometimes life-threatening problems. The youth uses the gang as a surrogate family, friend, and protector despite the fact that gang members live violent, criminal lives.

Some communities have found that gang prevention is most successful with a blend of three strategies:

- primary prevention — educating young people about gangs and providing alternatives to gang membership;
- intervention — persuading members out of gangs by providing attractive alternative activities and programs designed to help them give up their gang lifestyles; and
- suppression — responding with strong police action in communities where gangs are prevalent and ensuring swift and severe penalties for gang-related crimes.

To offer teens viable alternatives to gang membership, the community must address the causes of gang activity. The police department must enforce laws against gangs, and the juvenile justice system must cope with delinquent youths. The most effective gang prevention, however, must also involve parents, schools, community leaders, local government agencies, and teens.

Some teens are interested in unusual religious practices, including cult activities — e.g., Satanism, animal mutilation, and secret rituals. Cults have been the focus of much media attention, and their members, like gang members, are usually young people who feel alienated from mainstream society.

In this chapter, you will learn to teach young people ages 12 to 18 to:

- know the difference between the myths and realities of gang life;
- describe the criminal activities and characteristics of gangs;
- identify the consequences of gang membership;
- identify the characteristics of cults;
- recognize the signs of gang and cult activity in your community;
- explain how to report gang and cult activity to the proper authorities; and
- cite good alternatives to gang and cult membership.

What Do Gangs Do?

Gangs are organized groups involved in territory protection, criminal activities, violence, and/or drug use and sales. They often use special symbols on their clothing or to mark their territory, and they frequently have a strict code of behavior for their members.

Gangs are seen as substitutes for families by many young people because they offer identity and a sense of belonging. They offer a way to break from family but keep a support network. However, gangs do not provide their members with caring and safe environments. Many gangs require their members to steal, fight, or even murder. As gang members, young people run the risk of being arrested by police or hurt by rival gang members.

Gangs: Myth and Reality

Myth: A youth who joins a gang will be safe and protected.

Fact: It is estimated that thousands of young people are seriously hurt or killed each year in turf wars and other gang fights.

Myth: If a youth doesn't do well in school or in sports, it's best to drop out and hang out.

Fact: Young people who stay in school are less likely to hang out with gangs. Young people with poor academic performance can seek tutoring to pull up grades, and teens who are not star athletes can join youth clubs that focus on other talents.

Myth: There's nothing else to do but join a gang.

Fact: Most communities offer sports programs, youth clubs (such as Boys & Girls Clubs and Scouts), religious activities, and organized family activities, including picnics and concerts. Additionally, teens can help younger students with schoolwork, help elderly neighbors with chores, and become involved with community projects that will help keep gangs out of their neighborhood or make other improvements.

Myth: A youth can earn lots of money by joining a gang.

Fact: Many gang members sell drugs and get involved with other illegal activities that hold a promise of monetary profit, but the average drug dealer doesn't keep much of the money that he collects. Sometimes the money is seized by the leaders of the gang or stolen by other gang members. Getting money through illegal activities puts a gang member at risk of arrest and jail time.

Myth: If a teen's friend joins a gang, he or she will have to join, too.

Fact: Young people often feel pressure from their friends — and sometimes from family members — to join gangs. It can be hard to resist this pressure, but those who don't want to join a gang can seek support from other friends who are not gang members, as well as from school counselors or community agencies that deal with gang prevention.

Myth: A member can never leave a gang once he or she has joined.

Fact: Leaving a gang can be difficult, but it's not impossible. It is important for anyone wishing to leave a gang to have support from family, friends, and community organizations.

Why Teens Join Gangs

A young person who turns to gang membership may be motivated by some or all of these needs:

- **Surrogate family:** Young people join gangs to receive the attention, affirmation, and protection they may feel they are lacking at home.

- **Identity or recognition:** Some youth join gangs for status they may feel they are lacking if they are unemployed or performing poorly at school. If young people don't see themselves as the smart ones, the leaders, or the star athletes, they join a group where they feel they can excel.

- **Family history:** Many gang members carry on a family tradition established by their fathers, grandfathers, uncles, cousins, or brothers, whom they see as role models.

- **Protection:** Some young people join gangs to protect themselves. They may feel threatened by other people and may feel alienated from the police and other authorities. They rely on fellow gang members to help protect them from the violent cycle of attacks by outsiders seeking revenge for harm caused by third parties.
- **Intimidation:** Some young people feel pressure from friends to join a gang; some actually feel threatened to join by other gang members.
- **Money:** Gang members can share profits from drug trafficking and other illegal activities. To a teen, money is often translated into social status. A teenaged girl in Detroit remarked, "If a guy ain't got no crew [gang], he probably ain't got not cash. Guys with no paper don't interest us."

Profile of a Teen Gang Member

Teen gang members typically have weak ties to family, school, religion, and community. A gang provides identity and status, and the member develops a strong loyalty to the gang and adopts its lifestyle, values, attitudes, and code of behavior. It is often difficult for a gang member to break away from the gang, though it is possible.

Members of gangs are frequently arrested for burglary, attempted murder, or possession of firearms. Gang members sometimes engage in drug trafficking and extortion of small businesses and individuals. In many metropolitan areas, drug trafficking has allowed gangs to expand into the suburbs and outlying areas.

Vandalism is a crime very frequently committed by gang members. Although often viewed as a victimless crime, vandalism is destructive to communities and their residents. Vandalism creates a sense of fear and isolation among residents while damaging a neighborhood's sense of pride and self-esteem.

Types of Gangs

Gang organizations can be categorized in many ways. One useful way is to look at four kinds of gangs: cultural, territorial, corporate, and scavenger gangs:

- **Cultural gangs** base membership on nationality, heritage, ethnic group, or other distinctive personal traits. They often see themselves as defenders of their group's heritage.
- **Territorial gangs** are interested in protecting their neighborhood or "turf." They use intimidation and violence to keep rival gangs out of their territory.
- **Corporate gangs** are highly organized and exist primarily to generate money through illegal activities, such as drug dealing.
- **Scavenger gangs** are loosely organized groups that engage primarily in vandalism and acts of bias-motivated violence. For example, some scavenger gangs proclaim the supremacy of Caucasians; others share a common interest in motorcycle riding or punk-rock or heavy metal music.

Other Characteristics of Gangs

Gang members use graffiti, special clothes or emblems, hand signals, and tattoos to signify membership and to communicate their gang affiliation to others. Street gangs have their own signals, signs, colors, jewelry, and costumes that serve not only to identify gang members but also to promote group solidarity.

- It is very important to the gang that its symbols be protected from insults by rivals. Gangs are humiliated when their graffiti is degraded. A gang's emblem or identifying sign drawn upside down by a rival gang member can set off a gang war.
- Gangs vandalize private and public property to mark their territory.
- Some gang members wear tattoos that identify the wearer as a member of a particular gang. The tattoo usually includes the gang's name, initials, or symbols.
- Gangs use hand signals — or "throw signs" — as a means of communicating gang affiliations or challenging rival gangs. These signals or signs are made by forming letters or numbers with the hands and fingers, depicting the gang symbol or initials.
- most gangs are simply loosely affiliated small bands

of young people out for thrills, some are large, highly organized groups and even use state-of-the-art communication equipment, including police radio frequency monitors, and have complex organizational structures.

Consequences of Gang Membership

When teens seek membership in a gang, they often tend to focus on the companionship and excitement they feel the gang can offer. Many teens don't understand that their decision to join a gang will also result in many negative short-term and long-term consequences, such as:

- being injured by other members of the gang in violent gang initiation rites;
- being at risk of being beaten, knifed, or shot by rival gang members;
- putting their family and friends at risk of being caught in the crossfire of a gang shoot-out;
- being forced to commit crimes;
- facing arrest and time in jail;
- losing their individuality and ability to "hang out" with whomever they choose; and
- pressures to use or sell alcohol and other drugs.

Are Gangs In Your Community?

Signs and signals that gangs have moved into a community include:

- **An increase in violent crime and drug sales activity:** Many gangs in the 1990s possess high-power firearms and other weaponry. In many communities, gang-related activity has contributed to marked increases in violent crimes.
- **Fear and isolation among community members:** Increases in violent criminal activity create fear in a community. Residents are afraid to leave their homes to conduct routine daily activities.
- **Deterioration of public and private property:** Graffiti is often a signal that gangs are present. Used primarily to identify turf or insult another gang, graffiti and vandalism destroy a community's pride.
- **Loss of commerce:** Fear of gang violence affects the viability of businesses. If the safety of customers and employees cannot be guaranteed, merchants will move out of an area, resulting in damage to the local economy.

How To Report Gang Activity

Successful gang prevention requires cooperation among adults, school personnel, community leaders, and, most importantly, young people. Teens must learn that the police need their help in combating gangs. Explain to them that all illegal gang activities should be reported to a trusted adult. Here are some tips to encourage teens to report gang activity:

- If you see suspicious activity, think about these questions: What is happening? Is someone hurt? Could you or someone else get hurt? Is this is a crime?
- Tell an adult exactly what you saw or heard. Try to remember as many details as possible. (You might even want to write them down to help you remember.)
- Call 911 or the emergency number in your area if someone is being hurt or threatened.
- Tell a police officer or another adult if you feel afraid of retaliation by gang members. They can keep your information anonymous.

What Are Cults and Who Joins Them?

No one is sure of the extent of cult activity or the nature of all the activity properly classified as cult behavior. Research indicates that most instances of such behavior as grave robbery and animal mutilation are done by small groups of alienated young people.

Cults typically operate with a set of rigid practices and doctrines that dictate the members' lifestyle in great detail and require extreme secrecy as well as behaviors far from social norms.

Teens may be attracted to cult membership because they:

- lack self-esteem;
- are bored or restless;
- perform poorly in school, despite high intelligence;
- feel isolated; or
- cannot function well socially.

Cults are an issue for crime prevention if they force members to commit illegal acts, or if they illegally restrain members.

Warning Signs of Cult Behavior

Signals of the possible existence of cults in communities include:

- graffiti containing religious symbols that are distorted or turned upside down;
- representations of such images as horned demons, magical charms, and broken crosses on clothing, posters, publications, etc.
- vandalized cemeteries or churches; and
- evidence of animal mutilation.

Cults tend to be characterized by rigid control and refusal to permit members to make independent judgements. Many who have left cult groups report that they must re-learn decision-making skills, for example. Some cults require or reward acts that our society has declared illegal.

The line between religious practices and cult tactics is not a clear one. One person's religious doctrine may be seen by another person as a rigid control, but cults tend to closely supervise members, to compel them to spend all of their time subject to that supervision, and to expect members to carry out the orders of the leaders without discussion or understanding.

Remember that you as the presenter must be careful about maintaining our tradition of religious freedom and respect for others' beliefs while helping the teens understand that most non-cult religions encourage questioning and individual thought.

Alternatives to Gang and Cult Membership

Experts agree that teens are less likely to join a gang or a cult if:

- they are thoughtfully educated about the dangers of gang membership and cult behavior;
- they are involved in constructive activities; and
- they have a supportive environment that reinforces a healthy lifestyle.

To be effective, help teens look at their options — they need to know that there are many things they can do. They may need support in gaining decision-making skills. They should be encouraged to become involved with sports, hobbies, youth clubs, after-school activities, programs at religious institutions, and such community-building projects as neighborhood clean-up activities.

Make available:

- a list of alternative activities available in the community, with contact names and phone numbers; and
- a list of resources available to young people who need help in choosing not to join a gang or in leaving a gang.

Alternative activities might include:

- Boys & Girls Clubs;
- Scouts;
- Police Activities League;
- Campfire;
- programs at neighborhood recreational centers;
- programs at libraries;
- day camps;
- sports such as swimming, basketball, football, or soccer;

- community service projects;
- religious group activities;
- hobby clubs, such as model airplanes, hiking, or performing; and
- music, such as bands or rap groups.

Messages For Parents

- Teens as well as younger children, need to recognize and obey family rules. Set curfews and insist that teens abide by them.
- Know where your children are and whom they are with at all times.
- Know your children's friends.
- Keep informed about your child's performance in school. If he or she needs help, ask a school counselor about tutoring programs.
- Make sure your neighborhood doesn't invite gangs to move in. You can
  — clean up parks;
  — make sure broken street lights are replaced;
  — remove graffiti;
  — talk with other parents about teen activities in the neighborhood;
  — work with law enforcement by reporting drug or gang activity; and
  — organize neighborhood citizen patrols.
- All children have problems as they grow up. If your child has trouble dealing with his or her problems, it is important to seek help from community agencies. Ask a school counselor or social worker where to go for help.
- Beware of dramatic changes in behavior.

Sample Materials and Activities

Cults

Objective:
To assist participants to understand how easy it is to become involved in cult behaviors.

Time:
Five minutes.

Materials:
None.

It is important that you create a very safe environment for this exercise in order for it to be effective. You want people to follow your instructions without question.

First, tell the class that you possess special insight that enables you to make them happy. Instruct everyone to stand up and stand on their left foot. Explain that this promises balance in your life.

Next, instruct them to keep their right foot in the air while touching their right hand to the ground. Tell them that this symbolizes the promise of being in touch with the earth. Now tell everyone (still with their left foot and right hand on the ground and right foot in the air) to moo.

You then announce: "I'm happy to report we'll have steak for dinner tonight, since there's a herd of cattle in the room."

Discussion

- What happened?
- What did you learn?
- How could you apply this to cults?
- Why do you think cults are successful?
- How do you think you could reach out to young people attracted to cults?

Getting Caught in the Crossfire

Objective:
To discuss methods of reducing confrontations with gang members.

Time:
20 minutes.

Materials:
Copies of scenarios.

Each year, a number of innocent bystanders are caught in the crossfire of warring gang members. Some of these tragedies could easily have been prevented. In this activity, present the following scenarios to students and brainstorm effective responses that will lessen their chances of becoming victims of gang violence. Remind them that surviving any ordeal should be considered a victory.

1. As you are walking home, you notice a group of four gang members standing on the street corner. You think that they probably are drunk or high. When one of the four sees you, he yells and threatens you.

2. You live in a large apartment complex. Only recently the complex has become infested by drugs and dealing gang members. After dark, you witness your neighbor selling drugs to a group of younger children.

3. You are walking down a crowded street one afternoon. By accident, you nudge another person in the arm. You suddenly feel an arm on your shoulder. The person you nudged has grabbed you and is now giving you a menacing look. He is obviously a gang member.

4. While you are on an errand to a store, a number of gang members begin to harass you. One gangbanger asks you for your phone number and address so he can take you out on a date. Another asks you if you would go out with him tonight.

The Price

Objective:
To help students identify both apparent and hidden costs in joining a gang, and to present alternatives.

Time:
25-30 minutes.

Materials:
Flip chart, markers, paper, pens or pencils.

In this exercise, you challenge students to identify characteristics of acceptable groups of youth compared with gangs. You might ask students to name three to five acceptable groups, for example, a sports team, a religious group, a band, a Scout group. Have students break up into groups of four to five each and ask each group to develop two lists:

Positive Group

Benefits	Price Rating

Gang

Benefits	Price Rating

Ask them to identify and rate benefits 1 to 10 (10 = highest) and then do the same for the potential or actual costs. Add up ratings for each and list at bottom. Have groups share their ratings.

Cults and Gangs • Grade 7-12

Resources

State and Local Contacts

Juvenile Division, police department
Child Protective Services, Department of Human Services
County or state youth authority
Juvenile Court

National Contacts

Boys & Girls Clubs of America

See "General Resources" section.

Bureau of Justice Assistance

See "General Resources" section (BJA) Clearinghouse.

Chicago for Youth
Department of Human Services
510 North Peshtigo Court, Fourth Floor
Chicago, IL 60611
312-744-0297

Works to reduce juvenile delinquency in and around identified elementary and high schools, with emphasis on violence, substance abuse, gang recruitment, and school dropouts. CIN can provide a number of materials upon request.

Cult Awareness Network
117 South Cook Street
Suite 354
Barrington, IL 60010
800-556-3055

A national, nonprofit group founded to educate the public about the harmful effects of mind control as used by destructive cults. The organization provides a wide variety of briefing papers and books on cults as well as referrals to national cult experts.

Gang Violence Suppression Branch
Office of Criminal Justice Planning
1130 K Street, LL60
Sacramento, CA 95814
916-327-3682

State government office serving as a clearinghouse for information on anti-gang efforts throughout California. Documents include a report to the legislature on the Gang Violence Suppression (GVS) program, a summary of the projects currently funded by GVS, and a California Statewide Directory of Anti-Gang Efforts.

International Cult Education Program/ American Family Foundation
PO Box 2265
Bonita Springs, FL 34133
941-514-3081

Educates school staff and young people in high schools, colleges, and churches about cults and psychological manipulation. ICEP also maintains a speakers' bureau.

Juvenile Justice Clearinghouse

See "General Resources" Section.

National School Safety Center

See "General Resources" section.

Publications

Bing, Leon. *Do or Die.* 1991. New York: Harper and Collins.

Bryant, Dan. *Communitywide Responses Crucial for Dealing with Youth Gangs.* 1989. Department of Justice, Office of Justice Programs, Office of Juvenile Justice and Delinquency Prevention. Available from National Criminal Justice Resource Service, 800-851-3420.

National School Safety Center. *Gangs in Schools: Breaking Up Is Hard to Do.* 1993. Available from NSC, 805-373-9977.

Bias-Motivated Violence

Grades 7–12

Acts of bias-motivated (or prejudice-motivated) violence ranging from vandalism to murder are being reported in increasing numbers. At best, it is more accurate reporting that accounts for the sharp rise in incidents rather than increasing prejudice and violence on the part of our young people. Whatever the source, the great majority of adults deplore such attacks.

People of different races, ethnic origins, religions, or sexual orientations can be victims of prejudice-based violence. Law enforcement officers have even been targeted for bias-motivated violence merely because of their uniforms.

Education is vital to prevention of this kind of crime. This chapter is designed to help you acquaint teens with the nature and common characteristics of bias-motivated violence and to help them develop effective prevention strategies. After reading this chapter, you will be able to teach teens to:

- define bias-motivated violence and understand the risks it poses to the community;
- recognize and avoid biases and stereotypes that are often associated with bias-motivated behavior;
- cite common strategies that have successfully combated bias-motivated violence; and
- develop ways to combat bias-motivated violence in the community.

What is Bias-Motivated Violence?

- *Dennis Township, New Jersey:* A cross is burned at the home of a white woman whose children have a black friend.
- *Portsmouth, Virginia:* A white man fires shots at a racially mixed group of children while shouting racial slurs.
- *El Cajon, California:* A Jewish newspaper office is spray-painted with swastikas and firebombed on two separate occasions.
- *Rochester, New York:* Eight youths are arrested for beating a man because they thought he was gay.
- *San Francisco, California:* Feces are smeared on the Holocaust Memorial.
- *Knoxville, Tennessee:* An arsonist sets fire to a church ministering to gay and lesbian people.

- *Mount Clemens, Michigan:* Three white people beat a black teen to death.
- *Hopewell, Pennsylvania:* A white man whose organization helps black people is attacked and cut.
- *Seattle, Washington:* Three white men assault a 17-year-old Korean while yelling racial slurs.
- *Denver, Colorado:* A University of Denver student wearing an Arabic language shirt is brutally beaten as she walks across campus.

These examples illustrate that bias-motivated violence takes place in all kinds of communities, against all kinds of people. People are attacked, intimidated, taunted, or even murdered because of the group they are thought to belong to. No community, no group, no individual is safe from the threat.

Bias-motivated violence consists of acts, either physical or emotional, performed with the intent to intimidate or harm a person, based not on individual disagreement but on dislike of those in a category into which the victim fits.

The following three characteristics distinguish acts of bias-motivated violence:

- The offender(s) does physical or emotional harm to the victim or the victim's property.
- The offender(s) is motivated to action by hatred of a particular group, not by hatred of a specific individual.
- The offender(s) believes the victim to be a member of the hated group.

Factors that help identify a violent act as bias-motivated include:

- **Symbols or acts of hate:** A burning cross, hate-related graffiti such as swastikas and racial/ethnic slurs, desecration of venerated objects, and arson are examples of acts that damage or destroy property associated with the hated target group.
- **What offenders say:** Many acts of bias-motivated violence involve taunts, slurs, or derogatory comments about the target's race, ethnicity, religion, or sexual orientation.
- **The absence of other apparent motive:** Most bias-motivated violence is characterized by the fact that the victim is targeted because he or she represents the hated group rather than because of personal conflict with the offender(s).

The Hate Crimes Statistics Act of 1990 identifies the following as crimes that may be bias motivated:

- damage, destruction, or vandalism of property;
- arson;
- motor vehicle theft;
- larceny/theft;
- burglary;
- intimidation;
- simple assault;
- aggravated assault;
- robbery;
- forcible rape; and
- murder or negligent manslaughter.

Who Are the Targets of Bias-Motivated Violence?

Generally the targets of bias-motivated violence fall into four groups: people who are victimized for their race, for their ethnicity/national origin, for their religion, or for their sexual orientation. Under the Hate Crimes Statistics Act, quarterly reports include statistics on the following kinds of bias crimes:

- racial bias:
  - anti-white;
  - anti-black;
  - anti-American Indian/Alaskan native
  - anti-Asian/Pacific Islander; and
  - anti-multi-racial group.

- ethnicity/national origin bias:
  - anti-Arab;
  - anti-Hispanic; and
  - anti-other ethnicity/national origin.

- religious bias:
  - anti-Jewish;
  - anti-Catholic;
  - anti-Protestant;
  - anti-Islamic (Moslem);

— anti-other religion (e.g., Buddhism, Hinduism, Shintoism);
— anti-multi religious group; and
— anti-atheist/agnostic.

- **sexual orientation bias:**
    — anti-male homosexual (gay);
    — anti-female homosexual (lesbian);
    — anti-homosexual (gay and lesbian);
    — anti-heterosexual; and
    — anti-bisexual.

Bias-motivated violence has also occurred against fat people, poor people, members of motorcycle gangs, men with long hair, people who dress differently, people who are physically handicapped, smokers, and people with AIDS.

What Generates Bias-Motivated Violence?

Many experts point out that young people sometimes engage in bias-motivated violence because they are ignorant or misinformed about the target group. Education and one-on-one interaction with members of the group as individuals can help in such situations.

Researchers have found that these crimes have some characteristics that tend to differentiate them from other crimes:

- **They are far more lethal than other assaults.** Bias-crime victims are four times more likely to be hospitalized for their injuries than the victims of other assaults.
- **They are most often committed by groups of four or more people.** Researchers have found that many people who would not commit violent, bias-motivated acts by themselves express their hatred freely and violently in groups. Generally, the larger the group, the more vicious the crime.
- **They are crimes of youth.** Most perpetrators of bias crimes are in their teens or early twenties. Arrest records show that most of the bias-motivated crimes committed in the United States in the past seven years were committed by people under the age of 21. However, researchers believe that bias crimes are not acts of youthful rebellion, but rather are a violent expression of feelings shared by their families, friends, teachers, and/or communities.
- **They tend to be motivated by love or defense of one's own group.** Emotions bound to group identity are deep-seated and strong, especially during times of economic or political uncertainty or when a person has suffered emotional neglect as a child.

Experts on bias crimes think that a process called dehumanization leads to violent expressions of hatred against members of certain groups. In the process of dehumanizing another person or group, a person will:

- focus on individual differences, such as skin color, in a negative manner;
- refer to the target or group by a derogatory name, such as gook, nigger, or queer;
- stereotype by focusing on specific characteristics. (For example, all that might be noticed about a person is that he dresses like a gay person, or that he came out of a gay bar, not that he is a certain age, build, or social class.); and
- justify or explain their attitudes against those people who are deemed "wrong" because they are different.

When people are prejudiced, they prejudge the individual or group and tend to see only what they want to see.

Strategies To Stop or Reduce Bias-Motivated Violence

Individuals can use effective strategies to help reduce or prevent bias-motivated acts:

- Make sure your own actions, attitudes, and remarks set a good example for younger kids, friends, family, and neighbors.
- Educate the community against bias-motivated hatred, suspicion, and violence.
- Build community support and cooperation to organize hate-violence prevention and victim assistance efforts.

- Report crimes to local law enforcement and help the police make hate criminals responsible for their acts.
- Reduce or remove the opportunity for bias-motivated violence to occur.

Eleven-year-old Ashley Black of New Jersey decided to take action when she learned on TV about the dozens of German-language video games with Nazi and racist themes being sold in Germany and Austria. She organized a petition that read in part: "Video games should be fun. They should not promote racism, prejudice, hatred, and violence." She was able to gather 2,000 signatures from her peers and their parents in two weeks, focusing public and media attention on the spread of video games with Nazi themes. She was even able to get anti-hate legislation introduced in the New Jersey legislature. She received the 1991 Reebok "Youth in Action" human rights award, an international award given to young people who have made real contributions to improving the rights of people around them.

Schools and communities across the country have successfully reduced or prevented hate-crime violence. Some young people have written letters to the editor of the local newspaper or to a county government, urging them to set up a commission in their communities. Because young people have a significant effect on community attitudes and beliefs against bias-motivated violence, they are able to make a significant difference.

The Boy Scouts of America have established a merit badge in American cultures that is awarded to Scouts who learn about different cultural, religious, and ethnic groups in America.

Be Intolerant of Intolerance: Ways To Combat Bias Violence

- Start or join a bias-victim assistance group in your community, such as the Montgomery County, Maryland, Network of Teens/Network of Neighbors.
- Help organize a neighborhood or community group. Discuss the issues and causes of bias-motivated crime, the need for community support, and the actions you are willing to take to end hate violence in the community.
- Work with schools or the school board to introduce or improve cross-cultural education and activities.
- Volunteer to work with younger kids in and out of school to teach them to be tolerant and to respect and learn from people who are different from themselves.
- Establish a watch group in your neighborhood to help protect neighbors who have already been targets of bias-motivated violence or who are likely targets.
- Start a "tipster" fund to reward people for providing information leading to the arrest of hate criminals or information enabling the community to prevent a hate crime from occurring.
- Organize a poster, essay, or rap song contest on the theme of anti-racism or friendship and respect for all individuals and groups.
- Design a button or T-shirt celebrating multicultural friendship.
- Arrange an ethnic origins festival at your school or in your neighborhood. Encourage participants to wear the clothing of their ancestors and share regional food or traditions.
- Write letters to the editor or articles for your local or school newspaper to show the community or school that you won't tolerate hate violence or discrimination. Encourage family, friends, and classmates to participate in your letter-writing campaign.
- Visit a classmate or neighbor who has been a target of hate violence. Offer assistance and reassure the victim that the incident doesn't reflect the values of the community as a whole.
- Invite a speaker from a minority community to address your class or group about issues they face.
- Produce a performance celebrating ethnic music, plays, and/or dance.
- Paint over hate graffiti with a mural celebrating diversity.
- Become a trained peer counselor for victims of bias-motivated violence. You can help others through group sessions, one-on-one appointments, or hotlines.
- Produce a puppet show, skit, or video for peers or younger children, showing them how prejudice and discrimination threaten basic rights.

Messages For Parents

- Children learn by example and role models. Prejudiced comments, however unintentional, influence their attitudes.

- Bias-motivated crimes are against the law. Period. There is no excuse for bias-motivated violence.

- Help your child understand and appreciate the cultural diversity in your community and in your own heritage.

- Do not dismiss or take lightly bias-motivated remarks made by your child. Take time promptly to talk about why he or she believes this comment.

- The United States is becoming more diverse daily; this will provide a multitude of challenges and opportunities. Work to engage curiosity concerning diversity, not guilt. Curiosity moves the child toward additional learning.

- Differences are real. Do not attempt to explain them away.

- No one should ever be color-blind. We are who we are because of our heritage.

- When clashes arising from prejudice occur, what often matters is not what really happened, but what participants believe happened. Help your child understand the negative as well as positive roles perceptions can play, and how to check their own perceptions against the facts.

- This topic is value-laden, so never engage in activities without sufficient time for follow-up dialogue.

Sample Materials and Activities

Defining Bias-Motivated Crime

Objective:
To help teens define bias-motivated crime and understand how such acts affect their community.

Time:
15 minutes.

Materials:
Kooshball™ if desired.

This effective activity can be used at the beginning of a workshop, class, or discussion on bias-motivated violence. It lets teens use their own experience to define the crime and to understand its impact on their community.

The exercise can be structured several ways:

- Have an open discussion.

- Ask participants to write down their opinions and then discuss them with the group.

- Divide participants into groups of three to five people, and let them discuss the questions within their small groups and then present their ideas to everyone.

- Use a kooshball: The person holding the koosh speaks and then tosses it to another person or the facilitator.

Encourage everyone to participate in the discussion. If differences of opinion arise, encourage the group as a whole to explore all angles of the questions. If students are experiencing difficulty getting started, have them list only one or two items. The question thus becomes less threatening than an open-ended question.

Suggested topics:

- What acts or crimes do you think of as being motivated by hate or bias?

- Why do you think people commit bias-motivated crimes?

- What do you think influences people to feel hatred toward individuals or groups they perceive to be different from themselves?

- Do you know anyone who has been the target of an

Bias-Motivated Violence • Grades 7-12

act of bias-motivated violence or a hate crime? If so, what happened?

- How does bias-motivated crime affect individuals? the community?

Effects of Bias-Motivated Crime

Objective:
To identify and discuss the effects of bias-motivated crime on individuals and on the community.

Time:
At least 10 minutes for each scenario.

Materials:
Copies of scenarios.

Read and discuss any or all of the following scenarios. Discuss them as a group or divide into smaller subgroups to discuss a scenario and then present the ideas to everyone.

1. While waiting for the bus, John, the only black person in your class, is confronted by four older students who call him a "dirty nigger" and tell him "niggers are too dumb to go to our school — get out." He ignores them, and one student punches him in the groin and knocks him to the ground. The other three begin kicking him in the head, stomach, and back.

2. You walk past a cemetery on your way home from school. One day, you notice a terrible smell. looking around, you notice that many graves have swastikas and six-pointed stars painted on them with dried feces and blood. An old woman is standing in front of one of the gravestones with tears running down her face.

3. Angela, who is white, and Robert, whose mother's parents immigrated to the United States from China, are walking in the park holding hands when they find themselves surrounded by six neo-Nazi skinheads. Two of the skinheads grab Robert and physically restrain him. The other four start taunting Angela, calling her a "gook lover" and telling her it's "un-American" to go out with an Asian person.

4. Chris and four of his friends see a poster for a gay/lesbian support group meeting displayed on a bulletin board at school. They tear it down and talk about how much they hate queers and how "this AIDS thing" is all the fault of homosexuals. This inspires them to rip down posters from all the school bulletin boards and write anti-gay slurs on the torn remains.

5. Bob, a Caucasian, is walking home late one evening after working at his part-time job at the movie theater. About halfway home, in a predominantly black neighborhood, Bob is confronted by seven or eight black teens. They want to know what a "honky" is doing on their turf, and when he refuses to apologize, they beat him up.

Discussion

- How would you feel as the victim?
- How would you feel if you were a friend of the victim or of the offenders?
- Would you report the incident? Why or why not?
- How do you think this incident would affect the community?

Blues and Greens: Developing an Understanding of Discrimination

Objective:
To develop an understanding of discrimination and how it can become institutionalized in a society.

Time:
Up to one hour.

Materials:
Blue armbands and green armbands of ribbon, yarn, and paper, chalk board or flip chart.

Sometimes it is hard to understand prejudice and its potentially violent consequences if you are not a member of a group that is discriminated against. For example, police officers posing as gay men in Denver were surprised when they were attacked within hours of going out onto the street in a neighborhood frequented by gay men. This exercise is designed to give students a firsthand experience of discrimination.

Split the group randomly into two subgroups, one large and one small. Include most (80-90 percent) of the students in the larger subgroup. Give each of them a blue armband, and give each of the students in the smaller subgroup a green armband. Have the students put the armbands on their left arms. The blue group is the "superior" group and the green group is the "inferior" group. Choose three rules and two stereotypes that the green group will have to follow. Write them down on the chalk board. You can choose from the list below or make up your own.

Stereotypes

- Greens are not smart.
- Greens speak terrible English.
- Greens are physically stronger than Blues.
- Greens are greedy.
- Greens are clumsy and uncoordinated.
- Greens smell bad.

Rules

- Greens are only allowed to (choose one) sit in certain designated chairs/sit at the back of the room/sit with their backs to the front of the room.
- Greens must (choose one) speak only when spoken to are not allowed to ask questions.
- Greens are allowed only to call Blues by their full names or sir or madam; Blues can call Greens anything they want.
- Greens must start every sentence with the phrase "If it please your most honorable Blueness … "
- Greens must (choose one) hold their noses whenever they talk/talk with their teeth clenched together/talk with their tongues rolled behind their lower lips.
- Greens must (choose one) keep their right hands in their pockets/keep their right hands behind their backs.

The statements you write on the chalk board are the rules and customs of your society and must be obeyed. Run a ten-minute role-playing session where the rules are enforced. You can continue with other activities during the role-play if you wish. After ten minutes conduct a five-minute legislative session. All Blues can vote to modify or abolish any of the six rules. Greens cannot vote, but can lobby for changes. Majority vote wins. Conduct a ten-minute role-play under the new rules.

Now conduct a second legislative session, except this time let students know that after the vote and rule changes, you will randomly reassign the blue and green armbands. "Superior" Blues may or may not be reassigned as "inferior" Greens. Greens may or may not be reassigned as Blues.

Conduct the last ten-minute role-playing session with the most current rules.

Take back all of the armbands. Announce that the special rules no longer apply. Discuss the exercise and its relation to our society for 20 minutes. Possible discussion questions include:

- What was it like to be a member of the "superior" Blue group?
- What was it like to be a member of the "inferior" Green group?
- Why did Blues choose to modify or abolish some/all of the rules?
- How was their decision affected by the uncertainty of their status in the next round of play?
- How does this exercise relate to our society?
- What rules and stereotypes have you noticed in the real world?
- How does this exercise make you feel about prejudice and discrimination? Do you think others would feel the same way you do?
- Do you think people would be less likely to discriminate and engage in hate violence if they went through an exercise like this?
- Has this exercise given you any ideas about how to prevent or reduce bias-motivated violence?

The Orange

Objective:
To assist participants in understanding people's desire to associate with the familiar and that each individual is distinct.

Time:
15 minutes to one hour, depending upon how long you discuss the activity.

Materials:
One paper bag and an orange for every participant, plus six extra oranges.

Circulate among the students and have each one draw an orange from the bag. Tell them to study their orange and get to know its physical characteristics for about one to two minutes.

Have each participant turn to another. Each one should introduce his or her orange to the other young person's orange, giving it a little history and personality. (Allow four to five minutes, divided between the two.)

Now collect the oranges from all the participants. Throw them onto the floor with the extra oranges and have everyone find his or her orange. Then ask if anyone did not find his or her orange. Do they want to look at other people's oranges to see if someone has "orange-napped" it? Do they want to adopt another orange?

Discuss the Experience

- Ask people who could not find their orange how they felt about not getting their original orange.
- How did they feel when you took back the oranges and they had to find their orange?
- How would you apply this to being around people from cultures other than your own?
- How would you apply this to bias-motivated violence?

Resources

State and Local Contacts

Anti-Defamation League
Gay rights activist group
Human Rights Commission
National Association for the Advancement of Colored People
The Urban League

National Contacts

Anti-Defamation League of B'Nai B'rith
823 United Nations Plaza
New York, NY 10017
212-490-2525

A human relations agency dedicated to translating our country's heritage and democratic ideals into a way of life for all Americans. It battles bigotry and hatred by campaigning for strong laws to make discrimination illegal and punishable by law. One of the nation's largest distributors of human relations materials.

Center for Democratic Renewal (CDR)
PO Box 50469
Atlanta, GA 30302
404-221-0025

A national, multiracial, nonprofit organization that seeks to build public opposition to hate group activity and bigoted violence and to assist victims of bigoted violence. Conducts educational programs, research, victim assistance, community organizing, leadership training, and public policy advocacy. Speakers available.

National Association for the Advancement of Colored People (NAACP)
4805 Mount Hope Drive
Baltimore, MD 21215
410-358-8900

NAACP is one of America's oldest and largest organizations working to create racial equality. It has over 40,000 members who are either in high school or college. Young people are encouraged to join a local chapter or start their own. NAACP activities include campaigns to desegregate schools and voter registration drives.

National Gay and Lesbian Task Force
2320 17th Street, NW
Washington, DC 20009
202-332-6483

Provides individuals with information on organizing against violence and working with police, criminal justice, and social service agencies. They publish a list of anti-violence resources that includes many local groups. Also offers victim assistance through the National Gay/Lesbian Crisis line at 800-221-7044.

Southern Poverty Law Center
PO Box 548
Montgomery, AL 36101-0548
334-264-0286

Also known as Klanwatch Project, this national nonprofit organization's purpose is to gather and disseminate information about the Ku Klux Klan and to create a body of law to protect the rights of people attacked by the Klan. Collects information from 13,000 U.S. publications and other sources concerning the Klan. The Klanwatch Project has engaged in numerous successful lawsuits against white supremacists.

The Urban League
120 Wall Street, Eighth Floor
New York, NY 10005
212-310-9000

The Urban League works to increase opportunities for racial minorities. Chapters at 113 local affiliates in 34 states offer a variety of services including career counseling and help in resolving racial conflicts.

Publications

Anti-Defamation League. *Being Fair and Being Free.* 1986. Available from the Anti-Defamation League, 800-343-5540

Anti-Defamation League. *The Prejudice Book.* 1979. Available from the Anti-Defamation League, 800-343-5540.

Center for Democratic Renewal. *When Hate Groups Come to Town: A Handbook of Model Community Responses.* 1987. Available from CDR, 404-221-0025.

Conflict Management

Grades 7–12

Conflict is normal and often occurs when there are real differences — or differing perceptions — about issues, statements, acts, or events.

Because conflict can trigger emotion, teens sometimes hope that they can avoid an issue and it will just go away. However, an ignored or avoided conflict can become unmanageable and result in hurt feelings, disharmony, or irresponsible behavior — even violence. Unfortunately, there are no conflict cure-alls for disputes, but there are skills that can assist in successfully managing conflict.

This chapter will help you teach teens to:

- understand what conflict is;
- identify things that trigger anger and can lead to violence;
- learn about levels of conflict;
- differentiate between interest bargaining and position bargaining;
- learn skills to handle conflict constructively; and
- identify ways that conflict management skills can be used in their school and community.

What Is Conflict?

Put simply, conflict happens when people disagree. It stems from misinformation or from incompatible or opposing values, needs, or wishes. If ignored or handled incorrectly, disagreements can escalate to anger or even physical violence.

Conflict is destructive when it:

- takes energy away from important activities and issues;
- makes people feel bad;
- causes people to work against each other instead of working together; or
- produces irresponsible behavior, such as name-calling or violence.

But conflict can be constructive. The process of resolving differing views can help when it:

- results in solving problems;
- increases a person's involvement in issues that are important;
- promotes open, honest communication;
- helps relieve pent-up emotion, anxiety, fear, and stress;
- helps people learn more about each other and to work together; or
- helps teens grow personally and learn skills that they can apply to future situations.

Conflict Role Models

No one is born knowing how to handle conflict. Children learn to handle conflict by observing other people, such as parents, brothers and sisters, teachers, friends, or television or movie heroes. Some role models for conflict resolution are healthy, others are unhealthy.

Examples of healthy role models include people who:

- listen carefully and thoughtfully to the other person;
- negotiate with consideration for the needs of everyone involved;
- don't simply give in or compromise, but attempt to generate a range of solutions;
- provide constructive feedback; or
- help everyone to focus on solving the same problem.

Examples of unhealthy role models include people who:

- throw temper tantrums when they can't have what they want;
- threaten violence in order to get what they want;
- block solutions by refusing to discuss the problem;
- give in only because they think someone has more power; or
- refuse to be honest and open-minded about the problem and possible solutions.

Inhibitors of Effective Conflict Management

Many things can interfere with people's ability to effectively resolve their differences. Differences that aren't resolved can turn into arguments, and arguments can escalate into violence. Some of the things that can get in the way of resolving differences peacefully include:

- lack of understanding about the real nature of the conflict;
- the method or style used to communicate thoughts and feelings;
- inability to listen and understand;
- level of investment in resolving the problem in the individual's favor; and
- level of emotions, especially anger.

Triggers

An action or word can trigger an emotional response, and emotions can block or mask clear communication. Some people in conflict react to these trigger words or actions instead of focusing on the problem.

Examples of triggers (things that almost automatically cause anger) include:

- someone yells to argue a point;
- a person pounds on the table;
- the other person just walks away during a discussion; or
- the other person insults a third person.

It's important for people to recognize their own triggers to anger. These triggers can put a quick end to constructive communication, and communication is at the heart of effective conflict management.

Control or counter your reaction to these triggers by taking one or all of these simple steps:

- Count slowly to ten.
- Take a deep breath or two to calm yourself.
- Think about what you really want.
- Think about what the other person wants.
- If he or she is angry, ask for a time-out to help you both calm down.

Classes of Conflicts

Determining the kind of conflict can help assess how to manage the dispute. Information and data, process, goals, and values are four kinds of conflict.

Information/Data

The most basic type of conflict is when someone fails to get information or when two people get differing information. An example of an information conflict is when a teen violates rules and regulations that have not been written down or explained.

Process

In this second kind of conflict, everyone is getting the same information, but they disagree on interpretation. For example, after conducting a student survey, several teens may disagree about whether the results show that their crime prevention project is succeeding.

Goals

The third type of conflict occurs when people don't envision the same goal or results. Sometimes an outside facilitator can help to clarify the direction of a certain task or project. For example,

John thinks that the crime prevention project ought to make his classmates aware of school vandalism; Greta thinks that the project should encourage students to clean graffiti off the school walls on Saturday.

Values

The fourth category of conflict, values, is the most difficult to resolve. It frequently requires the training and skills of a third-party mediator. Examples of value-based disputes include those contesting religious doctrine, political opinions, or social traditions.

Negotiating: Interest, Not Position

Most people begin a conflict with a position, which is usually their solution to a problem or concern. This means they have determined their solution to the conflict without considering the other person's point of view. Both parties try to negotiate for their own solution, but they feel deadlocked when they argue about whose position to adopt.

Negotiating over positions is ineffective because it:

- often produces agreements that don't resolve the underlying problems;
- polarizes issues and can even end friendships;
- can be very complicated and result in a misunderstanding if there are several parties involved; and
- leaves no room for new alternatives.

A more effective way to approach a conflict is called interest negotiating. Interest negotiating means you consider the desires, concerns, goals, fears, or needs of the other party involved in a dispute. Sometimes teens discover that they have similar interests as they start to explore the levels of conflict.

Several methods can help identify interests:

- Question the other person about his or her concerns, goals, or fears.
- Ask the other person to define the problem under conflict. His definition might provide insight into his personal interest in the problem.
- Take a direct approach — ask what will it take to obtain his or her cooperation.
- Ask what is preventing him or her from agreeing to a certain solution. The reasons for not agreeing need to be taken into consideration when generating a list of potential solutions.
- Take note of any events or situations that generate conflict. These events will often disclose the underlying issues that are contributing to or causing the conflict.
- Determine what themes arise in discussion. Discussing these themes themselves sometimes exposes hidden issues that are contributing to the conflict.
- Determine why the other person wants to solve the conflict his or her way. Understanding his or reasons might help to clarify the problem and the interest.
- Determine if there are several interests that are contributing to this conflict. Multiple interests may provide a variety of alternatives to consider when problem-solving. One interest may be more negotiable than another.
- Keep a list of the interests that surface in a conflict discussion to refer to as solutions are considered.

Reaching Agreement

To manage conflict, a person needs to learn how to express what he or she wants from and for the other person. The following six-step process can help people reach agreement in a conflict:

Identify Your Problem

People in dispute often find that they are arguing about different problems. Write down the problem as each party defines it. Take a few minutes to brainstorm different ways of stating the problem. Sometimes you'll decide to redefine the problem after you have considered the options.

State the Need or Actual Problem, Not the Position

What are the needs, fears, desires, concerns, or goals of each party? Remember, position bargaining pushes a person into defending his proposed solution instead of considering others.

Ask the Other Party What S/He Needs

Identify the other person's needs. This will help to focus on the problem instead of the person.

Recognize Common Goal(s)

Although they are in conflict about an issue or an action, people may find that they are interested in the same cause, the same project outcome, or the same goals. If the discussion becomes tense or heated, take time out to talk about common goals.

Begin Problem-Solving With the Other Party, and Generate Alternative Ideas About How To Meet the Needs or Solve the Problem

Brainstorm a variety of ways to solve the problem, taking into consideration everyone's interests. After brainstorming the first set of alternatives, you may want to restate the problem and brainstorm again.

Decide Who Has Responsibility for Following Through on the Action Plan

Sometimes people are so relieved to resolve the issue, they don't create a follow-up mechanism to ensure that the solution is sustained. Take a few minutes to follow through by asking: What is going to happen next? Who will do it? By when? How are they going to do it? How will they know if they have accomplished what they set out to do?

Skills For Conflict Resolution

Basic communication skills help people become better at managing and successfully resolving conflict.

Active Listening and Constructive Talking

It is difficult for someone to listen effectively when angry, hungry, cold, or in an uncomfortable chair. Sometimes it's hard for a person to listen to someone he has a negative opinion about. Many factors influence what people hear from others, including past experiences, stereotypes, feelings, environment (temperature, seating, lighting, noise, etc.), and how they feel about the others.

Yet if people are going to be successful in resolving or managing a dispute, they must be effective communicators — listeners as well as talkers. Often someone delivers a monologue without really listening or responding to what the other person is saying. Some people in conflict simply talk past each other, with neither one listening. Instead, they can try to understand opposing points of view. Active listening involves amplifying, clarifying, countering, or agreeing with someone else's ideas. This process assists in identifying and understanding the other person's interests.

The key to active listening is for the listener to verify that he or she understands what the other party said and meant. This can be accomplished by "mirroring" the other person's statement.

Tanya might say to Ralph: "I hear you say that you want to change the deadline on this project because you're involved with the basketball tournament next week." If her "I hear" statement is an accurate reflection of Ralph's concern, then Ralph should confirm that the statement is true. If Tanya has misunderstood Ralph's communication, he has the responsibility to restate his point of view, and the mirroring should continue until there is agreement.

It is helpful if the information is presented without strong emotions that might get in the way. Sometimes when a person is angry, he or she seems to send "you" messages and generalizations that:

- blame or put down the other person, such as "You never finish your projects on time";
- make the other person feel guilty, such as "You were supposed to pick up the paint";
- make others feel that they or their needs are not important, such as "You don't need to come to our planning sessions";
- avoid responsibility for his or her own feelings, such as "You're not being fair," which indirectly tells the other person that the speaker is frustrated; or
- put the other person on the defensive, such as "You shouldn't have asked Betty to help us."

People need to learn to use "I" messages to communicate their feelings and experiences. "I" messages:

- enable the speaker to express thoughts or feelings accurately;
- avoid judging or criticizing the other person;
- avoid putting the message receiver on the defensive; and
- help people in conflict understand each other better.

With "I" messages, people learn to see each other as people with differing feelings and opinions. For example, this "I" message from Eileen:

"Peter, I am worried about our project being finished in time for the dance, because you haven't been able to come to any of our meetings."

An "I" message consists of three parts:

- The action or behavior by Peter that is causing the problem. (He hasn't come to any meetings.)
- How that behavior is affecting Eileen. (Their joint project might not get done in time for the dance.)
- What Eileen feels about Peter's action. (She is worried.)

A good way to practice "I" messages is to use this outline:

I feel _____

when _____

because _____

Leaving Judgments Out of the Process

When some people are involved in a dispute, they make personal judgments about others. As they listen to someone else's solution, they may say "She is stupid" or "He doesn't know what he's talking about." To avoid bringing such judgment to a conflict, Roger Fisher, author of *Getting to Yes,* advises people to be "hard on the problem and soft on the person." Conflict management is more effective if participants focus on the problem instead of blaming each other.

When resolving a problem, try to see it from the other person's point of view. One way to accomplish this is to role-play, with each person taking the position of the other. They can ask each other questions about their positions and interests in an effort to understand both sides of the dispute.

Tips On De-Escalating Conflict

In *Creative Conflict Resolution,* William J. Kriedler explains how conflicts can escalate and how people can de-escalate them. According to Kriedler, conflicts will escalate if:

- there is an increase in exposed emotion — for example, anger or frustration;
- there is an increase in perceived threat;
- more people get involved, choosing up sides;
- the people involved were not friends prior to the conflict; or
- the parties have few peacemaking skills at their disposal.

The conflict will de-escalate if:

- attention is focused on the problem, not the participants;
- there is a decrease in exposed emotion and perceived threat;
- the disputants were friends prior to the conflict;
- the parties involved know how to make peace, or have someone to help them do so; or
- needed skills are practiced daily. These abilities can improve your life and may save a life.

Messages For Parents

- Support and reward your child for using non-violent ways to settle disputes. Don't allow other adults or children to suggest that your child is a sissy or wimp for using non-violent methods.

- Get help — counseling, advice, therapy — if you are resorting to violence yourself. Free or low-cost counseling is available almost everywhere. If nothing else, talk to an understanding friend or to a religious leader.

- Find out if your child's school or a group in your neighborhood has a conflict resolution or mediation program — either one providing training or one offering help in settling disputes or one doing both. If there's no program, start one!

- Don't allow name-calling or other taunting. Teach children to respect the feelings and sensitivities of others.

- Check in your local library for books or magazine articles on how to help children manage conflict without using violence.

- Discuss with your child how to deal with rumors at school, including the dangers of accepting as fact things that are learned second-hand and third-hand.

- Help your child review and reinforce anger management and conflict resolution techniques.

- Work with your child to develop a range of healthy outlets for pent-up emotions, such as running, swimming, team sports. Keep an eye on your child's stress level and help him or her appropriately defuse anger that builds up.

- Ensure that your child knows that it's not acceptable to you for him or her to stand around and watch fights or to join in group violence.

- Refuse to accept or approve unhealthy interschool rivalries or ethnic, racial, or religious biases.

Sample Materials and Activities

Understanding Anger

Objective:
To identify healthy and unhealthy methods of dealing with anger.

Time:
20 to 30 minutes.

Materials:
Chalk board and chalk or flip chart and markers.

Groups:
This activity can be used in a large group discussion or in smaller groups. Ask each small group to report its findings.

Anger is part of everyone's life, and it's important for teens to know why they're angry. Understanding emotions is an important part of becoming a responsible adult.

Brainstorming
Discuss ways — healthy and unhealthy — to deal with anger.

- Ask students to list the ways they deal with anger. Write their responses on the board. (If the group is slow to get started, ask them how they have dealt with anger in the past, or how they have seen other people deal with anger.)

Discussion
- There are healthy and unhealthy methods of dealing with anger. What do you think are some differences?

- Looking at the list on the board, which of the methods we listed are healthy? (Put a + sign next to these.)

- Which methods are unhealthy? (Put a - sign next to these.)

- How can unhealthy responses to anger lead to violence?

- What healthy response might be used instead of an unhealthy one?

- What would you say to a friend who responds to anger in an unhealthy way?

Hot Buttons

Objective:
To help students understand and better control their angry reactions.

Time:
30 to 45 minutes.

Materials:
Pen or pencil, notebook paper.

Have students write down responses to each of the following questions.

- What are the words that hit my "hot button" — words that make me angry?
- What kind of body language (gestures, postures, etc.) pushes my hot button?
- How do I know I'm angry? What symptoms appear?
- How do I react when my hot buttons are pushed?
- Do I have a long fuse or a short fuse? How quickly do I lose my temper?

Discussion

- Ask for volunteers to name some hot buttons — both words and actions. Ask for a show of hands of those with the same hot buttons.
- Ask students why they believe they have hot buttons. What influenced them?
- Discuss short fuses and long fuses. What are the advantages of each? Can you change the length of your fuse?

It's All a Matter of Packaging

Objective:
To get participants to learn more constructive response patterns.

Time:
15 to 20 minutes.

Materials:
Paper, pencils, flip chart, and markers or chalk board and chalk.

Part of effective communication is providing messages in such a way that the other party accurately understands what you are saying. So many different factors can jumble a message. This exercise provides students an opportunity to frame their thoughts through "I feel" messages in a way that will contribute to effective communication.

Have students think about a recent personal conflict and jot a few notes concerning these questions:

- What happened?
- What is the problem?
- What behavior is causing the problem?
- How is that behavior affecting you?
- What feeling are you having about that effect?

Each person should next find a partner; the partners should briefly share their answers to the questions. They should then take the results of the first part of the activity and write "I" statements, coaching each other:

I feel _____
when _____
because _____

After completing the exercise, discuss how participants' views of the conflicts changed, what reactions they could or should expect from the other people involved in that conflict, and how "I" messages might have changed the conflict they were reflecting on.

Resources

State and Local Contacts

State and local Bar Associations
Department of Education
Department of Health

National Contacts

American Bar Association Standing Committee on Dispute Resolution
740 15th Street, NW, Ninth Floor
Washington, DC 20005
202-662-1000

The ABA Standing Committee on Dispute Resolution, established in 1978, sponsors over 400 dispute resolution programs nationwide. It also provides many other services including service as a clearinghouse for information on conflict mediation. The ABA also has a program that encourages law offices to adopt local high schools and assist them in implementing conflict mediation programs.

Community Board
1540 Market Street
Room 490
San Francisco, CA 94103
415-552-1250

One of the largest conflict mediation organizations in the country, Community Board works to foster mediation programs in schools, universities, businesses, and any other places where conflict may arise. It provides curriculum training and assists groups who wish to start conflict mediation programs.

Iowa Peace Institute
917 Tenth Avenue
PO Box 480
Grinnell, IA 50112
512-236-4880

Provides periodic training opportunities throughout the school year, as well as in the summer, and advises in developing training programs that meet the needs of a particular school.

Conflict Resolution Education Network
1726 M Street, NW, Suite 500
Washington, DC 20006
902-466-4764

Conflict Resolution Education Network is one of the largest mediation organizations in the United States. It provides curriculum training for high schools and is involved in many other activities to promote the field of conflict mediation.

National Coalition Building Institute (NCBI)
1835 K Street, NW
Washington, DC 20006
202-785-9400

NCBI is a national organization committed to building coalitions and reducing prejudice in a variety of different work places. It works with businesses, universities, schools and any other groups that have coalition potential. NCBI carries out its mission in part by sponsoring three institutes every year to educate the public about conflict mediation and prejudice reduction.

National Institute for Dispute Resolution
1726 M Street, NW
Washington, DC 20006
202-466-4764

Established by five foundations and corporations to encourage the growth and development of dispute resolution, the Institute funds projects to test the use of dispute resolution in untried settings, record its use, and encourage adoption of successful procedures.

Street Law, Inc.

See "General Resources" section

**U.S. Department of Justice
Community Relations Service**
600 E Street, NW, Suite 2000
Washington, DC 20530
202-305-2935

This division of the Justice Department was established in 1964 to assist communities experiencing racial strife. Today, the organization works in communities all around the country, mediating disputes that have arisen as a result of racial and other community problems.

Publications

Community Board. *Starting a Conflict Management Program.* 1992. Available from Community Board, 415-552-1250.

Henriquez, Marti, Meg Holmbera, and Gail Sadella. *Conflict Resolution: A Secondary School Curriculum.* 1992. Available from Community Board.

National Crime Prevention Council and Street Law, Inc. *Teens, Crime, and the Community* ("Conflict Management" chapter). 1997. Available from NCPC, 202-466-6272.

Building Blocks: Developing an Effective Presentation

The success of any presentation depends not only on the information being presented, but also on the skill and planning of the presenter. This chapter is designed to provide an overview of the knowledge and skills needed to make an effective presentation to children, teens, or parents. It includes information on:

- how people learn;
- things you need to understand about your audience;
- how to design a presentation; and
- how to be an effective presenter.

About Learning

Learning is a dynamic process that involves changes in knowledge, attitudes, and behaviors. The way in which children learn is different from the way teens and adults learn.

In elementary school, especially in lower grades, children learn by "Do as you're told" approaches. Generally, the child listens, observes, remembers, and applies the knowledge to a specific task.

As children get older, their methods and motivation for learning become more sophisticated. They learn more by thinking through situations and by problem-solving than by listening. They need to interact with the source of the information, the presenter.

Adults learn best if they see the information as personally useful, contributing to successful experiences, and associated with their prior knowledge. They respond well to an informal yet structured presentation style and learn most effectively as participants in an active, cooperative group learning process.

How Children Learn

Understanding the stages of mental and emotional growth children pass through can be enormously helpful in knowing your child/teen audience. The age ranges given here are not absolute guides, but they are good approximations.

Ages Three to Six

Children in preschool and kindergarten are still in the developmental stage that began when they were about two years old. They are:

- developing their language ability and increasing their vocabulary;
- beginning to understand and use symbols, images, and signs;
- learning to accept rules;
- beginning to imitate adult behavior through play-acting
- beginning to think logically;
- focused on the here-and-now, seeing beyond the immediate situation only with difficulty; and
- egocentric, finding it difficult to see another person's point of view and assuming that everyone shares their feelings, reactions, and perspectives.

Here are some hints for developing a presentation for children in this age group:

- Provide lots of structure.
- Offer immediate chances to practice new skills.
- Use concrete props and visual aids whenever possible.
- Be clear about the meanings of words you use.
- Repeat a few key ideas in different ways rather than many ideas once each.
- Use closely supervised activities.
- Provide immediate individual feedback.
- Maximize the use of hands-on activities.
- Make sure each child has a chance to experience success. Be tolerant of mistakes.

Ages Seven to 11

As children develop, they gain more sophisticated ways to look at the world and to process information.

Children seven to 11 years of age:

- can solve concrete (hands-on) problems logically;
- can understand classification — for example, that murder, auto theft, and stealing from stores are all crimes;
- can organize things in order — for example, lining up a set of blocks from the smallest to the largest, or putting pictures of how to bake a cake in logical order;
- begin to explore the world outside their homes; and
- place greater importance on neighborhood, school, and peer interactions.

Here are some hints for developing a presentation for youth in this age group:

- Provide clear structure.
- Offer immediate chances to practice new skills.
- Repeat key ideas in different ways, and ask children to restate them or apply them to their situations.
- Provide immediate feedback.
- Use a warm, friendly, and supportive presentation style.
- Use props and visual aids.
- Allow them to learn by doing.
- Use familiar examples to explain more complex ideas.
- Challenge them to use logical, analytical thinking. Use open-ended questions such as "What would you do if … ?"

Ages 12 to 15

Young people 12 to 15 years of age:

- can engage in complex, abstract, analytical thinking and learn from their own experiences, not depending mainly on others for ideas;
- are beginning to be concerned about broader community and social issues;
- explore and analyze their own beliefs and attitudes;
- experiment with their own identity, with relationships with other people, and with ideas;
- are concerned about how others see them;
- want to be accepted, especially by peers;
- understand the concept of being a part of a group and can allow group needs to supersede individual needs;
- feel that they can influence the direction of their own lives;
- want and need to participate in the community; and
- enjoy taking risks.

Here are some hints for developing a presentation for youth in this age group:

- Use more abstract visual aids such as charts, graphs, and diagrams.
- Challenge students to examine and analyze differing viewpoints and opinions.
- Whenever possible, teach reasons and concepts, not just rules and facts.
- Assist students in linking information to real-life situations.
- Help students generate ideas for solutions as well as problems.
- Give students feedback that rewards creativity, constructiveness, and risk-taking.

Experiential Learning Appeals to Teens

Many teens (and adults) learn best when they understand how the topic is relevant to their lives. This style is called experiential learning. Participants draw on experience, share, interpret, generalize, apply, and receive feedback.

Experience: The learning process begins with an experience that is real and gives them factual information about some event or situation. Ask some of the following questions:

- What is going on?
- How would you feel about that?
- Can you offer a solution to the problem?

Share: In this phase, the audience share their feelings and seek to understand the feelings of their peers.

- What happened in your experience?
- How do you feel about that?
- Who else had the same experience?
- Who reacted differently?
- Were any of you surprised at your experience?

Analyze: The audience is encouraged to think about the causes of the experience or event. What might have happened if someone had acted differently? Some questions to help make analysis easier:

- How did you account for that?
- What does that mean to you?
- How was that significant?
- What was important about that?
- How might the experience have been different?

Generalize: The audience is encouraged to consider their conclusions in relation to other and more general experiences. For example, the presenter can provide newspaper stories of other hate crimes in the community. The following questions will help with generalizing:

- What have you learned from your experience?
- What does this suggest about other similar experiences?
- Can that be applied to any other experience?
- What does that help explain?

Practice: The group is encouraged to apply what they have learned to real life situations. Questions are directed toward applying the generalized knowledge they have gained to their personal lives:

- How could you apply that in your own life?
- What are your options?
- How could you make the experience better?
- What would be the consequences of doing/not doing that?

Feedback: In this stage, the audience thinks about the entire experience. Questions are aimed at soliciting feedback:

- What did you feel about this experience?
- What was good or bad about the experience?
- How might it have been more meaningful?
- What are the benefits?
- If you had it to do over again, what would you do?
- What would you change?

The Role of the Presenter

The way you present your information is often as important as the information itself, in terms of whether or not the audience will learn. You want to:

Building Blocks: Developing an Effective Presentation

- have clear goals and objectives for the session;
- actively involve students;
- stimulate thinking;
- show how the learning applies to real life; and
- help young people develop and apply problem-solving skills.

To do so, you will have to do seven things:

- know your subject matter;
- know your audience;
- plan your presentation;
- establish an environment conducive to learning;
- manage the flow of the session;
- manage individual participation; and
- evaluate.

Know your subject matter. You don't have to know the answers to all the questions that may be asked. If you don't know, be honest about saying so. Don't save your pride at the expense of your credibility — but it is important that you know where you can find answers to questions outside your expertise. If you haven't presented a particular topic for a while, it's a good idea to brush up in advance. Keep abreast of current statistics and relevant developments in your community.

Know your audience. Get some key facts about your audience before you plan your presentation. How many will there be? Will your audience be kindergarten children, teens, or members of the YVA? Are you speaking as the result of a particular incident? Are there special needs or concerns to be aware of? Is your presentation part of a series? Does the audience know a little or a lot about the topic? Are certain kinds of activities more successful than others? The more you know about your audience, the better you can meet their needs.

Plan your presentation. Given the needs of your audience, what information do you want to convey? How much time will you have? Here are some tips for planning your presentation:

- Be familiar with the physical setting. Will you be in a classroom or an auditorium? Will the people be sitting at desks or tables, or on the floor? Can you rearrange the seating? If you want to use a visual prop or show a movie, can everyone see? What equipment will you need? Can you set it up in advance? A sample form is included at the end of this section to help you to gather this information.

If people are seated at desks in rows, it can be very difficult to make eye contact with the entire group, especially those in the back of the room. It also discourages discussion because people can't easily see each other. Arranging desks or chairs in a circle or semicircle makes it easier to bring the audience into active participation in the presentation.

- **Choose your learning objectives thoughtfully.** Be sure they address the needs of the group. You won't want to repeat materials that they've already heard. Allocate your time wisely. Don't try to pack too much information into too little time. It's better to cover one learning objective well than to cover four inadequately.

- **Present information in a focused, concise way.** Adult attention wanders after about 12 minutes; children's attention spans are even shorter.
  — Plan to periodically re-engage attention, based on the attention span of the audience.
  — Present information that directly supports and reinforces the learning objectives.
  — Rather than just lecturing, give examples. Use visual aids to emphasize your point.

- **Actively involve the group.** The more a person actively participates, the more likely he or she will retain information.
  — If you use several activities, vary the styles and methods. See the part of this chapter called "Choosing Activities for Your Presentation" for an overview of different kinds of activities. Here are some examples of activities:

Brainstorming	Case histories
Cartoons	Competitions
Crossword puzzles	Debates
Demonstrations	Discussions
Films/videos	Filmstrips/slides
Flannel boards	Games
Improvisations	Interviews

Jokes
Magic tricks
Memorization
News articles
Panel discussions
Picture studies
Raffles
Questions and answers
Reports
Testimonies
Storytelling
Lectures
Maps
Music
Overhead transparencies
Problem-solving
Plays
Quizzes
Skits
Role-playing
Stop and summarize

Successful activities begin with clear instructions. Be sure that everyone understands what to do and why they're supposed to do it before the activity begins. Stopping an activity to clarify instructions interrupts the flow of the activity and risks losing the group's attention and interest.

If your activity puts participants in small groups, you should circulate, observe, answer questions, and offer encouragement. Being aware of what is happening in the groups helps to bring out common themes. Be careful to avoid "taking over" as you visit each group.

- Choose effective examples to incorporate into the presentation. Presenting dry facts is often boring, so:
- Use relevant, real-life stories; share your own experiences, if appropriate; share events that have happened in your community.
- Invite audience members to share their own experiences.
- Reinforce your points. Emphasize key points by:
   — making the same point several different ways;
   — ending the presentation with a review or asking the audience what they've learned and how it applies to their own lives; and
   — asking the audience to recall key points that you write down.
- Allow for feedback. During your presentation:
   — check with the audience to see if you got your points across; and
   — ask questions and allow time in your schedule for questions from the audience at key intervals, not all at the end.

Create and maintain an atmosphere for learning. Ideally, an atmosphere that is conducive to learning is one in which each participant:

- knows that he or she is heard and taken seriously;
- senses that he or she is an equal and important member of the group;
- feels a sense of trust and safety in the group; and
- feels OK about making mistakes, taking risks, and expressing humor in the group.

Manage the flow of the session. You need to be prepared to manage the flow of the session, including transitions from one activity to another. Be prepared to cope with unplanned distractions, interruptions, or behavior problems during the session.

- Make sure that activities don't exceed the attention span of your audience. When an audience gets bored, they will lose interest in the remainder of the presentation.
- Have extra activities in reserve. If the group works faster than you anticipated, you won't run out of things to fill the rest of the session.
- Take your cues from your audience. If they seem to be losing interest, move the presentation on to a new activity.

Manage individual participation. Helping each participant be effective in the group can be a challenge. Here are some tips that may help:

- At the beginning, try to identify group members who might present behavior problems or those whose support will help you to engage the rest of the class. Get them involved, ask for their assistance, and try to get them personally invested in the presentation.
- Don't let a few people dominate the discussion. Encourage everyone to contribute.
- Call on a variety of audience members to answer questions.
- Thank each participant for his or her contribution.

Evaluate. The best way to learn is to continually assess your work and look for ways to be more effective. After your presentation, ask what was effective, what was not effective, and what should be changed.

How To Be the Best — A Summary

- Know your material and be clear about the message you want to leave with your audience.
- Rehearse your presentation.
- Make sure the first five minutes of your presentation are interesting. Tell a story, ask questions to pique interest, or present dramatic statistics from the community. Hook the audience by explaining why this information is relevant to them.
- Develop your own style. You can learn from watching others, but develop a style that makes you feel comfortable.
- Rehearse activities with children of the same age, if possible, before you use them in a classroom.
- Preview movies, video tapes, and other visual aids before you use them in the classroom.
- Be familiar with the facilities and equipment you'll be using.
- Know your audience.
- Don't talk too fast. Vary the level and tone of your voice to help keep the audience's attention.
- Listen to and accept ideas from your audience.
- Praise people as they learn.
- Use examples and situations that your audience can identify with.
- Determine the needs of the group and focus on them in your presentation.
- Be creative in your presentation.
- Make your presentation fun.
- Ask for feedback from the audience.

Asking Questions of Your Audience

The questions that a presenter should ask his or her audience depends on the age of the audience. However, here are some general rules for asking questions that you can use to guide a discussion:

- Try to ask questions that don't imply an expected answer. Ask "What do you think about someone who writes on your school books?" instead of "Wasn't it bad that someone wrote on your school book?"
- Don't ask questions that convey a judgment. Ask "How many of you have seen someone write on the walls?" instead of "How many of you failed to tell your teacher that you saw someone writing on the walls?"
- Use a non-intimidating question to coax a timid student to participate. For example, "Do you share his or her opinion that vandalism is a big problem in your school?" Use friendly questions to help the student feel comfortable.
- Ask questions of specific people in the audience. Use their names, if you know them. This technique helps to develop a friendly relationship between presenter and audience.
- Give the respondent time to complete the answer. Some questions require more time to think through.
- Avoid questions that can be answered with a simple "yes" or "no." They cut off discussion and don't demonstrate audience understanding.
- Don't embarrass the responder. If he or she seems uncomfortable with a question, call on someone else.
- Avoid asking two questions in one, which can cause the responder to get tangled up in answering.
- Avoid asking questions in long sentences with complicated prefaces.
- Use questions to move the discussion from one topic to another. For example, you can ask: "Do you know about acts of vandalism in other parts of the community?"

Choosing Activities for Your Presentation

You should choose activities that are appropriate for the age group of your audience and that complement your presentation and encourage the audience to participate. Here are some general guidelines for using activities in your presentation:

- If you are using handouts, be sure you have enough for everyone in the class. Leave a spare copy for the teacher.
- Read all of the directions and practice each activity before using it for the first time.
- Be enthusiastic. You'll generate enthusiasm in your audience.
- Encourage full participation.
- Be sure that the directions are clear to the students before beginning an activity.
- Be sure to end each activity with a summary of what the students have learned. Involve students in developing the summary and applying what they've learned to their daily lives.

Following are details on using four major types of activities — case studies, role-playing, interactive lecture, and small group activities and discussions.

Case Studies

Case studies describe events or situations that present problems to be solved. They provide the audience with the opportunity to focus on devising solutions.

Use a case study when you want a practical, hands-on experience for small groups to work on. Case studies can help students learn how to:

- understand and analyze facts in a complex situation;
- identify problems;
- recognize that there may be multiple valid approaches to resolving a problem; and
- develop alternative solutions to a problem.

Advantages

- actively involves all participants in dynamic discussion;
- involves use of many skills;
- uncovers different opinions, values, and attitudes; and
- allows discussion to be concrete rather than theoretical.

Disadvantages

- can be ineffective if not presented clearly and concisely;
- is not directly experiential — participants hear about the situation instead of personally experiencing it; and
- can take a lot of time.

Tips for Delivering a Case Study

- Make sure the case study is specific, believable, easy to understand, concise, and relevant to the age of the audience.
- Describe the purpose of the case study.
- Explain to the participants what they should to do after hearing or reading the case — for example, take notes, discuss it with a partner or with the group, write down three proposed solutions to the problems posed by the case.
- Have the case written on a handout, and give participants time to read it.
- After participants have read the case, have them review the instructions and/or discussion questions to get them started on their task.
- Be available to answer questions about the case.
- End the exercise with a discussion that airs all participants' ideas. Try to reach consensus on the top five solutions to the problems. Encourage the participants to apply their solutions to the generic problem.

Role-Playing

Role-playing requires participants to act out a specific role in a given scenario. Participants are typically given a description of the situation and the role they will play. The description presents a situation that needs to be resolved, but the solution is not scripted. Participants are encouraged to bring their own experiences to the roles.

Role-playing builds skills by allowing participants to practice the skill in a lifelike setting. It can also raise participants' awareness and sensitivity to other people's perspectives on a particular situation. Role-playing activities help participants learn by doing — they can then apply the lessons they have learned to their own lives.

Advantages

- is a high-interest activity and can be fun;
- allows participants to try out new behaviors in a safe environment;
- provides opportunity for participants to experience situations from another person's perspective; and
- can be conducted spontaneously and informally.

Disadvantages

- usually doesn't work well in large groups;
- can deteriorate into play;
- can exclude participants who are shy or self-conscious performing in front of others; and
- can be seen as superficial, phony, or irrelevant to real life.

Tips for Role-Playing

- Share background material with participants, and be sure they understand the scenario.
- Once players have been identified, allow time for them to become familiar with their roles.
- Set time limits for performing the scenario.
- Make sure there is enough space for the activity — move tables and chairs, if necessary.
- Make sure you have any necessary props to make the situation more realistic.
- When the participants begin role-playing, don't interrupt.
- Stop at the designated time and thank the players.
- Help the group understand what has been learned with the role play. You might want to ask some questions about:
  — How effective were specific strategies the players used to resolve the situation?
  — Has anyone in the class been in a similar situation? If so, how did they handle it?
  — What suggestions are there for other ways of handling the situation?

Interactive Lecture

The interactive lecture differs from the traditional lecture in that the presenter uses questions and open discussion to encourage participation and to check participants' understanding. The presenter encourages participants to relate the information to their own experiences and share their opinions with other group members. The interactive lecture is particularly effective with teens and adults.

Advantages

- actively involves the group;
- conveys information credibly and relevantly;
- capitalizes on the experience of the group;
- establishes two-way communication between the presenter and participants;
- clarifies the participants' understanding of the subject; and
- encourages participants to look within themselves for answers.

Disadvantages

- It may be difficult to move on from one point in the discussion to another if the participants become too involved.

Tips for Delivering an Interactive Lecture

Use one or more of these techniques:

- **Energizers:** Involve the group in an enjoyable physical activity to get their attention.
- **Associations:** Ask participants to identify ideas they associate with the topic, and list them on a chalk board or flip chart.
- **Reactions:** Ask participants to identify their initial reactions: "What is the first thing you think of when I say … ?"
- **Self-assessment:** Ask participants to apply the information to their own lives and share their insights.

Help participants by:

- listing major points on a chalk board or flip chart;
- using concrete examples they can easily identify with;
- regularly summarizing what you have covered;
- sharing your personal experiences; and

- soliciting comments from the group using a variety of methods including:
  - **Current events:** Ask for examples from the news to illustrate points in the lecture.
  - **Questions or review:** Stop from time to time to ask for restatement by a listener of a key point or concept. Distortions, misinterpretations, and omissions can then be clarified before continuing.

Small Group Activities/Discussions

Structured small group activities give the audience a chance to work with new information, learn from each other's experiences, and contribute to the session. Active involvement increases learning and retention.

Consider dividing a large group into smaller groups when the work calls for:

- problem-solving;
- a variety of solutions;
- close examination or exploration of an issue;
- building and strengthening working relationships; or
- brainstorming a variety of approaches to a problem or issue.

Before beginning a small group activity, identify:

- the purpose and intended result of the activity or discussion;
- the specific task(s) to be accomplished by the group;
- the time available for the activity or discussion; and
- how participants will share knowledge with other groups.

Advantages

- allows more individual participation;
- promotes group cohesiveness;
- allows work to be divided into manageable segments; and
- produces a variety of ideas and solutions.

Disadvantages

- The larger group does not benefit from small group discussions unless the groups are brought together again and their experiences are well-reported.

Audio-Visual Materials

Audio-visual aids increase learning by appealing to a variety of senses. Selecting or creating good audio-visual material doesn't have to be difficult or time-consuming, but it does require thoughtful planning. Some points to keep in mind are that they should:

- support the learning objectives of the presentation;
- be appropriate for your audience's age range and situation;
- reinforce, not repeat, your verbal message;
- be accurate; and
- be easy to use.

In addition, they should have:

- lettering that is clean, legible, and large enough to be easily seen by those in the back of the room; and
- bold colors to add interest and draw attention to key points.

There are a variety of audio-visual aids to choose from. In deciding whether and which to use, consider the following:

- **Circumstances:** Where will it be used? Will it be comfortably visible to all in the audience?
- **Subject:** How can audio-visual aids help the audience better understand this subject?
- **Cost:** How much money is available to invest in audio-visual materials?

When choosing a film or video, be sure to preview it in advance. Be familiar with the content to be sure that it supports the learning objectives of the presentation. Many "bargain" films and tapes contain information that is outdated. Also, be sensitive to your audience when choosing films and tapes; e.g., youth in a rural community will not relate as well to a film set in an urban environment, and an African-American or Asian audience may not relate readily to an all-white cast. The film should be long enough to convey the message you want to get across — perhaps 20 to 30 minutes — but shouldn't take up all of the presentation time allotted. Allow ample time for introductory activities, discussion, and processing.

Building Blocks: Developing an Effective Presentation

Preparation Checklist

Three or more weeks before the presentation:

- ❏ Select the date of the program.
- ❏ Find out what room you will be using — an auditorium, a classroom, a club meeting room, etc.
- ❏ Find out if you will have a power source for audio-visual materials.
- ❏ Confirm with panelists, if appropriate.
- ❏ Meet with or call teacher or contact person.
- ❏ If you are going to be meeting in a room that has little furniture, find out where you can get chairs.
- ❏ Confirm number of participants.
- ❏ Have handout materials printed.
- ❏ Make a list of all items you will need for the presentation.
- ❏ Locate audio-visual equipment and aids.

One week before the training program:

- ❏ Make sure you have supplies that may be needed — name tags (if a small group), felt-tip markers, pencils, notepads, props for skits or activities.
- ❏ Read over the materials you are presenting.
- ❏ Make sure you have a spare bulb for the projector.
- ❏ Check your itemized list to make sure you have all the items you need.
- ❏ Test all equipment.

Day of training session (a minimum of one hour before session begins):

- ❏ Recheck your list to be sure you're not missing anything.
- ❏ Organize materials so you can find them easily.
- ❏ Make sure room is set up properly.
- ❏ Tape electrical cords to the floor, if necessary.
- ❏ Test equipment again.

Presentation Overview

Day/Date of presentation:
_____

Set-up time:
_____

Beginning time:
_____

Ending time:
_____

Location:
_____

Contact person:
_____

Number of people:
_____

Age group:
_____

Topic:
_____

Special needs of the audience:
_____
_____
_____

Setting (e.g., classroom, auditorium, meeting room, etc.)
_____
_____
_____

Seating arrangement (e.g., fixed desks, moveable desks, tables and chairs, floor, etc.)
_____
_____
_____

Equipment (e.g., chalk board, microphone, easels, projector, screen, video player and monitor, electrical outlets, etc.)
_____
_____
_____

A Teaching Guide for Law Enforcement and Others

Building Blocks: Developing Youth-Led Projects

This chapter is designed to help you help teens develop both a sense of their role in the community and a sense of their power to effect positive change. Teens are vastly under-utilized as crime prevention and community-building resources: They, too, have a stake in their community and a meaningful role to play. Every teen can make a difference, and every community offers opportunities for the development of youth-led projects.

Successful partnerships between adults and youth involve knowledge of the specific crime prevention needs of the community, mutual respect and trust, and a working understanding of the nuts and bolts of program development. This chapter will help you meet these requirements.

This chapter will help you teach teens to:

- identify risks posed to the community by crime and crime-related behavior;
- identify ways that youth can be resources for community-building and crime prevention;
- recognize and counteract biases and stereotypes that influence teen and adult relationships;
- describe examples of youth-led crime prevention or victim assistance projects; and
- define four basic components of a successful youth-led project.

You will also be able to:

- communicate more effectively with teens in developing youth-led projects;
- develop methods to build teen involvement;
- help young people create action plans for successful projects in your community; and
- be familiar with a variety of youth-led projects that may be suitable for your community.

Crime and the Community

Crime affects not only the individual, but also the community. A community can be defined in a number of ways: a classroom, a school, a neighborhood, a city, or a county, for example. In each of these types of communities, the effect of crime is evident:

- People grow fearful and distrusting of outsiders and of their own neighbors.
- Environments begin to deteriorate.
- Insurance and operations costs increase as money is spent to repair or replace property damaged, destroyed, or lost because of criminal activities.
- Taxpayers pay for increased security costs, as well as the costs of sending criminals to court and to jail.
- The individual is less free either through fear of harm or because of rules and regulations (such as curfews) that are developed to prevent or limit criminal activity.

We can't be certain about the exact cause of any particular crime, and it's difficult to measure all of the costs, but we do know that much crime can be prevented if everyone works together. There are several proven strategies that will help curb crime in your community:

- Educate the community about crime.
- Remove or reduce the opportunity for crime to be committed.
- Report crimes to the police.
- Serve as a good role model for youth in the community.
- Build community support and cooperation in organizing crime prevention activities.

Here are some examples of crime prevention programs and the benefits they offer to a community:

- Block or Neighborhood Watch (and other variants): safer streets, more secure homes, child protection;
- community cleanup campaign: increased pride in the community, increased property values, reduced vandalism;
- after-school program: reduced juvenile delinquency, increased child safety;
- teen-employment program: reduced drop-out rate, reduced juvenile delinquency, increased teen self-esteem;
- teen victimization prevention course: reduced crime against teens; and
- school crime prevention program: safer schools, increased school pride, reduced school vandalism.

Building a Stronger Community Through Partnership

Young people are a vital resource in solving the problem of crime in the community. Their contributions are valuable to any crime prevention project. They bring:

- keen awareness of the effects of crime on the community;
- first-hand knowledge of the vulnerability felt by members of a highly victimized age group;
- idealism and creativity in their thinking;
- an affinity for risk-taking;
- an enormous amount of energy; and
- the desire to be part of a group.

Crime prevention efforts that overlook teens as resources are missing out on a valuable source of leaders, planners, and doers. Additionally, a community that makes an effort to involve teens in crime prevention will:

- reduce crime among a highly victimized population;
- change the negative image of teens held by many adults;
- foster an investment by teens in their communities;
- reduce community problems such as vandalism, littering, loitering, street crime, and drug trafficking;
- promote safer schools; and
- improve relationships between teens and community institutions.

Attitudes and Stereotypes: Barriers to Success

Adults sometimes hold negative attitudes and stereotypes about teens. These generalizations not only create a communication barrier, but also limit the creation of mutually beneficial partnerships. Let's look at some common attitudes adults have about teens, and, in contrast, the facts:

Myth: Teens are the problem, not part of the solution.

Fact: Although some teens are involved in delinquent acts, many more are involved in positive activities that benefit their communities. Teens welcome opportunities to direct their creativity, enthusiasm, and energy into positive channels.

Myth: Teens just want to have fun.

Fact: Teens do want to have fun, but they also want to be involved with the safety of their communities. Successful youth-led projects include a healthy balance of work and fun for youth. Having fun and helping the community are quite compatible.

Myth: Teens are unreliable.

Fact: Teens can be as reliable as adults.

Myth: Teens care only about themselves.

Fact: Adolescence is a time when young people begin to examine themselves as individuals. They're finding out just who they are, and they are laying the foundation for solid values and beliefs. They are also testing limits and asserting their individuality. But teens also have a sense of idealism and altruism that can be tapped by caring adults and other teens.

Myth: Teens need to be guided; they aren't old enough to make decisions.

Fact: Teens are capable of much more than we give them credit for. They make decisions every day. Some of their decisions are better than others, but adults make mistakes, too. Teens often think of solutions that adults overlook.

Myth: Teens have their hands full just getting through their adolescence. They can't handle additional responsibilities.

Fact: The teen years can be difficult, but precisely during those years, youth are looking for positive channels for their energy. Participation in a youth-led project offers teens a positive peer group, an opportunity to develop a partnership with a caring adult, and a chance to develop new skills. These are all needs teens must meet one way or another. Participation also builds self-esteem and self-confidence and gives teens the opportunity to use their new skills in a supportive environment.

The Needs and Tasks of Adolescence

Every teen is affected by a variety of particular influences as he or she grows up: Families, schools, friends, relatives, and living environments are all different. The adolescent years are a time of physical, social, emotional, and intellectual development involving specific developmental needs and tasks. When successfully guided, teens develop into mature and responsible citizens. According to experts on adolescent development, teens should have the opportunity, among other things, to:

- participate as equal partners, members of a household, workers, and responsible members of society, with power to influence the policies and practices of the groups in which they participate;
- gain experience in decision-making;
- understand themselves in relation to others;
- examine personal values;
- experiment with their own identity and try out different roles;
- develop a sense of self-esteem and confidence;
- discover personal strengths and be recognized by others for competence and skill;
- make a significant contribution to a group or to other individuals;

Building Blocks: Developing Youth-Led Projects

- expand their world by sharing experiences with persons of different social classes, cultures, and ages;
- have productive outlets for their immense physical energy;
- develop skills necessary for economic independence; and
- become involved in a cause and experience the results of their commitment and perseverance.

Youth-Led Projects Are Making a Difference

You don't need a magician to organize a successful youth-led project. You need good planning, openness to what teens want to do and how they want to do it, the commitment to accept teens as equal partners, the willingness to learn from them, and sensitivity to their special talents and needs. Here are some examples of projects developed by teens that have made a difference in their communities:

- *Dade County (Miami), Florida:* Students, school officials, teachers, and crime watch leaders organized a school crime watch program to report crime and suspicious behavior. Results have been dramatic: School crime was reduced by 50 percent in the first two years of the program.
- *Dallas, Texas; Bakersfield, California; Indianapolis, Indiana:* Teens Against Community Crime worked with the audio-visual section of the Dallas Police Department to produce a show for area high schools on how teens can prevent crime. Bakersfield teens made public service announcements against drunk driving and drug use. Teens in Indianapolis produced three public service announcements, including "You Can't Live Your Dreams If You're Behind Bars."
- *Flint, Michigan:* A high school anti-crime group explained the consequences of delinquency and crime to a group of high-risk elementary students and gave them tips on how to stay safe.
- *Virginia Beach, Virginia:* Young people hosted a neighborhood crime prevention fair complete with a dunking booth. Prizes for the events gave an anti-drug and anti-alcohol message.
- *New York, New York:* Young people painted a mural at a corner in East Harlem to discourage drug dealers from conducting business on the corner. Drug dealing on that corner stopped.
- *New Mexico:* Young Native Americans conducted a seat belt usage survey to raise public awareness of motor vehicle safety. They stopped each car coming into the school parking lot to ask if the passengers were using seat belts. A follow-up survey conducted three months later showed that seat belt usage had increased.
- *Boulder, Colorado:* Young men and women developed a presentation on acquaintance rape that was included in the University of Colorado's freshman orientation.
- *Philadelphia, Pennsylvania:* Junior high student councils work together to sponsor an annual crime prevention conference.
- *Knoxville, Tennessee:* A group of five schools conducted a contest for Victims' Rights Week by demonstrating their knowledge of and involvement in victims' assistance activities.
- *Detroit, Michigan:* Teens with 25 hours of training in conflict management set up a conflict resolution center where they meet weekly to help peers solve disputes.

The Four Rs of Successful Programs

The National Crime Prevention Council has identified four factors — the Four Rs — common to successful youth-led projects: Resources, Relationships, Responsibilities, and Rewards.

Resources

Resources are the crucial goods, services, and supports necessary to start and sustain the program. They include:

- an adult — mentor, coordinator, or leader — who acts as an institutional liaison, provides advocacy and support, and serves as a role model and partner;
- youth involvement in the identification and solution of local crime problems;
- support from such local adult institutions such as the

chamber of commerce, city council, school board, service clubs, civic associations, police department, and judicial system;

- in-kind or cash donations to purchase supplies or operate the program, such as a neighborhood printer producing a flier, a local resident or Rotary Club donating cash, or a local restaurant donating food;

- a permanent base of operation that provides youth with a sense of professionalism and lends credibility to the project in the community; and

- training that provides youth with the skills necessary to carry out their jobs, builds self-esteem, gives them credibility among adults and peers, and builds confidence in using their new skills.

Relationships

Relationships between young people and adults are pivotal to the success of youth-led programs. Other important relationships include those between teens and their peers and between teens and younger people.

It's important that adults treat teens as people evolving into adulthood and offer them appropriate respect and recognition. Adult leaders offer the following guidelines for developing positive relationships with youth:

- Provide a non-judgmental atmosphere, a place where teens are allowed to be themselves.
- Allow teens the opportunity to learn from their mistakes. Don't demand or expect perfection.
- Be patient — learning takes time.
- Allow teens to work out their own solutions to problems, but be there to provide support.
- Value the individual — don't stereotype.
- Listen and be receptive to teens' ideas and concerns.
- Be prepared to have your commitment, reliability, and sincerity tested.

Open, honest communication is important for a successful relationship. Teens need to feel that they will be listened to and that their ideas are valued. Here are some guidelines for building positive communication with teens in your community:

- Talk with teens; don't patronize them.
- Be honest.
- Be yourself.
- Listen to what is being said.
- Be attentive to nonverbal communication.
- Show your interest by asking questions.
- Take opportunities to talk one-on-one, in informal settings such as school halls, after-school club meetings, and neighborhood parks.
- Let teens know that you value their friendship and their contributions.

It is also important that teens treat adults with openness and respect. Here are some guidelines for teens who want to develop positive relationships with adults:

- Voice your opinions thoughtfully.
- Communicate your feelings.
- Treat adults as you would want to be treated.
- Be reliable.
- Dress the part — dressing nicely can set the tone, especially when working with adults.
- Respect confidentiality.

Responsibilities

Responsibilities will vary widely, ranging from providing services to running the organization itself. Here are several guidelines for setting responsibilities when working with youth:

- Have clear rules.
- Establish specific roles and job descriptions.
- Establish and maintain high standards and expectations.
- Determine and use specific talents and abilities — take advantage of the skills of a young artist, writer, mechanic, organizer, or musician.
- Let young people be responsible for decision-making.
- Allow for mistakes.

Rewards

Rewards include all kinds of pay-offs for group and individual endeavors and provide motivation for participation. The rewards offered by a project influence participants' feelings about whether a program is a good investment of their time and energy. Examples of rewards include:

- tangible results that are measurable and meaningful and that demonstrate how the project makes a difference in the community;
- recognition by peers and adults, through newspaper articles, television and radio coverage, and special certificates and/or award nights sponsored by adult groups or peers — even a simple "thank you" can be a recognition;
- social opportunities such as food and fun, meeting new people, spending time with old friends, and developing close relationships with adults; and
- personal satisfaction that comes from tangible results, recognition, and group interaction. This is also influenced by the teens' sense of self-worth and feelings of achievement, personal growth, and importance to the group.

Calling All Teens: Recruiting Youth

Recruiting teens is one of the most important elements in getting a project off the ground and keeping it running. Here are some ideas:

- Educate your audience about the problem in their community and solicit their ideas for solutions. Use classroom discussions, school assemblies, presentations at club meetings, meetings with the student council, etc.
- Provide examples of how other teens have made a difference in their communities.
- Ask for help — most people are willing to help if asked personally.
- Stress the results you expect from the project. Volunteers want to know that their involvement will be worthwhile.
- Ask youth to recruit friends who are willing to work with the group, but don't limit your recruitment. Strive for diversity.
- Recruit via personal contact with teens. Talk with them in the hallways, on the school grounds, or elsewhere in the community.

- Make it clear that work is balanced with fun. Allow time for socialization.
- Teens are generally risk takers: Offer them opportunities to take positive risks that can help them grow.
- Offer opportunities for teens to use their talents and learn new skills.
- Communicate that there is something for everyone — good listeners can mediate, artists can create murals, athletes can coach younger kids, and talkers can spread the message.

Planning for Success

The following Steps for Success model (APLAN) can assist you in organizing a youth-led project. Teens can design good projects without completing every step, but these five steps will help to make a good project even better.

Involving youth in all facets of planning and implementation generates interest, enthusiasm, commitment, and results. The degree of youth involvement can vary, but experience has shown that if youth involvement is strong, the program will be more successful.

The five *Steps for Success* are:

- **A**ssessing your community's needs and selecting a problem;
- **P**lanning a successful project;
- **L**ining up resources;
- **A**cting on your plan; and
- **N**urturing, monitoring, and evaluating.

These steps may be quick or lengthy, simple or complicated, depending on the problem and the situation. Young people interested in forming walking groups for security going to and from school may need only 15 to 20 minutes to plan their project and carry it out. Youth who want to create a hotline for peers may need ten to 15 hours of planning plus an equal amount of time in training. An assessment of needs may consist of a ten-minute classroom discussion or it may take several hours of research.

Building Blocks: Developing Youth-Led Projects

Step One: Assessing Your Community's Needs and Selecting a Problem

It's important that you first define your community. You might decide to focus on a classroom, a school, or a neighborhood, or on a special group of people such as latchkey children, disabled persons, or the elderly. Your community can be any size; it doesn't have to have geographic boundaries, but it does need boundaries.

- Define your community's boundaries to focus efforts and measure results.

If the community is a school, does it include the school grounds? If it's a neighborhood, how far does the area extend? If you're focusing on a special group, how do you define it?

- Research the community's crime and related problems.

Never assume that you know the problem. Get the facts. If appropriate, survey the community to gather information and develop a current picture of its needs.

Sources of community information include:

- reports from local planning and zoning departments, health departments, and other local government and private agencies and organizations;
- newspaper articles, especially those published in local or school newspapers;
- police records on crime and related problems;
- school records on security, disciplinary actions, and vandalism;
- surveys of the community by other groups; and
- interviews with key community leaders.

Step Two: Planning

Once you've defined your community and identified the problem you want to solve, it's time to develop the blueprint. Developing an operational plan will help you:

- identify specific tasks to be accomplished;
- assign responsibilities;
- generate interest and enthusiasm;
- determine what resources you'll need; and
- focus your group on its goal.

The energy, support, and commitment you generate early in the project will often carry over into the implementation stages. When you develop your plan, consider the following:

- Spell out goals and objectives. Goals are your reasons for doing the project — for example, to reduce crime in a local high school. Objectives are measurable steps you need to take to achieve your goals — for example, to make all the teens in the school aware of the crime problem and to persuade two-thirds of them to join a crime watch.
- Choose strategies to reach the objectives. For example, to convince students that crime is a problem in your school, you might conduct a survey and publish the results in the school newspaper.
- Set target dates for completing strategies.
- List specific tasks. For each strategy, determine job responsibilities — who will do what by when.
- Develop a plan for evaluating your project. This can be simple. For instance, we planned to do x, y, and z. Did we do x, y, and z? What did we learn?

Step Three: Lining Up Resources

It's important that you consider resource needs during the planning stage and have some idea of how you can secure them. Examples of resources are:

- people who are already addressing crime problems;
- key adult leaders in the community;
- the skills in your own group; and
- people and groups who can donate money, materials, and services (e.g., office space, desks, telephones, office supplies, printing, food, and transportation).

A project evaluation that shows what you've accomplished can help sustain existing contributions and generate new ones.

Step Four: Acting On Your Plan

Once you've developed your plan and secured resources, it's time to implement your project. Several things may help make your project run more smoothly: providing training, developing leadership, recognizing the contributions of volunteers, and securing public acknowledgment.

Training

Training should cover the following points:

- explanation of the goals and objectives of the project to generate enthusiasm and commitment and to ensure that each member of your team understands the purpose of the program and can explain it to others;
- explanation of the roles and responsibilities of each team member to clarify lines of responsibility and accountability; and
- explanation of any special rules to ensure the smooth operation of the project or to meet local laws.

In planning your training, consider drawing on resources within your group, as well as inviting outside speakers. In addition, your project may require such special skills as mediation training or training in counseling. That training should receive careful attention — who gets it, what's covered, where it's given.

Leadership

Leadership must be learned and practiced. Effective leadership will help keep the project on track and build a sense of camaraderie among group members. If leadership responsibilities are shared, teens will acquire and exercise leadership skills. Remember that youth — and adults — all have different levels of experience and expertise in leadership. Consider mentoring or formal training to build these skills.

Recognition

Recognizing the contributions of those who help with the project helps retain participants and build their self-esteem. Here are five ideas for recognizing volunteers:

- membership cards printed with your group's name and logo;
- a pizza party, sponsored by a local business, to say "thank you";
- teens as stars in public presentations and media interviews;
- have a group identity — perhaps T-shirts, jackets, hats with your name or logo; and
- publicity.

Step Five: Nurturing, Monitoring, and Evaluating

Though you may feel good about your progress, periodic formal checks provide an objective way to see how well you're doing. Ask whether you are using your resources wisely, if your action plan is running smoothly, and whether you are reaching your goals.

There are a variety of ways to conduct an evaluation. A key is deciding at the start what measurements will be useful and how those data will be collected. Be sure to make note of success stories, problems encountered, and suggestions for improvement.

Don't Forget

Working with teens places certain responsibilities on adult partners:

- Be familiar with relevant regulations, policies, and procedures of agencies involved in your project (e.g., schools, local law enforcement agency, sites at which you provide services).
- Because volunteers are generally minors, it's important that parents or guardians be aware of and approve their child's participation. Require permission forms, especially if participants will be involved in any hazardous activities. Keeping in touch with parents may encourage them to become involved in the project.

Publicizing Your Project

Getting publicity for your project can make people aware of it, give volunteers a boost, give the project credibility, help to recruit volunteers, and attract community sponsors.

Some publicity efforts require no money and little effort; others require greater resources:

- Place stories in the school newspaper.
- Issue a news release.
- Develop and distribute posters, fliers, or brochures announcing your project.
- Write public service announcements for local newspapers, television, and radio.
- Design "walking billboards" (T-shirts, caps, or buttons for your volunteers to wear in the community).

Sample Materials and Activities

School Attitude Survey on Crime

Person Answering: ❏ Male   ❏ Female _____
Grade ____
Date _____

This survey will help our school choose and design a project to improve safety. Your opinion is important and will remain confidential.

1. Crime in my school is (pick one):
   - ❏ Very serious
   - ❏ Serious
   - ❏ A problem, but not too serious
   - ❏ Not a problem

2. The most typical type of crime in my school is _____.

3. In the last year, crime in my school has (pick one):
   - ❏ Increased
   - ❏ Stayed about the same
   - ❏ Decreased

4. I feel in my school during the regular school day (pick one):
   - ❏ Very safe   ❏ Somewhat safe
   - ❏ Somewhat unsafe   ❏ Very unsafe

5. I feel in my school after school hours (pick one):
   - ❏ Very safe   ❏ Somewhat safe
   - ❏ Somewhat unsafe   ❏ Very unsafe

6. Someone I know ❏ was / ❏ was not the victim of a crime during the past semester.

   In or near school?   ❏ Yes   ❏ No
   In or near the neighborhood? ❏ Yes   ❏ No
   If no, go to question #7. *If yes:*

   a. What crime(s) _____.

   b. If it happened in or near school, or on the way to or from school, was the crime reported to school authorities?   ❏ Yes   ❏ No

   c. Was the crime reported to the police?
   ❏ Yes   ❏ No

7. If I saw a crime taking place in or near my school, I would (pick one):
   - ❏ Call the police
   - ❏ Call a teacher or friend
   - ❏ Try to catch the person
   - ❏ Do nothing

   Why?
   _____
   _____
   _____

8. If my schoolmates saw a crime taking place, they would (pick one):
   - ❏ Call the police
   - ❏ Call a teacher or friend
   - ❏ Try to catch the person
   - ❏ Do nothing

   Why?
   _____
   _____
   _____

9. Students and teachers in my school accept _____ responsibility for their personal safety (pick one):
   ❏ A lot of   ❏ Some   ❏ Little or no

10. The three biggest crime problems at or near my school are (check only three):
    - ❏ Fighting and assaults
    - ❏ Stealing/larceny
    - ❏ Vandalism
    - ❏ Drug abuse
    - ❏ Alcohol abuse
    - ❏ Truancy/skipping school
    - ❏ Harassment
    - ❏ Extortion
    - ❏ Abuse (including sexual abuse)
    - ❏ Shoplifting

11. I ❏ would / ❏ would not be interested in helping in an effort to reduce crime in my school.

Building Blocks: Developing Youth-Led Projects

Adult Guidance — To Have or Not To Have

Objective:
To identify when teens want and don't want adult guidance and what factors influence their decisions.

Time:
20 minutes, including discussion.

Materials:
A copy of the survey on the following page for each student who will participate.

Teens are usually capable of much more than adults (or they themselves) give them credit for and frequently think of innovative solutions and actions that adults may overlook.

In this activity, teens will fill out a short survey about their attitudes toward adult guidance on a variety of activities. Which activities in community efforts are teens capable of doing? How much adult support do they want or think is necessary? Give the students ten minutes to fill out the survey, then tabulate results and discuss them with the group. Did the teens mostly agree on when they need guidance? Why or why not? What attributes of the activity (e.g., perceived difficulty of the activity, familiarity with the activity, training) influenced how much support teens wanted on it? What opportunities would they most like to be given? Why might adults be hesitant to let them take on those responsibilities? What might they do to prove that they are ready to handle responsibilities?

Action Planning

Objective:
To identify strategies in which youth can be resources to the community in preventing crime and/or in community-building.

Time:
45 minutes.

Materials:
A hat and slips of paper.

This activity will give students a chance to brainstorm various solutions to problems that face the community. Before your presentation, use scissors to cut sheets of paper into small slips that can be folded and placed in a hat. On each slip, describe a problem that can affect a community (e.g., an increase in cases of vandalism). For ideas, refer to the bottom of this sheet. There should be one idea for every three teens participating. Once each group of three picks a slip, tell them to come up with a group project that will address this problem. Their solutions can be small-scale or large-scale, cost-free or expensive, but they must be realistic. Three to five ideas are okay if they're realistic. After a 15-20 minute brainstorm session within the group, ask for volunteers to present their group's ideas for general discussion.

Sample Problem Ideas

1. There is a growing presence of violent youth gangs in the community.
2. There has been a series of drunk-driving crashes involving students.
3. There have been reports of a man sexually assaulting women in the area around your school.
4. A predominantly African-American church has been vandalized by a neo-Nazi hate group.
5. A report says incidents of child abuse are increasing dramatically.
6. There have been reports of people selling drugs near local elementary schools and playgrounds.
7. Fights have broken out during lunch period every day of the last week. One student had to go to the hospital with a broken collarbone.
8. People are afraid to walk home after extracurricular activities because of the increased incidence of crime in the area.

Building Blocks: Developing Youth-Led Projects

Attitude Check

Please fill out the following survey, choosing either 1, 2, 3, or 4 for each activity.

Choosing:

"1" means you think teens can do this entirely on their own;
"2" means you think teens can do this with adult help;
"3" means you think teens can advise adults on this, but adults should make the final decisions and do it; and
"4" means you think adults should do this entirely on their own.

In a Nonprofit Organization

Hiring staff	1	2	3	4
Answering telephones	1	2	3	4
Sitting on the Board of Directors	1	2	3	4
Meeting with funds-givers	1	2	3	4
Planning projects and carrying them out	1	2	3	4
Serving refreshments at meetings	1	2	3	4

In a School

Counseling students	1	2	3	4
Evaluating teachers	1	2	3	4
Filing in the school office	1	2	3	4
Choosing school curriculum and textbooks	1	2	3	4
Setting rules and regulations	1	2	3	4
Taking attendance	1	2	3	4
Tutoring other students	1	2	3	4

In a Neighborhood

Conducting a community needs survey	1	2	3	4
Organizing a "speakout"	1	2	3	4
Cleaning a park	1	2	3	4
Rehabilitating abandoned housing	1	2	3	4
Organizing a block party	1	2	3	4

(Developed by Youth Force, Citizens Committee for New York City)

Resources

State and Local Contacts

Boys & Girls Clubs
Girl Scouts, Boy Scouts
4H Clubs
Volunteer clearinghouses
League of Women Voters
County Commission on Drug and Alcohol Use
United Way
PAL (Police Athletic League)
YWCA and YMCA

National Contacts

Center for Youth as Resources

See "General Resources" section at the end of this book.

National Crime Prevention Council

See "General Resources" section at the end of this book.

Youth Crime Watch of America

See "General Resources" section at the end of this book.

Youth Service America
1101 15th Street, NW
Suite 200
Washington, DC 20005
202-296-2992

Youth Service America is a national nonprofit organization that advocates for opportunities for young people to be engaged in youth service programs. The organization sponsors an annual conference and National Youth Service Day.

Publications

Independent Sector. *Youth Service: A Guidebook for Developing and Operating Effective Programs.* 1987. Available from Independent Sector, 202-223-8100.

Lewis, Barbara. *The Kid's Guide to Social Action: How to Solve the Social Problems You Choose and Turn Creative Thinking Into Positive Action.* 1991. Minneapolis: Free Spirit Publishing.

National Crime Prevention Council. *Changing Perspectives: Youth as Resources.* 1990. Available from NCPC, 202-466-6272.

National Crime Prevention Council. *Charting Success.* 1995. Available from NCPC, 202-466-6272.

Building Blocks:
When a Youth Reports a Crime

When you present a program on crime prevention, someone in the audience may report that he or she has been a crime victim. The disclosure may be accompanied by strong emotions. This chapter will help you deal with victimization disclosures by providing:

- an overview of the trauma of victimization;
- an outline of a method for handling the discussion effectively;
- an overview of reporting issues;
- suggestions for providing appropriate referrals; and
- tips for handling your reaction to a victimization disclosure.

Why Many Young People Don't Report Crime

Many young people are victimized and don't tell anyone, or they may have tried to tell someone, but weren't understood or believed. If a child or teen discloses victimization during or as a result of your crime prevention presentation, it's important that you help the victim feel comfortable, understood, and supported that he is doing something that is beneficial to himself, to his friends or family, and to law enforcement. If the victim senses a negative response to his disclosure, he may not disclose again.

This section is a brief summary of a complicated issue. We strongly recommend that you obtain a copy of NCPC's book, *When a Child Reports a Crime*, for a more in-depth and complete discussion.

Crimes committed against youth are the least reported. Here are some reasons why this may occur:

- **Lack of awareness:** The youth may not know that what happened was a crime.
- **Secondary victimization:** Sometimes, the systems that should be protecting youth (including schools, social service agencies, law enforcement agencies, and the legal system) exacerbate the young person's victimization by not believing the report, breaking confidentiality, adding to the his or her confusion, or not acting on the information given.
- **Fear:** Crime itself produces fear that is often compounded by other fears:

- fear of retaliation by the perpetrator;
- fear of not being believed;
- fear of parental disapproval or rejection if the perpetrator is someone the family knows or if the youth was in a place or engaging in a behavior that parents would disapprove;
- fear of punishment if the youth participated in the behavior;
- fear of being shut out by friends; and
- fear of law enforcement.

It is important to recognize these fears and help the young person deal with them. The fear won't be ignored just because you tell the child it's irrelevant or unimportant.

The Trauma of Victimization

To effectively handle disclosure of victimization by a young person, you need to be aware of the kinds of damage victims may suffer. Crimes can affect victims in a variety of ways. Some are easier to detect than others, but all cause trauma:

- physical injuries, such as cuts, bruises, and other wounds, or damaged or destroyed property;
- emotional injuries that can be serious and long-lasting — common symptoms in young people include:
  - insomnia, nightmares, fear of the dark, or fear of sleeping alone;
  - bed wetting or thumb sucking;
  - distrust and fear of strangers;
  - difficulty in concentrating or decreased school performance;
  - increased risk-taking behavior and recklessness;
  - confusion and guilt; and
  - depression or feelings of isolation from family members and friends.
- financial injuries, ranging from economic inconvenience to the devastation that the child's family may feel from these injuries:
  - medical expenses;
  - lost money or destroyed property;
  - legal fees;
  - lost income from having to take time off from work; and
  - costs of transportation, lodging, meals, child care, and other expenses incurred through hospital and doctor visits and attending legal meetings and court room procedures.

Recovery from Victimization

It's hard to tell how long it will take a victim to recover from a crime, but we know there are certain stages that most victims experience as they recover. The feelings and thoughts in each of these stages are normal and healthy. Some victims may stay in one stage for days, others for months or even years. A victim who becomes stuck in one stage for a long time may need professional counseling.

Depending on the crime, the environment, the support available, and the individual, a person's recovery from the effects of a criminal victimization may take anywhere from a day to a decade — or even a lifetime in the case of particularly heinous crimes. Adult reactions have been found to follow, in general, the pattern outlined below. Children and youth who are victims seem to follow similar patterns, but often show their reactions differently. For instance, an adult may verbalize his rage and express clearly the anger felt inside. A child may withdraw or "act out," unable or unwilling to put feelings into words.

Responses of Adult Victims

Adult victims generally pass through six stages:

- **Shock/denial:** Immediately after the crime, the victim feels out of control and has trouble believing what happened. The victim may refuse to talk about the event and may become confused or disoriented.
- **Anger/rage:** In this stage, the victim has accepted what has happened and may become very angry. He may be angry at himself, at his assailant, at someone close to him who he thinks should have been able to protect him, or even at the world for allowing bad things to happen to innocent people.

The victim needs to be able to talk with someone who will listen without making judgements or giving advice.

- **Powerlessness:** At the time of the crime, the perpetrator took control of the victim's life. If the crime was reported to the police, the criminal justice system may seem to have taken control. At times it may seem that the victim's feelings are taking over. Victims may feel that their lives will never again be the same. It often helps a victim regain a sense of control to report the crime, even if the case doesn't go to court.

- **Guilt:** The victim mentally replays the crime scene and wonders "Was it my fault?" "Did I make this happen?" "What did I do wrong?" "Did I deserve it?" "Is there something wrong with me?" "What would have happened if I had ... ?" It's important to assure the victim that he or she wasn't responsible for the crime. The blame belongs with the criminal.

- **Depression:** The victim may continue to feel fear, anxiety, and vulnerability. He or she may be afraid to go to sleep or to get out of bed, or have difficulty performing routine daily tasks.

- **Acceptance:** As time passes, the victim focuses more on day-to-day living. The problems may not have gone away entirely, but the victim feels OK about himself again and in control of his life.

Responses of Child Victims

Children of different ages will exhibit different behaviors in response to having their lives touched by crime. Although their general patterns of response are like those of adults, six- to nine-year-olds might be expected to exhibit some of these behaviors either immediately or eventually:

- clinging to adults;
- bed wetting or thumb sucking;
- changes in eating and sleeping habits;
- crying;
- irritability;
- confusion and guilt;
- distrust of others;
- fear;
- withdrawal/isolation;
- panic;
- fear of dying; and
- anger at the person who caused the crime to happen.

Ten- to 11-year-olds might be expected to exhibit these behaviors in response to victimization:

- shock;
- shortened attention span;
- unaccustomed listlessness or hyperactivity;
- decreased school performance;
- reckless play (e.g., playing chicken or Russian roulette, hitchhiking);
- internalized guilt;
- depression; and
- denial or intellectualization of the event.

Older children tend to act at some level between these and adult behaviors.

Reacting to a Disclosure in the Classroom

Whenever crime is the topic of a presentation, someone in the audience might remember a victimization and choose that moment to disclose the incident. The disclosure may involve a range of emotions. Your goal is to determine what happened, to help the victim feel as stable as possible, and to provide appropriate follow up:

- Know the policies for the school and your department.
- Arrange for privacy if at all possible.
- Let the victim tell the story. Take a sympathetic and supportive attitude.
- Let the victim know you're sorry about what happened and that he or she was right to talk with you.

A Checklist

Dr. Marlene Young of the National Organization for Victim Assistance has developed a crisis checklist that can be helpful in structuring your interviews with young victims. Though the first step may not apply to disclosures, the process is helpful in understanding what kinds of things you will want to do to help the victim. Depending on the crime, the time elapsed, and the individual victim, the discussion may take three minutes, 30 minutes, or three hours. However long it takes, you will find this checklist helpful in ensuring that you have helped meet the victim's needs in your handling of the disclosure.

- Deal with life, death, and injury.
- Ensure safety and security.
- Calm and comfort.
- Give back control.
- Help ventilate and validate.
- Reassure and respond.
- Surmount the "insurmountable" problems.
- Find solutions.
- Predict and prepare.
- Say goodbye.

Deal with life, death and injury: The first step is to respond to any emergency medical needs.

Ensure safety and security: You need to ensure that the young victim is physically safe and emotionally secure. Sometimes ensuring emotional security requires a private talk, reassurance, and a hug. Other times, if the victimization has been particularly traumatic, it may require a long time and professional counseling or the removal of the child from his/her home to a safer and more supportive environment, such as the home of a relative or another responsible adult.

A victim may not want to be touched: Always ask if it's OK for you to hold his/her hand or put your arm around him or her while you talk. You might consider buying an inexpensive stuffed animal to keep with you when making school visits. It can be given to the child to hold while you talk, and you can let him or her take it home for comfort and security.

Calm and comfort: Ask how the victim is feeling. At this point, the child may be experiencing many different feelings about what has been disclosed and where he or she chose to disclose it — in front of friends or classmates. By showing your concern and caring, you are providing an opportunity for the victim to think about what he or she is feeling.

Be aware that boys are generally not as verbal as girls; that girls often disclose victimization through a friend; and that privacy is important — youth are concerned about being embarrassed in front of others.

Expect the victim to check you out to determine whether you are someone he can trust. Be conscious of your body language and tone of voice. Beware of double messages: You may be saying that you care, but your tone or style might be intimidating. Here are some things that can help victims feel more comfortable:

- Sit while talking to the young person so you can make eye contact easily.
- Don't sit behind a desk — it creates a barrier.
- Use a comforting tone of voice.
- Establish positive rapport with the victim by talking about neutral subjects such as school work, friends, or sports.
- Believe the victim.
- Be creative in helping the victim talk about what happened. For example, encourage the child to tell a story in third person, such as: "There was a little girl who was home alone and … "
- let the victim know that talking about what happened to him or her is good, that you are there to help, and you believe what he/she is telling you.

Give back control: The victim often feels a loss of control. Loss of control can be more devastating for young people than for adults because much of their lives is already controlled by others. Remember, too, that a child's sense of control is damaged even further when he or she is victimized by someone who had been thought to be trustworthy. The young person's disclosure can be an opportunity to restore some of this control.

Ask the victim how he or she would like to be addressed. Where would he/she like to sit? Would he/she like a drink of water or a soda? The power to choose can provide an opportunity to get back the sense of control that was taken away by the perpetrator.

Help ventilate and validate: Allow the victim to talk about what happened, believe what he or she says, and praise him or her for disclosing. Be prepared to give as much time as the child needs to feel comfortable and to tell what happened.

Ideally, the victim should have the opportunity to tell the entire story and talk through feelings. You should be prepared to provide appropriate referrals and to comply with the school's and your jurisdiction's reporting requirements.

Disclosure may be very difficult and emotional for the victim during presentations on sexual assault, rape, or child abuse. You may want to consider making your presentation with a partner, so that one person can leave the room with the victim, or asking the teacher or another adult to remain in the classroom during the presentation.

Reassure and respond: This step provides comfort and demystifies the experience. Children are often frightened by their feelings and fear of the unknown. Let the victim know that feelings of anger, fear, and anxiety are OK. Talk about both physical and emotional injuries. Let the victim know that others have the same feelings and that talking to someone might help him or her feel less scared. Ask what worries or fears the victim has.

Surmount the "insurmountable" problem: The child has just disclosed a major event in life and may be faced with a variety of seemingly overwhelming problems because of the incident(s) — feeling that life has shattered and needing assistance in identifying and dealing with various problems. Ask the victim to help you make a list of questions, concerns, needs, or problems. Ask him or her to choose the top three most important concerns to address. This method will diffuse the feeling that the problems are too overwhelming to handle.

Find solutions: Ask questions to determine if the young person knows what to do about these concerns. Other personal experiences may assist him or her in solving the problem or help to identify ways to deal with the situation. You may want to ask what he or she would advise a family member or friend in a similar situation. By helping the victim find solutions, you are helping him or her regain control. Make note of any problems that should be referred to a social service agency.

Predict and prepare: Ask permission to tell someone else about the crime — the victim disclosed because he or she trusted you. Explain why you think that sharing with someone else would help or why you must share. If you're required by law to report the incident, you might say: "Because of my job, I need to share our talk with _____ someone who helps children with problems like yours."

When the victim agrees to involving other people, explain the next steps. Keep your explanation simple and use words appropriate for the child's age. Children can be easily overwhelmed by too much information. For example, you might say, "I'll share our talk with your school counselor. He'll probably ask you to come into his office to talk about what happened. I understand that this might make you feel a little uncomfortable. Explain what happened and let him know how you feel. Your counselor cares about you and wants to help. Do you have any questions about what will happen?" Encourage every adult who will talk with the child to keep the victim informed about each step in the process.

Say goodbye: It is now time to bring the interview to a close. Tell the child that you are sorry about what has happened and remind him that it wasn't his or her fault. If the victim feels comfortable with physical contact, a hug might be reassuring and thoughtful. Review the case with the assigned law enforcement officer or other concerned authorities and share the information you have gotten from the victim. Encourage them to call you if they have any questions or need additional help.

Back in the Classroom

It is important to be sensitive to the feelings of the other young people in the audience. It's often upsetting for them to see a friend in distress. If the disclosure situation warrants it, you, the teacher, or another responsible adult should:

- discuss what they can do to help their friend;
- remind them not to spread rumors about their friend that could hurt more or to discuss their

friend's situation casually; and

- emphasize that the support of friends is important; they shouldn't tease their friend. Tell them: "This person is your friend, and you certainly don't want to make him or her feel bad."

Providing Appropriate Referrals

It is critical to be familiar with your jurisdiction's policies and procedures regarding victimization disclosure. They may detail important steps to follow and require specific referrals. If the policies and procedures allow for your discretion, there are several guidelines that may help:

- The young person may be hesitant about reporting the crime. Fears about reporting may play a role in this hesitation. Answer questions truthfully and don't promise to "fix everything." Help the victim prepare for what is going to happen.

- Be familiar with the resources available in the community. Many communities have special groups that will assist young victims. Check with your local child protective services office, the prosecutor's office, or a victim assistance or rape crisis center for information about nearby resources.

- Refer the child to a child-centered organization that will not only believe the young victim but will also work in his or her best interest.

- If appropriate, follow up. Use reasonable judgment in determining the length and intensity of your involvement.

The Presenter's Reaction

When a young person reports a crime, you may feel discomfort, disbelief, or anger, or even sometimes amusement. The disclosure can also trigger your protective instincts. It's important to be aware of your own feelings and reactions. The victim will be watching closely for verbal and nonverbal cues signaling your response. If he or she senses that you're uncomfortable or not treating the report seriously, the victim may think that telling you was a mistake, that there is something wrong with him or her, or that the victimization was his or her fault. Your first priority is to attend to the immediate needs of the victim. If your feelings are getting in the way of helping, here are some tips:

- Excuse yourself for a few minutes. Take time to collect your thoughts, compose yourself, and take some deep breaths before you return.

- Ask the child if it's OK to invite the teacher (school counselor, principal, nurse) to join the discussion. This will give you a break and shift the child's focus from you to the other person.

For more information, assistance, or training, consult with your local victim service or child protective service providers.

General Resources

Audio-Visual Contacts

AIMS Media, 6901 Woodley Avenue, Van Nuys, CA 91406-4878, 800-785-4111

Barr Films, 12801 Schabarum Avenue, PO Box 1000, Irwindale, CA 91706-7878, 800-234-7878

Churchill Films, 12210 Nebraska Avenue, Los Angeles, CA 90025, 800-334-7830

Community Intervention Inc., 529 South Seventh Street, Suite 570, Minneapolis, MN 55415, 800-328-0417

Coronet/MTI, 108 Wilmot Road, Deerfield, IL 60015, 800-621-2131

Guidance Associates, PO Box 1000, Mount Kisco, NY 10549-0010, 800-431-1242

Kidsrights, 10100 Park Cedar Drive, Charlotte, NC 28210, 800-892-5437

Pyramid Films, Box 1048, Santa Monica, CA 90406, 800-828-7577

National Contacts

Association of Junior Leagues, Inc.

660 First Avenue, Second Floor
New York, NY 10016
212-683-1515

Headquarters of local educational and charitable organizations that promote volunteerism, participation in community affairs, and training community leaders. Develops service projects and advocacy efforts to address issues such as juvenile justice, mental health counseling, parenting, and substance abuse.

Boys & Girls Clubs of America

1230 West Peachtree Street, NW
Atlanta, GA 30309
404-815-5700

Helps young people gain competence, usefulness, and a sense of belonging through the Targeted Outreach Program, SMART Moves, and other efforts. A variety of resource materials are available.

Resources

Boy Scouts of America

Exploring Division
1325 Walnut Hill Lane
Irving, TX 75308-3096
972-580-2084

Provides young men and women with a variety of crime prevention and law enforcement projects that include character-building, citizenship, and fitness training. Good source of volunteers.

Bureau of Justice Assistance Clearinghouse

Box 6000
Rockville, MD 20850
800-688-4252

Provides information and publications on BJA-funded crime and drug programs, including formula grants, technical assistance, and training and demonstration programs.

Camp Fire, Inc.

4601 Madison Avenue
Kansas City, MO 64112
816-756-1950

Provides informal educational opportunities for youth to help them realize their potential and function effectively as caring, self-directed individuals, responsible to themselves and to others. Seeks to improve social conditions that affect youth.

4-H Extension Service

7100 Connecticut Avenue
Chevy Chase, MD 20815-4999
301-961-2820

Emphasizes "head, heart, hands, and health" through activities that include drug and alcohol education programs. Offers training at the local, county, state, and national levels.

Juvenile Justice Clearinghouse

NCJRS
Box 6000
Rockville, MD 20850
800-638-8736

Clearinghouse of programs and practices for juvenile justice professionals. Collects program descriptions, project reports, research studies, and evaluations and maintains information in a computerized database with on-line search and retrieval capabilities. Covers many subjects on prevention and treatment.

National Crime Prevention Council

1700 K Street, NW, Second Floor
Washington, DC 20006-3817
202-466-6272

The National Crime Prevention Council (NCPC) is a private, nonprofit, tax-exempt organization whose principal mission is to enable people to prevent crime and build safer, more caring communities. NCPC publishes books, brochures, program kits, reproducible materials, posters, and other items; operates demonstration programs, especially in community and youth issue areas, including Youth as Resources and Teens, Crime, and the Community; provides training on a wide range of topics; offers technical assistance and information and referral services; manages (with The Advertising Council, Inc. and the U.S. Department of Justice) the McGruff public education campaign; and coordinates the activities of the Crime Prevention Coalition of America (136 national, federal, and state organizations and agencies active in preventing crime).

National Criminal Justice Reference Service (NCJRS)

Box 6000
Rockville, MD 20850
800-851-3420 or
800-732-3277 (Statistics)

Provides free, up-to-date data and statistics on crime and drug-related crime. Maintains the largest criminal justice library in the world.

National Safety Council

Orders Department
PO Box 558
Itasca, IL 60143
800-621-7619

Promotes safety through publishing and distributing pamphlets, booklets, posters, and displays on such topics as drinking and driving, latchkey children, babysitting, and pedestrian safety. A free catalog is available.

National School Safety Center

4165 Thousand Oaks Boulevard
Westlake Village, CA 91362
805-373-9977

Provides a variety of materials on subjects ranging from gangs to vandalism prevention as well as technical assistance to school systems. Publications of particular interest are *Gangs in Schools: Breaking Up is Hard to Do* and the *Curriculum Standards Handbook*.

Office for Substance Abuse Prevention

National Clearinghouse for Alcohol and Drug Information
PO Box 2345
Rockville, MD 20847
800-729-6686

Services include a video tape loan program, the newsletter *Prevention Pipeline,* dissemination of grant announcements and application kits, database searches, and referrals. A free catalog of materials is available.

Street Law, Inc.

918 16th Street, NW, Suite 602
Washington, DC 20006
202-293-0088

Services include curriculum development, teacher training, and technical assistance to new and established law-related education programs.

Programs

Center for Youth as Resources

c/o National Crime Prevention Council
1700 K Street, NW
Second Floor, Washington, DC 20006-3817
202-466-6272

Begun in 1987 by NCPC and the Lilly Endowment, this unique program enlists young people to solve local problems and help build a stronger community. The YAR program helps youth to identify issues of greatest concern and then design programs to address these problems. Local YAR boards give grants to teens for program development.

Teens, Crime, and the Community

c/o National Crime Prevention Council
1700 K Street, NW
Washington, DC 20006-3817
202-466-6272

TCC is an innovative crime prevention curriculum that combines education and action. Classroom lessons are coupled with opportunities to work in the school or community to actually reduce or eliminate specific crime problems. Building on the community emphasis in the curriculum text, students are encouraged to design action projects that meet the needs of the local area.

Youth Crime Watch of America

9300 South Dadeland Boulevard, Suite 100
Miami, FL 33156
305-670-2409

A dynamic, student-led program that began in Florida and has quickly spread across the nation. Youth Crime Watch is a popular, widespread, and comprehensive program, targeting crime and drug prevention education as well as dropout and gang prevention techniques.

Publications

National Crime Prevention Council. *Keeping Kids Safe Kit*. 1997. Available from NCPC, 202-466-6272.

U.S. Department of Justice, Office of Justice Programs, Bureau of Justice Statistics. *Lifetime Likelihood of Victimization*. (Annually updated.) Available from NCJRS, 800-732-3277.

U.S. Department of Justice, Federal Bureau of Investigation, *Uniform Crime Report*. (Annually updated.) Available from NCJRS, 202-514-3151.

U.S. Department of Justice, Office of Justice Programs, Bureau of Justice Statistics. *Criminal Victimization in the United States*. (Annually updated.) Available from NCJRS, 202-514-3151